Neo Delhi and the Politics of Postcolonial Urbanism

This book is augmented by an interactive website (neodelhi.net). During research trips to Delhi and Gurgaon between 2008 and 2015 the author produced a multi-media urban archive that includes full color photos, an essay film, ethnographic videos, field notes and more pertaining to the arguments and ideas presented in this book. The reader is encouraged to actively engage with the website alongside this text.

This book challenges the prevailing metro-centric view of globalization. Rather than privileging the experiences of cities and urban regions in the industrialized world, it argues that cities in the so-called "developing" world present opportunities for scholars to re-think entrenched ideas of globalization, urban development and political community. Kalyan presents a trans-disciplinary exploration of the manifold possibilities and challenges that confront a "globalizing" megacity like New Delhi.

Combining theoretical scholarship, ethnographic exploration, media archival research and textual and visual analysis, the book foregrounds complex urban dynamics in and around the region and raises critical questions about changing urban life for postcolonial cities across the Global South. Kalyan employs methodological approaches from political economy, urban studies and visual culture to render a vivid portrait of changing urban life in India's largest conurbation.

The book will be of interest to students and scholars of urban studies, postcolonial studies and inter-disciplinary studies.

Rohan Kalyan is Assistant Professor of ASPECT (Alliance for Social, Political, Ethical and Cultural Thought), Political Science and International Studies at Virginia Tech, USA.

Interventions
Edited by:
Jenny Edkins
Aberystwyth University
and
Nick Vaughan-Williams
University of Warwick

The series provides a forum for innovative and interdisciplinary work that engages with alternative critical, post-structural, feminist, postcolonial, psycho-analytic and cultural approaches to international relations and global politics. In our first 5 years we have published 60 volumes.

We aim to advance understanding of the key areas in which scholars working within broad critical post-structural traditions have chosen to make their interventions, and to present innovative analyses of important topics. Titles in the series engage with critical thinkers in philosophy, sociology, politics and other disciplines and provide situated historical, empirical and textual studies in international politics.

For a full list of available titles please visit www.routledge.com/series/INT
The most recent titles in this series are:

Disorienting Democracy
Politics of Emancipation
Clare Woodford

Democracy Promotion as Foreign Policy
Temporal Othering in International Relations
Cathy Elliott

Asylum Seekers, Sovereignty, and the Senses of the International
A Politico-corporeal Struggle
Eeva Puumala

Global Powers of Horror
Security, Politics, and the Body in Pieces
François Debrix

East-Asian Marxisms and their Trajectories
Edited by Joyce C.H. Liu and Viren Murthy

The Evolution of Migration Management in the Global North
Christina Oelgemöller

Neo **Delhi and the Politics of Postcolonial Urbanism**
Rohan Kalyan

The Political Afterlife of Sites of Monumental Destruction
Reconstructing Affect in Mostar and New York
Andrea Connor

Neo Delhi and the Politics of Postcolonial Urbanism

Rohan Kalyan

LONDON AND NEW YORK

First published 2017
by Routledge
2 Park Square, Milton Park, Abingdon, Oxon OX14 4RN

and by Routledge
711 Third Avenue, New York, NY 10017

Routledge is an imprint of the Taylor & Francis Group, an informa business

© 2017 Rohan Kalyan

The right of Rohan Kalyan to be identified as author of this work has been
asserted by him in accordance with sections 77 and 78 of the Copyright,
Designs and Patents Act 1988.

All rights reserved. No part of this book may be reprinted or reproduced or
utilized in any form or by any electronic, mechanical, or other means, now
known or hereafter invented, including photocopying and recording, or in
any information storage or retrieval system, without permission in writing
from the publishers.

Trademark notice: Product or corporate names may be trademarks or
registered trademarks, and are used only for identification and explanation
without intent to infringe.

British Library Cataloguing in Publication Data
A catalogue record for this book is available from the British Library

Library of Congress Cataloging in Publication Data
A catalog record for this book has been requested

ISBN: 978-0-415-78835-9 (hbk)
ISBN: 978-1-31522-535-7 (ebk)

Typeset in Times New Roman
by Wearset Ltd, Boldon, Tyne and Wear

Contents

List of figures	vi
List of maps	vii
List of tables	viii
Acknowledgments	ix
Introduction: *Neo* Delhi as an image of thought	1

PART I
Distance and proximity in Delhi — 35

1 The urban — 43

2 The neighborhood — 76

PART II
Aura and trace in Gurgaon — 105

3 The district — 121

4 The enclave — 148

5 The village — 175

Conclusion: partitioned communities of sense — 206

Index — 210

Figures

0.1	Panorama of Delhi as seen from minaret at Jama Masjid	2
0.2	Interior, Ambience Mall, Gurgaon	7
0.3	Chaupal, Chakkarpur Village, Gurgaon	9
0.4	Street scene in Old Delhi	10
0.5	Street scene in New Delhi	13
0.6	Wires and visible infrastructure in Old Delhi	16
0.7	Lane in Old Delhi	19
0.8	Panorama of Chakkarpur Village and surrounding areas, Gurgaon	26
1.1	Official slogan of 2010 Delhi Commonwealth Games: "Come Out and Play"	46
1.2	Presidential complex in New Delhi	53
II.1	Unrealized Mall of India project in Gurgaon	106
II.2	Unrealized Mall of India project in Gurgaon	107
II.3	Unrealized Mall of India project in Gurgaon	110
II.4	Unrealized Mall of India project in Gurgaon	112
II.5	Unrealized Mall of India project in Gurgaon	114
II.6	Unrealized Mall of India project in Gurgaon	117
3.1	DLF Limited headquarters, New Delhi	137
3.2	Property broker office in Chakkarpur, Gurgaon	139
3.3	Man in front of construction in Gurgaon	141
4.1	DLF Gateway Tower in Gurgaon	148
4.2	*HT* headquarters in Park Centra Building, Gurgaon	153
4.3	"Experience the perfect life"	155
4.4	Real estate billboard, Gurgaon	166
5.1	View from MG Road Metro Station 1, Gurgaon	176
5.2	View from MG Road Metro Station 2, Gurgaon	178
5.3	The road into Chakkarpur Village, Gurgaon	182
5.4	Interior, *nambardar* office, Chakkarpur Village	184
5.5	*Jhuggi*, Chakkarpur Village	189
5.6	Uttaranchal Hotel, Chakkarpur Village	192
5.7	Numbers 90 and 91, Chakkarpur Village	194
5.8	Number 91, Chakkarpur Village	195
5.9	Old *haveli* and cow, Chakkarpur Village	199

Maps

1	National capital territory of Delhi	xi
2	Gurgaon (old and new parts)	xi
3	Chakkarpur Village, Gurgaon	xii

Tables

0.1	Population of Delhi (Union Territory) 1901–2011	28
1.1	Foreign direct investment: financial year-wise equity inflows between April 2000 and February 2011	45
3.1	Population of Gurgaon District (1901–2011)	122
3.2	Land acquisition by DLF in Gurgaon	128

Acknowledgments

It is a privilege to get to thank so many people and organizations for helping in the production of this book, in whatever small or big way. It is also a pleasure since this opportunity comes along too rarely. I would first like to thank The J. Watamull Foundation in Honolulu, Hawaii for funding my first year of field research in Gurgaon and Delhi in 2008–2009. Thanks to the University of Hawaii for funding a return trip in 2010. The University of the South funded trips to Delhi and Gurgaon in 2012 and 2013, and the Institute of Society, Culture and Environment at Virginia Tech funded a final trip to Delhi in 2015. Thank you to each of these institutions for supporting my research.

Thanks to my teachers. This book is in so many ways shaped by the conversations, incitements, arguments and provocations we shared in and out of the classroom or office at the University of Hawaii (as a grad student) and Vassar College (as an undergrad) or as a professor at the University of the South and Virginia Tech. My deepest admiration, affection and gratitude goes to Sankaran Krishna, Mike Shapiro, Himadeep Muppidi, S. Charusheela, Jon Goldberg-Hiller, Nevzat Soguk, Noenoe Silva, S. Shankar, Kazi Ashraf, Kathy Ferguson, Monisha Das Gupta, Monica Ghosh, Gorav Kalyan, Ashish Kapoor, Marwan Sehwail, Milan Dale, Sami Majeed, Sidney Plotkin, Katie Hite, Andy Davison, Ravi Sundaram, Mara Sydney, Manny Ness, Christian Kroll, Jeremy Sather, Manuel Chinchilla, Mila Dragojevic, Taylor Spence, Raji Soni, Ralph Calbert, Nick Copeland, Francois Debrix, Tim Luke, Scott Nelson, Mario Khreiche, Alex Stubberfield, Anthony Szczurek, Christine Labuski, Emily Satterwhite, Vinodh Venkatesh, Matt Gabrielle and more. Your mentorship and friendship, your exemplary academic work and creativity, your ideas and insight, and perhaps most of all your generosity and trust, are things I try to bring into my encounters with new colleagues and students.

In graduate school in Honolulu I had the insanely fortunate experience of being able to genuinely say that the weather and the surfing weren't the best part of my seven years there. Thank you to the Aloha School in Manoa for being a dynamic, vibrant, fun, challenging and endearing community of scholars, activists, artists and friends. Some of us are no longer in the city by the sea but our overlapping geohistories in Honolulu from 2005 to 2012 will

x   *Acknowledgments*

remain impressed into my mind and spirit (and reinforced through social media) forever. Thanks to Lorenzo Rinelli, Noah Viernes, Amy Donahue, Jimmy Weir, Jason Adams, Bianca Isaki, Sam Opondo, Melisa Casumbal-Salazar, Iokepa Casumbal-Salazar, Willy Kauai, Ashley Lukens, Kelii Collier, Rujunko Pugh, Carmen Nolte, John Maus, Brianne Gallagher, Chad Shamura, Konrad Ng, Melli Wilson, David Toohey, Mike Cawdery, Ed Coates, Ben Schrader, Jake Dunagan, Stuart Candy, Fabiano Mielniczuk, Keanu Sai and Ned Bertz. There are many others to be included here. I hope to continue thinking with you lot in the years ahead.

Thanks to my Delhi friends and comrades whom I met during the course of my research. I am indebted to you for your hospitality and for injecting me, an awkward South Asian-North American, into the always-simmering political and cultural life of Delhi. You brought me to political meetings, demonstrations, speeches and rallies, film screenings, to conduct surveys and interviews for progressive knowledge, to drink chai and smoke cigarettes, attend concerts and plays, and talk about everything. Tara, Praveen, Naveen, Lucky, Bono, Ish, Leo, Kailash, Ashish, Namrata, thanks for playing host and allowing me to tag along. I hope to return these to you some day. Very special thanks also goes to my family in Delhi and Haryana, especially my cousin Rubal in Gurgaon. Thanks for making me feel at home. I would also like to thank my research contacts and informants in Delhi and Gurgaon. Without your generosity of time this research would have been impossible. Many of my informants were from low-income communities and led lives filled with everyday challenges and existential struggles. I hope I have done an adequate job in documenting some of these issues and contributing in some small part to their alleviation.

Thanks to Jenny Edkins and Nick Vaughan-Williams, the series editors of Routledge Interventions. They originally invited me to submit my proposal and manuscript and I am happy to have found a home for this research there. Thanks also to Lydia de Cruz, Nicola Parkin, the anonymous reviewers and everyone else at Routledge who helped in transforming the manuscript into a book.

Thanks to Danielle for being with me through the final months of this project. Thanks especially for reading rough drafts of some of the chapters, for being a critical and always insightful thinker. You inspire me.

This book is dedicated to my family: Sulekha, Narender and Gorav Kalyan. Thanks for being my intellectual base and for sparking my curiosity in the world. Your unconditional love and support for my work inspired me to see it through to the end. I hope it does you proud.

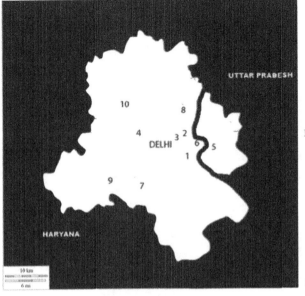

Map 1 National capital territory of Delhi.
Source: created by author.

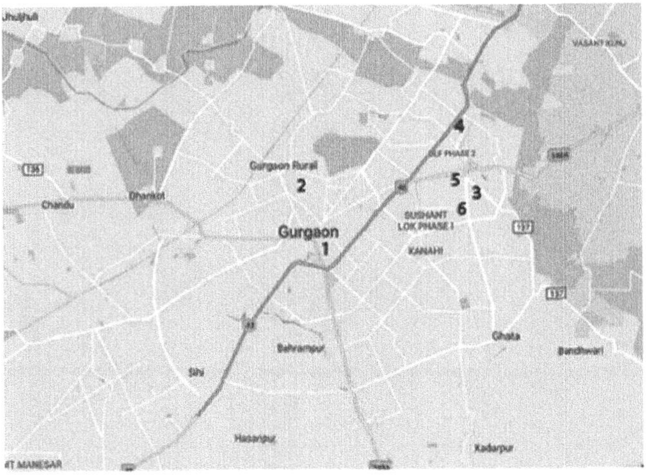

Key
1 New Delhi
2 Old Delhi (Shahjahanabad)
3 Paharganj
4 Shadipur (Kathputli Colony)
5 Commonwealth Games Village
6 Yamuna Pushta
7 Indira Gandhi International Airport
8 Delhi University (North Campus)
9 Dwarka
10 Rohini

Map 2 Gurgaon (old and new parts).
Source: edited from Google maps.

Key
1 Old Gurgaon (existing town)
2 Gurgaon Village
3 DLF City
4 DLF Cyber City
5 Chakkarpur Village
6 DLF Qutab Enclave

Map 3 Chakkarpur Village, Gurgaon.
Source: edited from Google Earth.

Key
1 MG Road Metro Station
2 Deepak's Tiki Stand
3 Sahara Mall
4 Ashish's Barber Stall
5 *Nambardar* Market
6 Kadam Singh's *Jhuggi*
7 Uttaranchal Hotel
8 Numbers 90 and 91
9 Chaupal/*Haveli*

Introduction

Neo Delhi as an image of thought

> This book is augmented by an interactive website (neodelhi.net). During research trips to Delhi and Gurgaon between 2008 and 2015 the author produced a multi-media urban archive that includes full color photos, an essay film, ethnographic videos, field notes and more pertaining to the arguments and ideas presented in this book. The reader is encouraged to actively engage with the website alongside this text.

The integrity of the image

We are said to live in a post-analogue era of "computational photography," in which the very idea of an "original" exposure becomes an increasingly suspect notion.[1] Thus the "integrity of the image" is called into question, as avenues for digital manipulation multiply with each new generation of digital photography and visual art. So let me begin with a (perhaps redundant) warning before settling into this book's main thesis: do not get too enamored with the image you see in Figure 0.1. There is both more—and less—to the image than meets the eye.

The image is very much an illusion, and not just in the sense that all images are merely visual representations and not the thing-in-itself. A friend of mine, proficient with digital photographic editing software, merged together four separate images that I had captured with a camera back in 2008, at the beginning of my fieldwork in Delhi.[2] From the top of a minaret at Jama Masjid, the exquisite seventeenth-century mosque located in the heart of Shahjahanabad (now commonly called Old Delhi), I took photographs in the four cardinal directions, enchanted by the city's dense and seemingly limitless urban horizon.[3]

I had just arrived in the city, having returned to the country of my parents' birth after a gap of around ten years, and for the first time as an adult. In the meantime, growing up in the U.S. I had read of India's economic "miracle" from a distance, following "liberal" reforms announced by the central government in the early 1990s. Many of the effects of these reforms, I had read, were especially visible in India's large and growing National Capital Territory of Delhi (NCTD), and the high-tech suburb of Gurgaon in the bordering state of Haryana. The last

Figure 0.1 Panorama of Delhi as seen from minaret at Jama Masjid.

Source: Photo taken by author, edited by Lorenzo Rinelli.

Introduction 3

time I had been to the region I was fourteen, and all my life before that I had visited about once every two or three years. On these trips I would note the myriad complex and simple changes taking place in a landscape that was so starkly different from the suburban New Jersey town in which I had grown up. Some of my earliest childhood memories were as this kind of amateur ethnographer in Delhi and Haryana, the state from where my family traced its ancestry.

That day at the top of the minaret at Jama Masjid, my eyes were caught by the endless urban sprawl of Delhi. There was an allure to this visuality, the seduction of epistemic mastery and independence, however naïve and momentary. The four landscape images I took that day comprise the digital panorama you see above.

The image is an illusion at multiple levels. First, there is a sense of the image as a seductive fiction. Michel de Certeau wrote about this kind of experience on the 110th floor of the World Trade Center, before those twin towers were ultimately felled.[4] Upon reflecting on the view of Manhattan afforded from such heights, de Certeau pondered:

> To what erotics of knowledge does the ecstasy of reading such a cosmos belong? Having taken voluptuous pleasure in it, I wonder what is the source of this pleasure of "seeing the whole," looking down on, totalizing the most immoderate of human texts.[5]

The view from 1350 feet rendered the city a "gigantic immobilized mass." But what exactly was erotic about this view from the top? For de Certeau it bespoke of a "scopic and gnostic drive: the fiction of knowledge is related to this lust to be a viewpoint and nothing more."[6] Visual knowledge was tied to power, to be sure, but both knowledge and power were mediated by something else: by desire, carnal and impure.[7]

De Certeau thus described the panoptic image of Manhattan as a "fiction of knowledge." But wasn't the city that was visible from the top of the World Trade Center *real*, as geographical and historical as any other? De Certeau responded by suggesting the existence of two separate orders of urban reality that were put into stark relief from this aerial view of the city. First, there was the "panorama-city" which gained visibility from the top floor. The ability to perceive the city as a whole was a privilege once reserved for power and authority. Their desire was to visualize and understand the city as a whole in order to better rule over it. The panorama-city could be contrasted with the city "down below," belonging to "ordinary practitioners ... below the threshold at which visibility begins."[8] In contrast to the "all-seeing power" of the "eye/I" that gazed at the city from high above, de Certeau presented the walkers of the streets who experienced a different city altogether, one that was perceived through everyday movements and immersive encounters, in improvised instants and interactions. Here "bodies follow the thicks and thins of an urban 'text' they write without being able to read it."[9] These two orders of reality—the panoramic-city and the city of everyday life—were obviously related and overlapped, yet what was significant for de Certeau was that,

4   *Introduction*

perhaps for the first time, ordinary people on the streets of New York could come up and access the visual position of power, at least temporarily. They could forget about the now-invisible realities "down below." Perhaps this was part of its seduction, that the panoramic-image could help one experience anew the everyday, the mundane, the ordinary, paradoxically through escape.

This brings me back to the digital photograph of Delhi in Figure 0.1. With its inherent privileging of a top-down, static representation of the city—Delhi in its panoptic totality—did the image not reveal itself as a modernist illusion in precisely the same way that de Certeau decries above? Did it not reproduce the fictional knowledge of the voyeur-god who sought universal knowledge in and through the visual? It did this, I'll allow, but it also did something else, something far more mysterious and unexpected.

One day I accidentally discovered an entirely new level of deception in the panoramic image of Delhi, something that had previously escaped my attention. It had to do with the spatial juxtaposition between the mosque's central dome in the foreground of the panorama and the distant skyscrapers far off in the background. I wondered if the visual contrast wasn't a bit too convenient. What were those tall buildings on the horizon doing *there*, positioned as if directly behind the dome? This main dome was on the western side of the mosque. If one were up in the minaret looking at the space behind the dome, one would see not the skyscrapers around Connaught Circus and central New Delhi, which were actually positioned a few kilometers to the south. Rather, one would witness the dense low-rise sprawl of west Delhi: the rough and tumble neighborhood of Paharganj just past the Old Delhi Railway station, stretching out to the middle-class colonies of Karol Bagh and Rohini, extending as far as visibility spreads out on the hazy horizon. Clearly there was something strangely amiss about the image.

I went back to the raster graphics software that my friend used to combine the separate stills into one panoramic image. For Photoshop's "photomerge" effect to work, in order for it to produce a single image from several disparate photos, there should ideally be no spatial gaps between the images that are being merged together.[10] Rather, portions of each image should overlap so the algorithm can match up similar visual content. Of course, I did not think of this when I was up on the minaret at Jama Masjid taking the original photos back in 2008. Instead I simply fired off shots in what seemed to be the four cardinal directions, with the idea of printing them out later and arranging them in a kind of disjointed collage. As a result the gaps in between these images were filled in *virtually* through the software's algorithm, which searched for overlapping visual data but approximated and even distorted this content, albeit nearly imperceptibly, when there were significant gaps. The images thus appeared to blend together in a seamless, yet impossible panoramic whole, one that could never exist in "actuality." That is, the visage could never exist independently of the camera and the digital imaging technology that rendered it an image.

But while there might have been a certain infidelity, or a noticeable "flaw," in the visual representation of Delhi, perhaps there was also a kind of power immanent to this very act of imaging and distorting. The image staged a temporal drama that was false yet nevertheless insightful, namely, the visual and spatial juxtaposition of medieval Old Delhi (symbolized by Jama Masjid's marble dome in the foreground) with the modernist skyscrapers of New Delhi in the background. This "false" juxtaposition generated an image of thought that was to become the central argument of this book. Between foreground and background, mosque and skyscrapers, there emerged a "depth of field" within the image. But the depth was no longer merely spatial, it was temporal. The image became, following Deleuze, a "time-image."[11]

I'll return to the concept of time-images and the "powers of the false" they engender before the end of this Introduction, underlining their implication for the study of cities like *Neo* Delhi. But for now let it suffice to assert that after we falsify the actual image of Delhi we can move from a strictly spatial analysis of the city to one that is decidedly inter-temporal. As I'll show in different scenes within contemporary Delhi and Gurgaon, dominant projections of the city perpetually privilege the "erotic" visuality of the panoramic-city at the expense of the radically heterogeneous times of the city "down below," the city of everyday life. How can we produce images of changing urban life in cities like Delhi that render both orders of reality simultaneously, while analyzing the inherent tensions, exclusions and mediations between them?

In this book I propose to study a virtual city, that is, a city that does not exist in actuality. I call it *Neo* Delhi. But it is not that *Neo* Delhi does not exist as such. Rather *Neo* Delhi names a field of possible urban experiences, spaces and times which come to shape and structure the actuality of the city and urban region. It is this actuality that constitutes the dominant image of cities like Delhi as they are usually approached in contemporary urban studies. To study the virtual city is to think beyond this actuality, to think with the possibilities and impossibilities which structure the actual.

My purpose in writing this book and producing the visual media featured on the accompanying website (www.neodelhi.net) is to help generate alternative images of thought regarding world cities like Delhi.[12] As I argue in this Introduction, what I call an "image of thought" is not necessarily a visual construct. It is first and foremost a way of critically rendering the abstract presuppositions that go into the production of knowledge, power and desire within common sense discourses of cities, particularly non-Western or "developing" ones. The dominant image of thought for cities like Delhi, expressed in discourses of development and globality, as I show in Chapter 1, portray these cities more in terms of what they are *not*, or not *yet*—that is, properly "developed" cities—than in terms of what they *are*, or what they might be in the process of *becoming*. The substantive chapters in this book are experiments in how we might study changing urban life, its potentialities and its limits, in ways that challenge existing ideas of cities, urbanism and even globalization. But *Neo* Delhi only becomes intelligible as a virtual city once we let go of some of the abstract presuppositions that mainstream urban studies, such as it is, continues to hold. This introductory chapter explores how cities become visualized and conceptually

6 *Introduction*

imagined within contemporary urban theory. In particular, I present eight images of thought that are simultaneously sites of contestation and intellectual exchange among theorists in four broad fields: (1) mainstream/liberal urban studies, (2) radical urban theory, (3) assemblage urbanism and (4) postcolonial theories of cities. Rather than each image representing a separate school of thought, I stage eight conceptual encounters between contrasting urban theories that are sequenced so as to build upon the ground work laid by the previous images. This Introduction thus elaborates increasingly complex images of thought that crystallize into a virtual city: *Neo* Delhi.

One last note before beginning this conceptual montage, the images vary in terms of the emphasis they each give toward viewing the city primarily as "place" versus as "process." As we will see, this duality remains a major tension within contemporary urban studies. In practice these binary approaches are not always mutually exclusive. And it is certainly not impossible to generate a critical image of thought regarding cities like Delhi that is both at once, that is, place-based and process-oriented. In fact this will be one of my major tasks in the chapters ahead: to render a theoretical image of the city that is conceptually stereoscopic: place and process, actual and virtual, spatial and temporal, at once. To render this image of thought, I employ a decidedly cinematic strategy for mediating between space and time, place and process, in the postcolonial city. This strategy yields what I call an "urban depth of field," which I'll define toward the end of this introduction and elaborate in the chapters that follow. In the contrast and sequencing of these dominant and critical images of thought, then, I clear a conceptual space for *Neo* Delhi.

The global city

Sometime in the first decade of the twenty-first century it became commonplace to read about our increasingly "urbanized" world. For the first time, we were told, a majority of the planet's population resided in what could be called, for lack of a better term, "cities."[13] This produced a sharpened focus on cities and urban regions and what was happening to them in an era marked by global urbanization. The paradox of these seemingly unrelenting processes—globalization and urbanization—famously examined by the likes of Saskia Sassen and Manuel Castells, was that the geographic dispersal implied by globalization required the place-based labor of coordination and management in order to function efficiently.[14] Such specialized service-labor would inevitably take root in certain "global cities," where the requisite human capital and material infrastructure were in place. Thus global dispersal entailed spatial concentration in cities.

Equally inevitable, however, was the reality that for less historically privileged cities seeking to become "global" in this way, existing urban infrastructures would have to be greatly modified in order to accommodate "global city" functions, like playing host to multi-national corporations and their white collar workers. The resulting conflicts between white collar and working-class residents

Figure 0.2 Interior, Ambience Mall, Gurgaon.
Source: Photo by author.

led to popular debate about the effects of gentrification and "urban renewal," local identity versus capital mobility, property speculation, income inequality and the right to the city.[15]

In the so-called "developing world," global urbanism as intensified spatial concentration was marked by a somewhat different trend. Here globalization entailed the proliferation of "informal" spaces in the form of dense slums, favelas, shanty-towns and illicit or non-legal economies in sprawling "megacities."[16] These new formations consisted mostly (but not exclusively) of a growing under-class of under-employed workers and socially marginalized groups, displaced by globalized agriculture.[17] Much of the world experienced widespread enclosures of farm and pastoral lands, which were sold off to powerful resource-extraction companies and big agricultural businesses.[18] This process of "accumulation by dispossession" sent displaced farmers and rural workers into rapidly expanding urban regions.[19] Once there, they often struggled to improvise a day-to-day existence in a city that was woefully unprepared for their arrival. Moreover, these urban migrants were greeted by an entrenched civil society (comprising middle and upper classes) that often despised the former's low-grade presence, even if it quickly became reliant on their low-cost labor.

8   *Introduction*

These two relatively new forms of spatial concentration—of intensifying high-end agglomeration in "global cities" and low-grade informality in "developing cities"—were obviously connected, even deeply entangled. "Global cities" like New York or London, for example, contained not only highly specialized labor in the form of financial, legal and technological services, but also lower-wage local and informal economies (including underground sweat shops and black markets) that were often "under the table" or otherwise hidden in plain sight.[20] Even as "globalized" as cities like London or New York were, the vast majority of their urban economic activity still occurred within national boundaries.[21] Meanwhile, so-called "developing cities," ever eager to "catch up," increasingly sought out foreign direct investment in order to produce their own "global" enclaves and accumulation zones within cities or just outside of them.[22] In this way even these peripheral and historically distant places began forming financial, industrial and commercial links with other, more central capitalist cities and regions.

An urbanized planet

But beyond this intensifying concentration of so-called "global" and "developmental" city-spaces across the capitalist world, a second branch of theoretical research on global urbanism focused less on the new place-based realities associated with this phenomenon and more on the expansive economies of scale and networks of exchange that structured this spatially dispersed process, albeit ambivalently and always at a distance.[23]

This contrasting approach moved away from theories of spatial concentration and agglomeration in *place* in favor of a more de-territorialized analysis of urbanization as *process*. Researchers foregrounded the emergent properties of many of the same kind of new commercial spaces highlighted by the Global Cities camp, but the theoretical emphasis was different. Thus process-oriented scholars too highlighted sprawling urban/suburban regions, new technological corridors, and zones of de-territorialized economic production, but their focus was simultaneously on the networked infrastructures that virtually synchronized these disparate sites at multiple scales—local, regional, national, global—into a singular process. This process effectively brought the entire planet into relation with a single, albeit uneven and frayed, urban fabric.

Critical urban theorists like Neil Brenner called this process "planetary urbanization," containing "two dialectically intertwined moments—concentration and extension."[24] Thus, the more existing cities and towns grew and intensified as centers of attraction for people, capital and technology, the more the "urban process" of necessity expanded outwards in the search for increasingly remote bio-chemical "supply zones" that could fuel and sustain it. These connections over vast geographic expanses were not merely synchronically structured through digital networks and markets, as Global Cities scholars had already argued. They were simultaneously to be thought of diachronically, that is, in terms of the production process that connected geographically distant supply zones with the city's present and future. Since the production of the city as place

Figure 0.3 Chaupal, Chakkarpur Village, Gurgaon.
Source: Photo by author.

entailed a direct impact on these geographically distant but temporally connected zones, the latter had to be thought of as part of the same planetary "urban" process. In this way, according to Brenner, "the urban can no longer be viewed as a distinct, relatively bounded site."[25] The precise line that once marked where "the city" as such began and ended was now being blurred beyond recognition.

The essence of cities

Such expansive, de-territorialized theories of planetary urbanization, if taken to their logical conclusion, questioned the very coherence of the idea of "the city."

10 *Introduction*

Figure 0.4 Street scene in Old Delhi.
Source: Photo by author.

If the whole planet was now effectively "urbanized," as theorists like Brenner argued, then what were we to make of the idea of the city as such? Was it time to move beyond spatial conceptions of cities as the confluence of territory, demography and density in a specific geographic place, as had been the tradition in mainstream urban studies since Louis Wirth's famous 1938 essay "Urbanism as a way of life"?[26] Was it time to move toward a de-territorialized focus on dispersed global or planetary processes that shaped urban formations and their proliferating supply zones?

Introduction 11

Answering forcefully in the negative, Michael Storper and Allen Scott critiqued the work of Brenner and others for dissolving the very idea of the city "into a sort of overarching global plasma as theorists of 'planetary urbanism' proclaim."[27] In contrast these authors argued for an essentially territorialized conception of cities as the unambiguous object of urban theory and knowledge production. That is, they proposed, or re-proposed, a fairly common sense conception of cities as "a very specific scale of economic and social interaction generated by agglomeration processes and focused on the imperative of proximity."[28] For Storper and Scott urban theory had to "capture the essence of cities as concrete social phenomena" in order to "shed light on the observable empirical diversity of cities over space and time."[29] For them, this essence boiled down to what they called the "urban land nexus," which was a confluence of political, economic, ecological and cultural forces that acted as a sort of geohistorical center of gravity for cities over long periods of historical and pre-historical time. They defined the urban land nexus as "a spatially extensive lattice or patchwork, but one whose overall logic is still structured by agglomeration, convergence, and the need for proximity."[30] As an analytical concept, the urban land nexus was both broad enough to handle the rich diversity of world historical cities, but robust enough to tell us something specific and analytically useful about what cities were, what precisely happened in cities and why. This concept thus "provides a distinctive place for urban analysis in the academic division of labor and ... together with the appropriate analytical machinery, endows it with a central mission."[31]

But in their desire to defend the distinctive "place" of urban analysis within academia and perpetuate a place of employment in statist knowledge production, mainstream theorists betrayed a classically modernist impulse to assert epistemic mastery over social reality through distinction, classification and enumeration. At some level this was inevitable given the analysts' intended audience, but it ended up freezing cities in their "nominal essence," taking this current geohistorical form as necessary, pre-given and more or less immutable. It thus removed the city and its built environment from its constitutive essence, or the various processes through which urban topographies were made and unmade. Thus mainstream urbanists effectively limited knowledge production to the optimization requirements of cities in their current capitalist spatial form, with the presumed dominance of private property and the capitalist state. This sanctioned ignorance came at the expense of alternative conceptions of urban productions that corresponded not to what cities were in their present capitalist form, that is, how they functioned and how to optimize them for "the market," but rather how they could be imaged and lived otherwise. Knowledge production about the urban was in this way profoundly political.

Rather than beginning with a pre-constituted urban essence and limiting the political to its effective management and control, Ash Amin approached urban regions as processes undergoing multi-layered transformations. These transformations could not be approached merely spatially; they had to be interpreted in ways that were sensitive to the many temporalities of changing urban life, including

12   *Introduction*

everyday rhythms (social, biological, ecological) and the historicity of the city as such. Amin suggested a different agenda for urban studies that assumed neither a universal definition of the urban, nor a singular epistemological ground from which to study the politics of the urban. Amin argued instead for

> a politics of place that works ... by bringing into play sentiments, ethics, emotions, aesthetics, ambiguity and uncertainty into the field of what counts as political. It becomes an act of developing a sense of place and place attachment that works with difference and distance, assuming no indigeneity or privileged set of claims.[32]

Amin's was a "non-territorial reading of the politics of place."[33] He argued against theorizing urban regions, cities and towns as more or less permanent settlements, "places" that urbanists took for granted and whose management they sought to optimize. Amin argued "against the assumption that there is a defined geographic territory out there over which local actors have effective control and can manage as a social and political space."[34] For any nominal urban "essence" was always already shaped in innumerable ways by forces, relations and conditions that were distant from the urban present of the analyst, distant not only in space but in time. It was thus necessary to inquire into what haunted the nominal essence of cities. What escaped inclusion into "the urban" and was relegated to the "non-urban"? What happened when these exclusions "returned" to the urban scene (from which they never really left) in order to make their spectral presences known, albeit at a haunting distance? These distant relations were not necessarily intelligible as such to analysts despite their best efforts at holistic theorizations of cities. They were untimely presences that had no name inside the nominal essence of the city.

Urban productions

Process-oriented urbanists like Brenner and Amin probably owed much in their thinking to the French Marxian philosopher Henri Lefebvre. In his 1970 book *The Urban Revolution*, Lefebvre began with the following provocation: "An *urban society* is a society that results from a process of complete urbanization. This urbanization is virtual today, but will become real in the future."[35] Lefebvre's work here foreshadowed the process of planetary urbanization that Brenner would later pick up on and theorize along with other urban researchers some four decades later.[36] For Lefebvre this virtual urban society would be "post-industrial" in a specific sense. Rather than industrial capitalism driving the growth of cities and urbanization more broadly, the process would be reversed. The urban would not only dominate the rural as it had done since the advent of industrialized farming, but the urban would emerge as a mode of production in its own right, one whose proper scale was the planet itself.[37]

In his next book, *The Production of Space*, Lefebvre theorized this process of urbanization within a more complete philosophical framework. Lefebvre's major

Introduction 13

Figure 0.5 Street scene in New Delhi.
Source: Photo by author.

thesis here was that space was not a pre-given, neutral, static entity, as long presupposed after Newtonian physics and Cartesian geometry.[38] Rather, space was socially produced. This social production happened "in two ways, as a social formation (a mode of production), and as a mental construction (a conception)."[39] Lefebvre offered his now-famous conceptual triad that complicated this dialectical process: (1) representations of space (i.e., conceived spaces), (2) representational spaces (perceived spaces) and (3) spatial practices (lived spaces). Conceived, perceived and lived spaces did not designate mutually exclusive topographies, but rather overlapping processes and ways of theorizing, encountering and producing space.

Conceived spaces were abstract representations drawn up and projected by powerful institutions, including urban planners and policy makers. They composed a "far order," as Lefebvre described it elsewhere, that materialized through spatial practices on the ground. The far order was projected onto diverse everyday spaces, public plazas, residential and commercial districts, traffic codes and transportation infrastructure, historical monuments and formal institutional spaces. These "bureaucratic" conceptions of space projected an abstract, impersonal, rationalized distance that state institutions required in order to be seen as functioning legitimately and authoritatively, that is, at a distance.[40]

14   *Introduction*

Perceived spaces, on the other hand, composed what Lefebvre would else-where call the "near order."[41] They were representational insofar as they included "complex symbolisms, sometimes coded, sometimes not, linked to the clandes-tine or under-ground side of social life, as also to art."[42] That is, representational spaces were spaces that ordinary urban dwellers interpreted in their everyday lives, coding these perceptions in terms that made sense to them. They were the narratives and common discourses that people used to make sense of the spaces around them. These common sense discourses were shaped, but not legislated by the conceptual "far order" of the state, for there was always some room for crea-tive subversion and invention in spite of the dominance of conceived spaces in the city. Artists explored and reveled in this subterranean layer of changing urban life.

In the gap between the far order of state institutions (conceived space) and the near order of everyday social life (perceived space), there intervened the crucial third term of Lefebvre's conceptual triad: spatial practice, or lived space. For Lefebvre spatial practice rooted the urban encounter between perceived and con-ceived spaces on firm materialist ground: the built environment or urban fabric of the city itself. Thus, spatial practice "embraces production and reproduction, and the particular locations and spatial sets characteristic of each formation. Spatial practice ensures continuity and some degree of cohesion."[43] Spatial prac-tice mediated between abstract conceptions of space and more quotidian percep-tions of space in daily life. It was the "practico-material reality," as Lefebvre called it elsewhere, upon which the "far order" was projected and the "near order" perceived.[44] Yet the continuity and cohesion tied to spatial practice did not preclude the possibility for alteration, subversion and creative appropriation of socially produced space. The potential for counter-uses and non-normative practices served to politicize the production of space. This was a key point for Lefebvre, who famously argued, "there is a politics of space because space is political."[45]

Lefebvre's major philosophical contribution in *The Production of Space* was to challenge the long-held Newtonian image of space as passive and empty. He replaced this static conception of space with a more dynamic and emergent image of spatial production that was actively mediated by the practices of powerful institutions and everyday urban dwellers alike. As Doreen Massey argued, in Newtonian conceptions of space, "space is a passive arena, the setting for objects and their interaction."[46] Such conceptions were also indebted to Car-tesian ideas of geometrical space. As Elden noted, "Descartes importantly sug-gests that all problems in geometry can be reduced to the angle of some straight lines, to the values of the roots of the equations, thereby turning space into some-thing that is quantitatively measureable, calculable, numerical."[47] For Massey, such abstract concepts of space as merely a neutral container for social activity were problematic, for they "effectively depoliticize the realm of the spatial."[48] Worse, space came to be defined simply as "not-time," where "time is defined by such things as change, movement, history, and dynamism; while space, rather lamely by comparison, is simply the absence of these things."[49] Space became,

Introduction 15

by implication, the realm of stasis, structure, repetition, ordered movement and the like, that is, outside the realm of History.[50]

Yet in Lefebvre's *Production of Space*, as well as in his earlier *Urban Revolution*, it became clear that, far from being the mere passive setting for the progression of History, space was actively made and remade "through social relations and material social practices."[51] This active construction of space became especially visible in the modern context through what David Harvey called "the urbanization of capital."[52] For Harvey, capitalism had to purposively "urbanize" space in order to stabilize itself as a surplus-producing economic system seeking to avoid over-accumulation. Thus the urbanization process mapped "how capital flows into the construction of the built environment," providing opportunities for over-accumulated capital in profitable sectors of the economy to be absorbed into "public" investments that stabilized economic growth over the long-term.[53] These included investments in public goods that no private capitalist would be willing to finance (because they were most likely unprofitable) like urban infrastructure (roads, electrical grids, sewage systems) and social services (schools, hospitals, prisons). Yet for whatever stability was achieved through this "spatial fix" (i.e., reinvestment of surplus capital into the built environment for continued capitalist growth), "the structure of social relations prevailing in a capitalist society" meant that the achievement of truly "balanced growth" was never ultimately realized.[54] So that the history of the urbanization of capital was beset with instances of over-speculation and over-investment in the built environment, leading first to property-market inflation and inevitable market crash. If urbanization mediated this otherwise turbulent process of capital accumulation, it did so only at the cost of great social violence and instability that could always lead to political revolution.[55] For Harvey, this revolutionary potential in the modern capitalist city was what continued to make it a key site of class struggle in the early decades of the twenty-first century.

The city as assemblage

For scholars like Brenner, Harvey and others, the underlying process that structured urbanization was unquestionably that of capitalism, defined as a historically specific set of social forces and relations of production in which the interests of private property occupied the commanding heights of both the state and the economy.[56] In contrast, assemblage urbanists held onto a slightly altered conception of capitalism and its relation to modern cities. They held that capitalism was but one of the many social and political processes and sets of relations through which cities and urban formations were made and unmade. This contributed to an image of thought that rendered the city as process, only now that process was conceptualized as much more open-ended and heterogeneous than the universal becoming of capitalism on a (now) planetary scale.

Disrupting the Marxian image of the urban as belonging to a pre-defined "social totality," urban assemblages were conceived as contingent part–whole relations that worked at multiple-scales of urban life, where neither part nor

16 *Introduction*

Figure 0.6 Wires and visible infrastructure in Old Delhi.
Source: Photo by author.

whole was taken as a pre-given and immutable identity. Rather both were formed through a process of interaction among heterogeneous elements, including humans, organizations, tools, objects, technologies, texts, organisms and other cities.[57]

This mode of thinking owed much to the work of Mexican-American philosopher Manuel Delanda. Drawing on the philosophy of Gilles Deleuze, Delanda argued that "all that exists in the actual world is singular individual entities (individual atoms, cells, organisms, persons, organizations, cities, and so on) whose main difference from each other is spatio-temporal scale."[58] But what *assembled* these heterogeneous elements into particular part-to-whole relations in any given scale? For Delanda, there was no essential causal agent or universal structure at work here, only singular entities whose affective capacities (i.e., capacity to affect and to be affected) could be mapped at multiple overlapping scales. Thus "wholes that are both irreducible and decomposable are referred to as assemblages."[59] Assemblages were decomposable insofar as they were formed out of the myriad interactions of parts, and did not precede these interactions. They were irreducible insofar as any whole could simultaneously interact with other wholes and thus become the parts of a larger assemblage. Thus "lower scale entities form the working parts of a larger scale whole, a whole which emerges (and needs to be continuously maintained) by the interactions between the parts."[60]

Introduction   17

Delanda conceptualized these multi-scalar assemblages of parts and wholes as "nested sets," in which "wholes at one scale are the parts of wholes at the next scale."[61] Thus "interacting persons yield institutional organizations; interacting organizations yield cities; interacting cities organize a space in which nation-states emerge and so on."[62] Here we might note the contrast with the image of the ancient city as a "whole" found in Aristotle's city-state. Aristotelean conceptions of the city and political community began from the top—an essential form or metaphysical ideal—and subsequently moved down to particular manifestations of this essence on the ground.[63] Thus the city was a whole that existed prior to and independently of its individual citizens and households. This a priori status was necessary for the metaphysical conceits of justice to obtain as an eternal philosophical truth. In contrast, Delanda's ontology worked in the opposite direction. By locating part–whole relations at multiple scales of existence (including human and non-human life), Delanda's bottom-up approach allowed for a view of reality as composed of increasingly complex assemblages with different affective capacities that related to multiple larger and smaller-scale "wholes." This ontology resisted reductive analysis of cities to their "nominal essence" or their economic structure, that is, to some foundational and immutable "whole." The assemblage was derived not from its immutable essence (as a metaphysical ideal) or its location within the structural totality (of capitalism), but from its "emergent properties," where the latter was "a property of the whole that is caused by the interactions among its parts."[64]

Delanda's conceptualization of cities as multi-scalar assemblages has found resonance within contemporary urban theory. In the scholarship of Ignacio Farias, for instance, assemblage theory changed the focus of urban research "from 'the' space of the city to the multiple urban assemblages in which urban topologies are made and remade."[65] For Farias, assemblage theory helped theorists "unfreeze" the idea of the city or the urban form from some unchanging place-based essence. It also dislodged the city from the determinist relationship it was so often posited as being in with capitalism, creating the possibility for understanding cities as both part of the capitalist world, yet not determined by the totality of this structure. "By looking at cities," Farias argued, "we can learn more about capitalism as a form of life, although not as a global abstract logic imposing its forms into local spaces, but as a concrete process assuming multiple forms even within a city."[66] From this perspective, cities were more than economic units or the products and/or facilitators of capitalist production. They were virtual objects that had shifting, contingent borders and belonged to multiple nested sets of part–whole relations, comprising interactive networks at different scales.

Critical urban theorists like Brenner, although supportive of efforts to move beyond strictly territorialized or place-centric theorizations of cities and urban life, nevertheless criticized assemblage urbanism on a number of issues: its seeming obsession with objects and the multiplicity of space, the prioritization of non-linear histories over historical processes of capitalist development. Above all Brenner opposed the "theoretical indeterminacy" of the very concept of

18   *Introduction*

assemblage, whereby "the concept of the urban is attached to an extraordinarily diffuse array of referents, connotations, and conditions, all too frequently derived from everyday categories of practice, which are then unreflectively converted into analytical commitments."[67] As a critical urban theorist with a Marxian orientation, Brenner was interested in the (capitalist) process that produced the urban as an ideological effect, giving the urban the appearance of a geographically bound, demographically condensed, historically stable entity. But for Brenner, part of the problem with assemblage urbanism was that it took these heterogeneous processes too far, uncritically embracing multiple de-centered part–whole relationalities at the expense of a clearer analysis that could pave the path to revolutionary class-based struggle.

Among the assemblage urbanists, Farias furnished the strongest rebuke of this kind of criticism. Farias responded that the political project of assemblage theory "is certainly radical, but not in the sense critical urban scholars imagine radicalism to be."[68] The difference was in the analytical task that assemblage theorists set for themselves, in stark contrast to critical urbanists like Brenner and Harvey. Assemblage theory was more about open-ended "inquiry" vis-à-vis the urban than about the "critique" of the capitalist mode of production as such. For Farias, this "is connected with a redefinition of democracy towards participatory practices that might eventually recognize and represent humans and nonhumans as political actors."[69] Such a redefinition of the politics of urban democracy challenged dogmatic conceptions of the political in mainstream and critical theory. For mainstream theorists, the urban was a unit-like entity to be managed and optimized for market competition. The task of urban theory was to produce knowledge that could turn the city's use-values into exchange-values, even if this meant policing the border between the urban and the non-urban. For critical urbanists, the city was an expression of the social totality of capitalism, a now-planetary mode of economic production and social reproduction that was the driving force of global urbanization. While not denying the influence of capitalism as a global force, assemblage theory allowed for the possibility of theorizing plural normative horizons that kept the question of the political open to its radical democratic potentialities. It was open to the unexpected arrival of new political actors and subjectivities, expanding the domain of the political beyond an exclusive focus on class-based struggle.

Postcolonial cities

Postcolonial urban theorists shared with assemblage urbanists a desire to pluralize the normative horizons of cities. These theoretical approaches framed the immanent relationality of cities for an anti-essentialist analysis. In other words, postcolonial and assemblage urbanists not only wanted to resist reducing cities or urban formations to their nominal essence; they also resisted enclosing the city and its theoretical possibilities within a constitutive essence, that is, within the social totality of capitalism as a global process. But postcolonial theory had slightly different reasons for this resistance to orthodox Marxian analytics. At

Figure 0.7 Lane in Old Delhi.
Source: Photo by author.

the risk of over-generalization, postcolonial theory held Marxian analyses of capitalism as a world historical process to be necessary yet insufficient, particularly with regard to the analysis of capitalism and economic transformations in the "postcolonial" world. The fact that Marxian theory remained to some degree necessary was a testament to the enduring legacy of Euro-centrism, as not only an intellectual project but a materialized set of trans-continental political economic relations and social practices. This was a legacy that postcolonial theory, broadly conceived, took as the focus of its critical scholarship. Before describing this project in more detail, with particular emphasis on how postcolonial theory conceptualized cities and urban processes, a few words of clarification on the

20   *Introduction*

term "postcolonial"—for I have already oscillated between two quite different connotations, and this was precisely the problem found in many contemporary critiques of postcolonial scholarship.

First, there was a relatively straightforward, historical sense of the post-colonial, whereby it referred to the time period of a specific nation or community in the period following its decolonization from European colonial rule. This strictly temporal sense of the postcolonial was of limited value since it included such a wide range of ostensibly "decolonized" nations (from those in the Americas that gained independence from European empires in the late eighteenth and early nineteenth centuries to those in Africa and Asia that were decolonized only in the middle decades of the twentieth). Moreover, such a concept of the post-colonial had little to offer those peoples and places of the world that remained colonized by more powerful "outside" entities, such as Hawaii or Palestine.

The second, more critical sense of the postcolonial was defined less by the sup-posedly by-gone period of colonialism from which it proceeded as a "post," and more by a critical engagement with the legacies of "coloniality" in the present.[70] In this second sense, the postcolonial referred not to the historical period of time beginning after decolonization in those particular societies that were once colonized. Rather, it referred to a political project of critique that began in the immediate wake of the colonial encounter itself and was thus not "after" colonialism but coterminous with it. This sense of the postcolonial performed an immanent critique of modernity itself, except instead of locating modernity's origins squarely in Europe, modernity was defined as the constitutive encounter between "the West" and what became "the non-West." That is, both colonizer and colonized were jointly created as modern subjects through the colonial encounter, though in radically different ways. This ongoing coeval and coextensive—albeit historically differentiated—relationship defined the condition of coloniality and was directly evoked in each recitation of the postcolonial.[71]

Two implications followed from this critical insight. First, there was no longer any question of a linear trajectory that posited non-European societies as "historically behind" Europe and thus meant to "catch up," an implicit temporality most often projected in social theories of development and modernization. Rather, the processes we called "development" (of modern economic, political and social institutions) and "under-development" (of the same) were essentially coeval. That is, Europe "developed" thanks in significant part to wealth extraction from the colonies and empires and the uneven transformation of many of the latter into vast external supply zones over the course of several centuries. This only served to ensure that the colonies themselves were actively and intentionally kept "under-developed."[72] In many cases, robust civilizations in Africa and Asia moved from being relatively self-sufficient and industrious in their own right to becoming not only economically dependent upon European colonizers but politically subservient to them as well in the neo-imperial post-war international arena.

The second implication was that all the philosophical concepts and social theories exported from Europe and imported to non-European lands had to be

Introduction 21

critically interrogated and reassessed. Part of the legacy of Euro-centrism, as postcolonial theorist Dipesh Chakrabarty powerfully argued, was the idea that non-European subjects and nations felt compelled to employ theories derived from specifically European experiences in order to interpret social processes unfolding outside of Europe.[73] In contemporary social theory these included, most prominently, the normative models of the liberal democratic state and free-market capitalism as progressive historical forces or even end points of history, universals that were usually translated intact into life-worlds that were never part of the empirical material that informed these theories in the first place. At a minimum, any practice of applying such "universal" European models outside of Europe necessitated a critical practice of cultural translation in which the models themselves were seen as simultaneously indispensable (since they had already been internalized and institutionalized on a global scale) yet inadequate for fully understanding life-worlds that existed outside of their historical provenance, or even within it. This critical practice informed Chakrabarty's now well-known idea of "provincializing Europe."

Chakrabarty made his argument by locating a critical tension in Karl Marx's own writings on capitalism's historical expansion. Chakrabarty found that there were "two histories of capitalism" suggested in Marx's work: History 1 and History 2. The first was the familiar history of capitalist transition, where capitalism was posited as a universal, progressive, if also disruptive, force. This History 1 of capitalism originated in Europe and subsequently came to structure the world, as Marx and Engels famously declared in *The Communist Manifesto.* This universalizing transition was materialized through colonial expansion, imperialism and now economic globalization, or what many call neo-colonialism. For Chakrabarty, History 1 was nominally "universal" but materially "global." In the gap between the universal and the global, one found traces of capitalism's alternative histories, namely those of what Chakrabarty called History 2. For History 1's universalizing narratives produced exclusions in the very act of "creating the world after its own image."[74] These exclusions formed the material substance of History 2, or what Chakrabarty theorized as capitalism's "historical difference." These were alternative histories that drew strength from their capacity to resist becoming "forms of [globalizing capitalism's] own life-processes."[75]

Why did this distinction between capital's "two histories" matter for the study of postcolonial cities and their histories? In Chakrabarty's reading of Marx, capitalism could be seen as a world historical force that worked through a particular hermeneutic, or mode of interpretation. This was a hermeneutic that interpreted human and social activity through the post-Enlightenment concept of "abstract labor." This concept in turn allowed capitalists to draw up abstract equivalences between things that were historically different, such that these differences could be subsumed into expanding "market" relations of production and commodity trade. History 2 was the excess that was left unabstracted in these interpretive processes of production and exchange because it posited a subtle, often invisible resistance to the abstract labor of capitalist subsumption.

22 Introduction

Thus, if History 1 was "the universal and necessary history we associate with capital" as a universalizing economic structure guided by a global logic of abstraction, History 2 constituted a history of resistant substrates that "does not belong to capital's life-process," that is, "it does not contribute to the self-reproduction of capital."[76] The point was that "History 2s are thus not pasts separate from capital; they inhere in capital and yet interrupt and punctuate the run of capital's own logic."[77]

Between History 1 and History 2 lay a whole field of interpretive politics and mediation that was largely ignored in modern social thought. Yet it was not that History 2s were absent in these analyses, rather they were surreptitiously repressed, hidden from view, and rendered unrecognizable as such. History 2s that appeared suddenly within the temporal optic of History 1 had to now be framed as "anachronistic" or otherwise untimely. Their difference became anathema to world historical progress. For Chakrabarty rendering History 2 as archaic in this way was a part of the larger practice of "historicism," or "the idea that to understand anything it has to be seen both as a unity and in its historical development."[78] It made the historical difference represented by the untimely appearances of History 2s as so many appearances of "pre-modern" practices that were bound to disappear in time, following the universal historical trajectory of "the West." Historicism in the context of Euro-centrism thus operated under a very specific interpretive schema: "first in Europe, then elsewhere."[79] In this way, historicism was "what made modernity or capitalism look not simply global but rather as something that became global *over time*, by originating in one place (Europe) and then spreading outside it."[80]

The practice of historicism was common in mainstream social theory, including urban theories pertaining to the so-called "developing" world. Jennifer Robinson argued that a problematic division of intellectual labor existed in contemporary urban theory between cities that were seen as "theoretical" sites of knowledge production and those that were treated as merely "empirical." The latter were often seen through the rubric of "developmentalism, an approach which broadly understands these places to be lacking in qualities of city-ness, and which is concerned to improve capacities of governance, service provision and productivity."[81] The problem with this theory/development binary was that it conceived of non-Western cities in terms of their derivation and deviation from ostensibly "theoretical" Western norms, telling us more about what the former were *not*, rather than what they were, or could become.

Adopting Chakrabarty's aforementioned strategy of "provincialization" within urban theory, postcolonial scholars of cities sought to "demonstrate the parochial character of universal knowledge claims" regarding world cities and histories of urban development in the global South.[82] Global urbanism as an academic subfield within urban theory broadly valorized History 1s at the expense of History 2s. Sheppard et al. suggested the modified Geohistory 1 (GH1) and Geohistory 2 (GH2), combining insights from critical urban theory, assemblage urbanism and postcolonial theory:

Introduction 23

Geohistory 1 imagines places as bounded territorial units progressing at different speeds along the same linear development trajectory, following the advice of those ahead of them. Interactions between these places are imagined as mutually beneficial and reinforcing ... accelerating the convergence of backward towards advanced territories, and culminating in a flattened geography of equal opportunity. In contrast ... geohistories 2 entail differentiated places interpenetrated by uneven, emergent connectivities. These relational, contingent geographies tendentially reinforce pre-existing inequalities, interrupted on occasions by qualitative shifts in power relations ... differentiation emerges at every scale, shaped by how residents of any place, living prosperously or precariously, are differently positioned within and through the trans-local processes.[83]

GH2s incorporated the history of colonial under-development that continued to affect nominally "postcolonial" nations and their largest cities in the present. They framed such inter-temporal processes of under-development not as evidence of "incomplete transition" to modernity, but as alternative, co-existing forms of the modern that had to be understood in their own terms, through non-Euro-centric and non-metro-centric analyses. The difference between Chakrabarty's and Sheppard et al.'s approaches was that GH1, unlike History 1, was not merely an abstract mode of interpretation regarding the historiography of "the past." Geohistories were concretized abstractions of capitalist "development" or state-led "modernization" in contemporary urban landscapes. They were performative in their spatio-temporal presence and duration in the urban present. Within the field of postcolonial urbanism, scholars began to explore the performative frictions between GH1s and GH2s in the context of non-normative urban developments, like slums, underground economies, but also special economic zones and special export processing zones. These were all spatial formations that stood in radical difference, that is, out of time, with global norms of "city-ness" and spatio-temporal continuity derived largely from the now-mythologized experience of urban modernity in "the West."[84] In the chapters that follow, I map several sites and processes of mediation between GH1 and GH2, rendered through what I call an urban depth of field.

Urban depth of field

My concept of "image of thought" is adapted from Gilles Deleuze's complex philosophy. Though eclectic in his treatment of artistic, scientific and philosophical materials, Deleuze employed the concept-metaphor "image of thought" throughout his oeuvre to critique dogmatic presuppositions within Western philosophy.[85] Similarly, the eight images of thought presented in this introduction could be understood as critiques of dogmatic urban theory in its dominant and critical iterations.

More specifically, Deleuze differentiated between two images of thought. The first was that of "common sense," or *doxa*. This was the unquestioned

24   *Introduction*

recognition of a reality that existed prior to and independently of its various representations (for example, the image/idea of a person or a city). This image of thought was dogmatically expressed through the familiar expression, "Everyone knows ..." (for example, "Everyone knows that is a city").[86] But for Deleuze this image of thought was never simply given as "common sense." Rather, common sense was an achievement in itself. For it included not only the recognition of what was supposedly already common, but all the abstract presuppositions that were necessary in order for common sense to actually *make* sense, that is, to generate such recognition in a world that was in reality quite indifferent to our sense of it. This led Deleuze to a second, more "critical," image of thought. It was an image that confounded the various presuppositions through which dogmatic representation, commonly recognizable to "everyone," was achieved.

In his later work on the history and philosophy of cinema, Deleuze argued that movies constituted their own image of thought, one whose potential exceeded the affective capacities of all the other arts. One of the most vivid examples of cinema's radical artistic potential was the deep focus or depth of field shot developed in the middle of the twentieth century. This innovative cinematographic technique produced one of the first self-conscious "time-images" in the modern cinema, marking an evolution from the more spatially-oriented "movement-images" which characterized the era of classical cinema.[87] Through non-linear story-telling and montage editing, through recurring flash-backs and symbolic foreshadowing, for instance, but most radically through the depth of field shot, which I describe below, time-images began to crystallize in post-war European and non-European cinema alike. These "un-timely" images presented unexplored regions of the past, invisible lives in the present, and potential pathways toward the future, articulating a specifically cinematic "politics of now-time."[88] The time-image emerged not just as a progression within the history of modern cinema but became part of an immanent critique of modernity that was potentially radical in its political implications.

In *Cinema 2: The Time-Image* Deleuze argued that it was Orson Welles' *Citizen Kane* (1941) that served as a major pivot point between the two ages of cinema, from the movement-image which dominated pre-war films and the time-image which increasingly reigned thereafter. In the movement-image time was represented indirectly and thus chronologically. It was derived from the movements of bodies or objects across more or less homogeneous and static cinematic space. But in the time-image "time became out of joint and reversed its dependent relation to movement; temporality showed itself as it really was for the first time, but in the form of a coexistence of large regions to be explored."[89] *Citizen Kane* famously dramatized the coexistence of the past and present as heterogeneous regions of time that came into virtual contact in inter-temporal cinematic space. In one famous depth of field shot the viewer saw the film's main protagonist, the reporter Jerry Thompson, obscured in shadows but firmly planted in the foreground of the frame.[90] Thompson is positioned very much in the film's present, even if he is "in the dark" regarding his investigation into the mysterious life and times of the recently deceased Charles Foster Kane.

Introduction   25

Meanwhile, Thompson's interview subject in this scene, Kane's erstwhile lover Susan Alexander, is well lit but positioned at some distance in the background, sitting quietly at a table weeping. But it was not the spatial distance between Thompson and Alexander that marked the significance of the deep focus or depth of field shot here, rather it was the temporal distance between Thompson, positioned very much in the narrative present of the film, and Alexander, lost in memories of the past, that rendered this a time-image. As Deleuze would put it, between Thompson and Alexander, foreground and background, "the unbridled depth is of time and no longer of space."[91]

In the context of the contemporary postcolonial city, what I call the "urban depth of field" is useful for theorizing the productive encounters between GH1s and GH2s, revealing how cities are shaped by forces that are near and far, where distance and proximity are no longer merely spatial but temporal. The depth becomes spatial because the "here" and "now" of the city, any city, is always structured by an "elsewhere," whether this elsewhere is near or far.[92] So the city is always about the distance (imagined or real) between the foreground, or the "immediate" sensory experiences of the city, and the background, that is, the distant infrastructures and logics, the invisible supply zones, markets and social relations that fueled the city's urban ecology.

But an urban depth of the field is also temporal in the sense that "elsewhere" isn't always a geographical or physical place. Sometimes it is a vivid memory that is collectively shared, sometimes it is lodged in the more distant past, already half-forgotten. Sometimes "elsewhere" is not in the past at all but belongs to the future, a distant one that may one day become more proximate. The point of the urban depth of field perspective is to bring these relations of distance and proximity into analytical view, and to define the city and its political life through this changing set of spatio-temporal relations. That is, the politics of the city is manifest in the ongoing mediations between near and far orders in everyday city life, mediations that become visible through an urban depth of field lens in which the depth or distance is both spatial and temporal at once. My cinematic approach allows me to theorize *Neo* Delhi as a *virtual* space and time that immanently critiques dogmatic ways of theorizing cities within the field of urban studies.

Neo Delhi

Thus what I call *Neo* Delhi is several things at once. First, it is the national capital territory (NCTD) and metropolitan region of an economically "rebirthed" India. That is, it spatially and symbolically represents an India that has incrementally shifted its postcolonial economy over the past three decades: from state-led development to state-mediated globality. As I will argue in Chapter 1, the post-economic reform state increasingly mediates between the domestic economy and the newly accessible "global" economy.[93] *Neo* Delhi is a useful place to deploy an urban depth of field analysis that looks at the inter-temporal space between existing discourses of "development" and incipient ones of

Figure 0.8 Panorama of Chakkarpur Village and surrounding areas, Gurgaon.
Source: Photo by author.

"globality." These contrasting discourses embody heterogeneous temporal logics that are rarely, if ever, treated in mainstream or critical urban studies. *Neo* Delhi is an apt entry point into a larger conversation that would likely include other Southern cities with complex pre-colonial, colonial and postcolonial pasts co-existing in the present, like Cairo, Hong Kong or Mexico City. For like these other large postcolonial cities *Neo* Delhi is not a singular entity but rather a multitude of times, spaces and urban experiences, each with their own rhythms and durations.

The NCTD is located in the north Indian gangetic plain, just south of the sloping foothills of the Himalayas. For centuries the triangular area between the Yamuna river to the east and the Aravalli hills to the west has served as a center for commerce and trade in the region. It has also long served as a political center. Before becoming the capital of independent India in 1947 New Delhi was made the capital of British India in 1911, and before that became the capital of the Mughal Empire in 1639. But even prior to this walled-city of Shahjahanabad, Delhi was the location of numerous ancient kingdoms and settlements. Remnants of some of these older sites are still discernable today.[94]

Compared with other Indian cities, *Neo* Delhi takes on a singular political and economic importance for merely contingent reasons. First, as India's political capital, its space both symbolically and materially "represents" the nation in ways that are unique, as I will show in Chapter 1. Second, Delhi is also an intellectual and artistic hub. It is home to dozens of colleges, universities and research institutes, national museums and performance arts spaces. This concentration of intellectual and artistic activity in Delhi results in the prodigious output of material *about* Delhi. I will treat some of this vast output in the chapters ahead. But Delhi is also much more than merely the sum of its images and representations. The whole metro area—which includes parts of Uttar Pradesh and Haryana—is a sprawling metropolitan region comprising more than twenty-four million residents, the largest urban agglomeration in India today and still growing (Table 0.1 outlines the population growth [1901–2011] in the NCTD alone). By some estimates, over the next two to three decades Delhi's National Capital Region (NCR) will surpass the Tokyo metropolitan region as the largest conurbation in the world.[95]

The name "New Delhi" officially refers to the central bureaucratic district of the world's largest democracy, as well as the diplomatic enclaves and consulates of foreign emissaries. The name "Delhi" refers to a Union Territory (i.e., National Capital Territory of Delhi—NCTD) that is akin to a city-state. This territory has its own level of government, but is complexly intertwined with higher national branches of federal government and local informal systems of power and authority at the neighborhood and street levels. Including New Delhi, this Indian union territory is spread out over some 570 square miles (for comparison's sake New York City—all five boroughs—adds up to around 300 square miles). This territory is relatively wealthy, having the third highest per capita income among India's twenty-eight states and four union territories.[96] But the NCTD is not evenly urbanized. Rather, conventionally "urbanized" lands are

28   *Introduction*

Table 0.1 Population of Delhi (Union Territory) 1901–2011

Year	Population	% variation since preceding decade
1901	405,819	–
1911	413,851	+1.98
1921	488,452	+18.03
1931	636,246	+30.26
1941	917,939	+44.27
1951	1,744,072	+90.00
1961	2,658,612	+52.44
1971	4,065,698	+52.93
1981	6,220,406	+53.00
1991	9,420,406	+51.45
2001	13,850,507	+47.02
2011	16,787,941	+21.21

Source: Government of National Capital Territory of Delhi, *Statistical Abstract of Delhi 2014* (Delhi: Directorate of Economics and Statistics, Delhi, 2014).

surrounded by vast open spaces, abandoned historical relics and ruins, preexisting agricultural villages and rustic farmhouses that serve to make up Delhi's patchy and parched terrain. The urban landscape includes planned and unplanned residential settlements, a sprawling military cantonment and international airport, national parks, diplomatic enclaves and government administrative spaces, corporate campuses, industrial zones and factories, parks and commuter hubs, street markets and underground economies and much more.

"Delhi" also refers to the even more spread out National Capital Region (NCR) that exceeds the boundaries of the union territory. The NCR includes the NCTD but also several additional ring towns located in the neighboring states of Haryana and Uttar Pradesh. Because of this territorial heterogeneity, multiple political institutions, operating according to different jurisdictions and scales of representation, different protocols and procedures, resource-allocations, governing intelligences and spatio-temporal logics, administer the Delhi metropolitan region. These institutions often work at cross-purposes, as we will see frequently in the chapters ahead.[97]

This book is not an exhaustive account of the metropolitan capital region. Rather, it is interested in the collection of parts and wholes at ascending and descending scales that make up a virtual city called *Neo* Delhi. This is a city that is an urban assemblage in Delanda's sense of the word, except that this assemblage is conceptualized not merely spatially but temporally, that is, through the concept of geohistorical difference. *Neo* Delhi shows how geohistorical difference mediates the distance between near and far orders at different spatio-temporal scales: between society and state, but also between private and public spheres, rich and poor, urban and rural, autonomous and regulated zones, spaces of development and spaces of globality. Thus the study foregrounds multiple scales of mediation within the Delhi conurbation—the urban, the neighborhood,

Introduction 29

the district, the enclave, the village—analyzing socio-spatial and temporal relations between different near and far orders at each scalar site/intervention. These relations in turn map a virtual city, one that is defined not by what it *is* or *is not* or *is not yet*, but by its potentiality.

The chapters that follow are composed cinematically, that is, as dynamic juxtapositions between near and far orders at different scales of changing urban life: they jump from the *urban* region of Delhi itself (Chapter 1) to the slum *neighborhood* of Shadipur in central Delhi (Chapter 2). These first two chapters comprise Part I. Part II cuts between the *district* of Gurgaon (Chapter 3), some of the private *enclave* spaces within it (Chapter 4) and an urbanized *village* called Chakkarpur (Chapter 5). Each scale of investigation and analysis thus stages urban mediations between higher-scale far orders and lower-scale near orders. To study these mediations I combine analytical tools and concepts from the literatures reviewed in this Introduction. The resulting studies are necessarily experimental, but collectively articulate a virtual city I call *Neo* Delhi.[98]

Conclusion

After returning to Delhi in 2008 following an absence of nearly a decade, I began to visit the city and region more frequently over the next several years as a researcher. But I remained haunted by the inadequacies of time, my limitations as a scholar, my geohistorical distance from the sensible milieus of Delhi and Gurgaon. The chapters that follow are experiments in studying cities that seem to defy disciplinary understanding. For this reason, augmenting the chapters ahead are a collection of artistic and ethnographic media interventions that can be engaged alongside the book at the website (www.neodelhi.net). This site contains videos, images, blog posts and commentaries that more or less follow the arguments and sites presented in the chapters. Collectively, they tour a virtual city whose online presence is both an extension of the analysis contained in this book and a contribution to Delhi's cultural archive.

Notes

1 David Campbell, *The Integrity of the Image: A World Press Photo Research Project* (Amsterdam: World Press Photo Academy, 2014).
2 Special thanks to Dr. Lorenzo Rinelli for stitching together these four images to create the virtual panorama of Delhi.
3 These images can be seen on the book's accompanying website, www.neodelhi.com. This website contains additional photographs, videos, commentaries, blog posts and music that are part of the multi-media assemblage I call *Neo* Delhi. In whatever small and probably insignificant way, I wanted to not merely study, but participate in changing urban life in Delhi from 2008 to 2015. The book's website documents from alternative perspectives many of the scenes of investigation opened up in the chapters ahead.
4 Michel de Certeau, *The Practice of Everyday Life* (Berkeley, CA: University of California Press, 1984), 92.
5 Ibid.

30   *Introduction*

6 Ibid.
7 Jacques Derrida, *Specters of Marx* (London: Routledge, 1994), 34.
8 De Certeau, *The Practice of Everyday Life*, 92.
9 Ibid.
10 For more on this "photomerge" feature, see, accessed September 23, 2014, https://helpx.adobe.com/photoshop/using/create-panoramic-images-photomerge.html.
11 Gilles Deleuze, *Cinema 2: The Time-Image* (Minneapolis, MN: University of Minnesota Press, 1989).
12 This website features videos, photographs, field notes and maps that augment the material presented in this text: www.neodelhi.net.
13 Mike Davis, *Planet of Slums* (New York: Verso, 2006), 1.
14 See Saskia Sassen, *Global Cities: New York, London, Tokyo* (Princeton, NJ: Princeton University Press, 2001) and Manuel Castells, *The Rise of Network Society: The Information Age: Economy, Society, and Culture* (London: Wiley Blackwell, 2011).
15 David Harvey, *Rebel Cities: From the Right to the City to the Urban Revolution* (London: Verso, 2012).
16 Davis, *Planet of Slums* and Janice Perlman, *Favela: Four Decades of Living on the Edge in Rio de Janeiro* (Oxford: Oxford University Press, 2010).
17 See James Ferguson, *Give a Man a Fish: Reflections on the New Politics of Distribution* (Durham, NC: Duke University Press, 2015).
18 See Vinay Gidwani and Amita Baviskar, "Urban commons." *Economic and Political Weekly* 46.50 (2011), 42–43.
19 David Harvey, *Spaces of Global Capitalism: Towards a Theory of Uneven Development* (London: Verso, 2006), 41–50.
20 Saskia Sassen-Koob, *New York City's Informal Economy*. ISSR Working Papers 4.9 (1988).
21 Jennifer Robinson, "Global and world cities: A view from off the map." *International Journal of Urban and Regional Research* 26.3 (2002), 536.
22 Aihwa Ong, *Neoliberalism as Exception: Mutations in Citizenship and Sovereignty* (Durham, NC: Duke University Press, 2006).
23 David Harvey, "Between space and time: Reflections on the geographical imagination." *Annals of the Association of American Geographers* 80.3 (1990), 428.
24 Neil Brenner, "Theses on urbanization." *Public Culture* 25.1 (2013), 102.
25 Neil Brenner, "What is critical urban theory?" *City* 13.2–3 (2009), 206.
26 See Louis Wirth, "Urbanism as a way of life." *American Journal of Sociology* 44:1 (1938), 1. Wirth famously defined the city as "a relatively large, dense and permanent settlement of socially heterogeneous individuals." In addition he defined urbanism as "a way of life" that was made possible by the city and its physical, social and ideological characteristics.
27 Michael Storper and Allen Scott, "Current debates in urban theory: A critical assessment." *Urban Studies* 53:6 (2016), 1119.
28 Ibid.
29 Ibid., 1116.
30 Ibid.
31 Ibid., 1118.
32 Ash Amin, "Regions unbound: Towards a new politics of place." *Geografiska Annaler: Series B, Human Geography* 86(1) (2004), 40.
33 Ibid., 33.
34 Ibid., 36.
35 Henri Lefebvre, *The Urban Revolution* (Minneapolis, MN: University of Minnesota Press, 2003 [1970]), 1.
36 Neil Brenner (ed.), *Implosions/Explosions: Towards a Study of Planetary Urbanization* (Berlin: Jovis, 2014).
37 Lefebvre, *The Urban Revolution*, 13.

Introduction 31

38 Doreen Massey, "Politics and space/time." *New Left Review* (1992), Online version.
39 Stuart Elden, "Between Marx and Heidegger: Politics, philosophy and Lefebvre's *The Production of Space.*" *Antipode* 36.1 (2004), 95.
40 Henri Lefebvre, *Writings on Cities* (Oxford: Blackwell, 1996), 101.
41 Ibid.
42 Henri Lefebvre, *The Production of Space* (Oxford: Blackwell, 1991 [1973]), 33.
43 Ibid.
44 Lefebvre, *Writings on Cities*, 101.
45 Elden, "Between Marx and Heidegger," 93.
46 Massey, "Politics and space/time."
47 Elden, "Between Marx and Heidegger," 92.
48 Massey, "Politics and space/time."
49 Ibid.
50 Ibid.
51 Ibid.
52 David Harvey, *The Urbanization of Capital: Studies in the History and Theory of Capitalist Development* (Baltimore, MD: Johns Hopkins University Press, 1985).
53 Ibid., 5.
54 Ibid., 11.
55 Harvey, *Rebel Cities.*
56 Brenner, "What is critical urban theory?" 198–207; Harvey, *The Urbanization of Capital, Spaces of Global Capitalism*, and *Rebel Cities.*
57 Jane M. Jacobs, "Urban geographies I: Still thinking cities relationally." *Progress in Human Geography* 36.3 (2012), 412–422.
58 Manuel Delanda, "Parameterising the social." *Architectural Design* 86.2 (2016), 124.
59 Ibid., 124.
60 Manuel Delanda, John Protevi and Torkild Thanem, "Deleuzian interrogations: A conversation with Manuel Delanda and John Protevi." *Tamara: Journal for Critical Organizational Inquiry* 3.4 (2005), 68.
61 Neil Leach, "The limits of urban simulation: An interview with Manuel Delanda." *Architectural Design* 79.4 (2009), 53.
62 Delanda, Protevi and Thanem, "Deleuzian interrogations," 68.
63 C. D. C. Reeve, *Aristotle: Politics* (Indianapolis, IN: Hackett, 1998).
64 Delanda, "Paramterising the social," 124.
65 Ignacio Farias, "The politics of urban assemblages." *City* 15.3–4 (2011), 370.
66 Ibid., 368–369.
67 Brenner, "Theses on urbanization," 92.
68 Farias, "The politics of urban assemblages," 371.
69 Ibid.
70 Amy Donahue and Rohan Kalyan, "Introduction: On the imperative, challenges, and prospects of decolonizing comparative methodologies." *Comparative and Continental Philosophy* 7:2 (2015), 124–137.
71 Ibid.
72 Sankaran Krishna, *Globalization and Postcolonialism: Hegemony and Resistance in the Twenty-First Century* (New York: Rowman & Littlefield, 2009), 7–30.
73 Dipesh Chakrabarty, *Provincializing Europe: Postcolonial Thought and Historical Difference* (Princeton, NJ: Princeton University Press, 2000).
74 David McLellan (ed.), "The Communist Manifesto," in *Karl Marx: Selected Writings* (Oxford: Oxford University Press, 2001), 245–272.
75 Chakrabarty, *Provincializing Europe*, 63.
76 Ibid., 64.
77 Ibid.
78 Ibid., 6.
79 Ibid., 7.

32 Introduction

80 Ibid.
81 Robinson, "Global and world cities," 531.
82 Eric Sheppard, Helga Leitner and Anant Maringanti, "Provincializing global urbanism: A manifesto." *Urban Geography* 34.7 (2013), 895.
83 Ibid., 896.
84 Robinson, "Global and world cities."
85 Gilles Deleuze, *Difference and Repetition* (New York: Columbia University Press, 1994).
86 Gilles Deleuze and Felix Guattari, *What Is Philosophy?* (New York: Columbia University Press, 1994), 26.
87 Jean-Louis Comolli, "Technique and ideology: Camera, perspective, depth of field." *Narrative, Apparatus, Ideology* (1986): 421–443.
88 Michael J. Shapiro, "Towards a politics of now-time," in *Cinematic Political Thought* (New York: NYU Press, 1999), 10–38. See also Walter Benjamin, *The Arcades Project* (Cambridge, MA: Harvard University Press, 2002).
89 Deleuze, *Cinema 2*, 105.
90 See www.neodelhi.net/blog/ to view a still from this motion picture.
91 Deleuze, *Cinema 2*, 108.
92 Jane Jacobs, *Cities and the Wealth of Nations: Principles of Economic Life* (New York: Vintage Press, 1985), 59–71.
93 See Himadeep Muppidi, *The Politics of the Global* (Minneapolis, MN: University of Minnesota Press, 2004).
94 Romila Thapar, "Rambling through some of the pasts of Delhi," in Romi Khosla (ed.) *The Idea of Delhi* (Mumbai: Marg Publications, 2005), 22–31.
95 Gerhard Heilig, *World Urbanization Prospects: 2014 Revision* (New York: United Nations Department of Economic and Social Affairs, 2014), 5.
96 EPW Research Foundation, *India: A Pocket Book of Data Series 2012* (New Delhi: Academic Foundation, 2012).
97 Sheila Dixit, "Government of National Capital Territory of Delhi Speech of Smt. Sheila Dikshit, Chief Minister, Delhi at National Development Council Meeting," December 9, 2006 in New Delhi.
98 See for instance, Ahmed Kanna, *Dubai: The City as Corporation* (Minneapolis, MN: University of Minnesota Press, 2011). See also Gyan Prakash, *Mumbai Fables: A History of an Enchanted City* (Princeton, NJ: Princeton University Press, 2010). See also Abdoumaliq Simone, *City Life from Jakarta to Dakar: Movements at the Crossroads* (London: Routledge, 2010).

Bibliography

Amin, Ash. "Regions unbound: Towards a new politics of place." *Geografiska Annaler: Series B, Human Geography* 86.1 (2004): 33–44.
Benjamin, Walter. *The Arcades Project*. Cambridge, MA: Harvard University Press, 2002.
Brenner, Neil. "What is critical urban theory?" *City* 13.2–3 (2009): 198–207.
Brenner, Neil "Theses on urbanization." *Public Culture* 25.1 (2013): 85–114.
Brenner, Neil (ed.) *Implosions/Explosions: Towards a Study of Planetary Urbanization*. Berlin: Jovis, 2014.
Campbell, David. *The Integrity of the Image: A World Press Photo Research Project*. Amsterdam: World Press Photo Academy, 2014.
Castells, Manuel. *The Rise of Network Society: The Information Age: Economy, Society, and Culture*. London: Wiley Blackwell, 2011.
Chakrabarty, Dipesh. *Provincializing Europe: Postcolonial Thought and Historical Difference*. Princeton, NJ: Princeton University Press, 2000.

Comolli, Jean-Louis. "Technique and ideology: Camera, perspective, depth of field," in Philip Rosen (ed.) *Narrative, Apparatus, Ideology*. New York: Columbia University Press, 1986: 421–443.

Davis, Mike. *Planet of Slums*. New York: Verso, 2006.

de Certeau, Michel. *The Practice of Everyday Life*. Berkeley, CA: University of California Press, 1984.

Delanda, Manuel. "Parameterising the social." *Architectural Design* 86.2 (2016): 124–127.

Delanda, Manuel, John Protevi and Torkild Thanem. "Deleuzian interrogations: A conversation with Manuel Delanda and John Protevi." *Tamara: Journal for Critical Organizational Inquiry* 3.4 (2005): 65–88.

Deleuze, Gilles. *Cinema 2: The Time-Image*. Minneapolis, MN: University of Minnesota Press, 1989.

Deleuze, Gilles. *Difference and Repetition*. New York: Columbia University Press, 1994.

Deleuze, Gilles and Felix Guattari. *What Is Philosophy?* New York: Columbia University Press, 1994.

Derrida, Jacques. *Specters of Marx*. London: Routledge, 1994.

Dixit, Sheila. "Government of National Capital Territory of Delhi Speech of Smt. Sheila Dikshit, Chief Minister, Delhi at National Development Council Meeting," December 9, 2006, New Delhi, India.

Donahue, Amy and Rohan Kalyan. "Introduction: On the imperative, challenges, and prospects of decolonizing comparative methodologies." *Comparative and Continental Philosophy* 7:2 (2015): 124–137.

Elden, Stuart. "Between Marx and Heidegger: Politics, philosophy and Lefebvre's *The Production of Space*." *Antipode* 36.1 (2004): 86–105.

EPW Research Foundation, *India: A Pocket Book of Data Series 2012* (New Delhi: Academic Foundation, 2012).

Farias, Ignacio. "The politics of urban assemblages." *City* 15.3–4 (2011): 365–374.

Ferguson, James. *Give a Man a Fish: Reflections on the New Politics of Distribution*. Durham, NC: Duke University Press, 2015.

Gidwani, Vinay and Amita Baviskar. "Urban commons." *Economic and Political Weekly* 46.50 (2011), 42–43.

Harvey, David. *The Urbanization of Capital: Studies in the History and Theory of Capitalist Development*. Baltimore, MD: Johns Hopkins University Press, 1985.

Harvey, David. "Between space and time: Reflections on the geographical imagination." *Annals of the Association of American Geographers* 80.3 (1990): 418–434.

Harvey, David. *Spaces of Global Capitalism: Towards a Theory of Uneven Development*. London: Verso, 2006.

Harvey, David. *Rebel Cities: From the Right to the City to the Urban Revolution*. London: Verso, 2012.

Heilig, Gerhard. *World Urbanization Prospects: 2014 Revision*. New York: United Nations Department of Economic and Social Affairs, 2014.

Jacobs, Jane. *Cities and the Wealth of Nations: Principles of Economic Life*. New York: Vintage Press, 1985.

Jacobs, Jane M. "Urban geographies I: Still thinking cities relationally." *Progress in Human Geography* 36.3 (2012): 412–422.

Kanna, Ahmed. *Dubai: The City as Corporation*. Minneapolis, MN: University of Minnesota Press, 2011.

Krishna, Sankaran. *Globalization and Postcolonialism: Hegemony and Resistance in the Twenty-First Century*. New York: Rowman & Littlefield, 2009.

34   *Introduction*

Leach, Neil. "The limits of urban simulation: An interview with Manuel Delanda." *Architectural Design* 79.4 (2009): 50–55.

Lefebvre, Henri. *The Production of Space*. Oxford: Blackwell, 1991.

Lefebvre, Henri. *Writings on Cities*. Oxford: Blackwell, 1996.

Lefebvre, Henri. *The Urban Revolution*. Minneapolis, MN: University of Minnesota Press, 2003.

McLellan, David (ed.) "The Communist Manifesto," in *Karl Marx: Selected Writings*. Oxford: Oxford University Press, 2001: 245–272.

Massey, Doreen. "Politics and space/time." *New Left Review* (1992). Online Version.

Muppidi, Himadeep. *The Politics of the Global*. Minneapolis, MN: University of Minnesota Press, 2004.

Ong, Aihwa. *Neoliberalism as Exception: Mutations in Citizenship and Sovereignty*. Durham, NC: Duke University Press, 2006.

Perlman, Janice. *Favela: Four Decades of Living on the Edge in Rio de Janeiro*. Oxford: Oxford University Press, 2010.

Prakash, Gyan. *Mumbai Fables: A History of an Enchanted City*. Princeton, NJ: Princeton University Press, 2010.

Ranciere, Jacques. *Film Fables*. Oxford: Berg Publishers, 2006.

Reeve, C. D. C. *Aristotle: Politics*. Indianapolis, IN: Hackett, 1998.

Robinson, Jennifer. "Global and world cities: A view from off the map." *International Journal of Urban and Regional Research* 26.3 (2002): 531–554.

Sassen-Koob, Saskia. *New York City's Informal Economy*. ISSR Working Papers 4.9 (1988).

Sassen, Saskia. *Global Cities: New York, London, Tokyo*. Princeton, NJ: Princeton University Press, 2001.

Shapiro, Michael J. "Towards a politics of now-time," in *Cinematic Political Thought*. New York: NYU Press, 1999: 10–38.

Sheppard, Eric, Helga Leitner and Anant Maringanti. "Provincializing global urbanism: A manifesto." *Urban Geography* 34.7 (2013): 893–900.

Simone, Abdoumaliq. *City Life from Jakarta to Dakar: Movements at the Crossroads*. London: Routledge, 2010.

Storper, Michael and Allen Scott. "Current debates in urban theory: A critical assessment." *Urban Studies* 53:6 (2016): 1523–1541.

Thapar, Romila. "Rambling through some of the pasts of Delhi," in Romi Khosla (ed.) *The Idea of Delhi*. Mumbai: Marg Publications, 2005: 22–31.

Wirth, Louis. "Urbanism as a way of life." *American Journal of Sociology* 44:1 (1938): 1–24.

Part I

Distance and proximity in Delhi

> Before beginning Part I: Distance and proximity in Delhi, the reader is encouraged to watch the short essay film *Letter to the City Yet to Come* (11 min). Directed by Gorav Kalyan and Rohan Kalyan and originally screened in 2015, the film offers a contemplative space for reflection on the rapid changes taking place in the capital city. To view the film, visit: www.neodelhi.net/videos/.

In December 2012, during a trip to the field in central Delhi, I was pickpocketed by a magician. It happened so fast that I didn't even recognize what was going on at the time. My eyes and ears were not equipped to interpret the event as it unfolded. And because, as Lee Siegel reminds us, "any object becomes invisible when no one's looking at it," the thief pulled off the ultimate conjuring trick.[1] I didn't even know I got ripped off.

It happened during a journey into Paharganj, the pre-colonial *mohalla* (neighborhood) located just west of the New Delhi Railway Station.[2] My brother and I were there to shoot documentary footage of street life in this notoriously seedy, but lively and rambunctious neighborhood. As we traversed a crowded bazaar that afternoon I accidentally stepped on a young man's foot. He in turn grabbed the back of my shirt as I passed him by and yanked me backwards, violently knocking me out of my rhythm and bringing me face to face with him. He pointed down emphatically at his violated foot, yelling and demanding an apology. I can distinctly remember looking down at his worn out rubber sandals and dusty toes, immediately juxtaposed with my running shoes, the latter embarrassingly clean and white. I said in the most austere Hindi I could muster: *Mujhe maaf ki jiye*. I am very sorry. But this wasn't enough. He raised his hand high above his head, as if getting ready to strike a blow. His other hand was still clenching my shirt. I can remember looking up at his open palm as I braced myself for the hit.

Meanwhile, in the back of my mind I was wondering: why is this guy so mad? This was a crowded pedestrian thoroughfare in one of the busier markets of the neighborhood. Surely people were bumping into each other all of the time, stepping on toes and sandals, shouldering past anonymous passersby. None of this was intentional. Why wouldn't this young man accept my apology?

36 *Distance and proximity in Delhi*

Survival instinct kicked in. I took a step away from him, hoping to put some distance between the two of us and let the situation calm down. He continued to glare at me, although I might have now noticed a sly grin. I can still clearly recall his eyes, bloodshot and piercing. I looked in my brother's direction. He was about ten feet ahead of me in the market, but facing the other way and busy interacting with a nearby shopkeeper. When I turned back toward my antagonist I was surprised to learn that he was already gone, quickly dissolving into the crowded street market.

I stood staring, dumbfounded. My brother walked up to me and asked, "What happened? What did that guy want?"

"I have no clue," I responded.

We turned and kept moving in the direction we had started on that afternoon. We had been navigating this old neighborhood with my smart phone, or more precisely, Google Maps.[3] We were searching for a central intersection in Paharganj where we could shoot the mélange of cars, bicycles, three-wheelers, pedestrians, cows and other actors jostling for space and recognition in the street. The premise of our collaborative documentary, entitled *Letter to the City Yet to Come*, was that of a cinematic time capsule of the city, featuring a collection of love letters written and read out loud by present-day residents of Delhi.[4] These individuals wrote letters addressed to loved ones in the city's future, telling them about the city as it was in the present. The narrations would be anonymous, with voices played over scenes of changing urban life, as if they belonged to the intersubjective voice of the city and not to any one individual. In the distance between audio and visual landscapes, our film would present an image of thought that was difficult, if not impossible, to render in traditional academic discourse. This was an image of thought that would be essentially temporal, a time-image[5] of a postcolonial megacity of more than twenty million.

But changing urban life is itself unpredictable. And as it happened, we ended up landing in New Delhi to begin shooting our film just days after news broke of the shocking, ultra-violent rape of a young woman by a gang of young men in the capital. The victims and the assailants were all in their early-twenties or thirties, with the exception of the youngest of the gang, who was determined to be a juvenile at seventeen. The men had tricked the woman and her male companion into a nightmarish ride through south Delhi on a privately owned and operated bus. The violence was enacted while the vehicle was still on the move. The couple was eventually dumped on the side of the road: battered, bruised and naked. The young woman, brutalized with an iron rod, succumbed to her injuries a few weeks later.[6]

The event cast an ominous shadow on the National Capital Region of Delhi and the nation more generally. It reinforced the idea of Delhi as an unloved and unloving city, violent and unforgiving.[7] For a diasporic researcher and filmmaker interacting with people in the dark days following the event, the macabre violence was all anyone could seem to talk about. The publicized brutality of the gang rape forced people to imagine the worst of what young urbanized men were capable of doing under the influence of untimely spirits and sadistic masculinity.

Distance and proximity in Delhi 37

Quite indirectly, this tension cut across the urban encounter I found myself embroiled in that afternoon in Paharganj, with another young urbanized man. Afterwards, his bloodshot eyes remained salient in my memory, even as I attempted to remember my own privilege and mobility in this encounter.

My brother and I had walked a full 100 yards away from that brief but torrid confrontation when I reached for my smart phone. I wanted to check the map to determine where we were. I reached into my front pocket. My phone wasn't there. I checked the other pocket. I stopped walking, now checking other possible locations: my jacket, the sound equipment bag, my brother's things; it was nowhere to be found. Then it hit me: the angry young man had stolen it right before my very eyes.

I sprinted back to where the encounter had taken place. I looked around, albeit with a different gaze than before, now scanning for each and every corner someone might possibly hide, every nook and cranny in the vicinity. I looked into the alleys, underneath stairways and balconies. I asked several shopkeepers if they saw someone running through the street. I described the pickpocket. All I could remember was that he was intense, wiry, perhaps in his mid-twenties, with red eyes. My brother and I walked around the area for a good twenty minutes, waiting in vain for the man to come back, for something to happen. But we knew he wouldn't return. Why would someone who was smart enough to steal a man's phone right in front of him return to the scene of the crime?

In addition to shooting the documentary that winter with my brother, I had also come to Delhi to continue my own field research on changing urban life in and around the metro region. These studies will be presented in the chapters ahead: two chapters on Delhi proper and three on the elite suburb of Gurgaon in the southwest corner of the NCR. In the event described above, however, I quickly became very much a *part* of the changing life I was in Delhi to research. But I was also quite clearly *apart* from this life. For there was a profound gulf that separated me from my assailant. And the unbridled distance was not merely spatial, it was also deeply temporal. I will argue in the pages ahead that this temporal depth of field that opened up between us was specifically urban. More, it was what set the scene for the pickpocket magician's skillful performance. For I had come to Delhi and Paharganj from "the West" (more specifically Honolulu, Hawaii), that is, from far away. But at our shared moment of encounter we came into close physical and spatial proximity, even direct contact—his one hand was on me throughout the ordeal, even as the other was raised high above as if poised to strike a blow. Yet I did not then understand the nature of the encounter. My proprioception, my body's sense of itself, was momentarily altered by the physicality of the encounter, which the young man had dominated from the outset.[8] I was distracted not only by the clamor of the bustling market, a foreign domain for me even if I came to the city as a returning researcher, but also by my own fear, that is, my own subjectivity.[9] In the encounter with the young man with the bloodshot eyes, the spatial environment around us grew strangely distant and cacophonous. It was a muddle of far-off voices and sounds, discordant and discombobulated. At this temporal distance, the pickpocket operated with efficiency

38 *Distance and proximity in Delhi*

and prowess, while the "researcher" was too distracted and blinded by the encounter itself. This corporeal displacement, this proximate distance, made me a *part* of—yet *apart* from—this specifically urban encounter.

Two minutes later I would return to the very same spot with a different set of eyes, a different body, one that was more discerning and reactive than before. It was a body that was prepared for action, in contrast to my prior paralysis. But what caused my inattentiveness during the event itself? What was it that inhibited any purposeful action? I came to the encounter from a distant geohistorical space, from a "far order," to invoke the terminology of urban theorist Henri Lefebvre, even if I was only an ambiguous "Westerner" (an Indian-American) from an ambiguously Western place (Hawaii).[10] My presence was thus underwritten by a certain kind of discernable absence, or a spatio-temporal distance. This was surely noticed by the pickpocket magician. This was, in fact, his urban *metis*.[11] Isn't it a minimum requirement for successful magicians and pickpockets alike to be able to target the most gullible in the crowd? To somehow know who are most distant in their very presence?

For my part, I had been performing urban research in and around Delhi intermittently since 2008 as a doctoral student. This "expertise" included visual ethnography, archival research, expert and ordinary life interviews, participant observation and experimental, cinematic explorations of changing urban life. While I had conducted research in several different parts of Delhi, this specific neighborhood of Paharganj, its people, places and their relations were foreign to me, just as I was foreign to them. Isn't it a minimum requirement of the transnational researcher to mediate this distance and proximity, to somehow transform it into academic knowledge? My relative distance from this place embodied paradoxically the very signs of my disciplinary access and privilege. It was a research methodology in its own right. As an urban researcher I could travel all the way from Honolulu to Newark to New Delhi to immerse myself for a limited period of time and study this city because I promised to reproduce a distant, dispassionate, detached analysis of the subject matter for my home audience. In some ways, the camera, audio-recorder and ethnographic notebook were there to reproduce this distance, this "objectivity," even at close proximity. As the anthropologist Johannes Fabian once observed, this distance was temporal more than it was spatial.[12]

But if modern ethnography was historically structured through modes of temporal distancing, perhaps I could mediate this geohistorical distance differently. I would attempt to gain access to what Lefebvre once called "the near order" of the modern city, its everyday life and its heterogeneous, inter-active rhythms.[13] Yet this near order was animated by rhythms I could not see and forces I could not feel until it was too late, precisely because I was at once immersed and entangled in these rhythms, yet still foreign, still distant, still off tempo. This urban arrhythmia too was part of the specificity of the city. And here came the near order—so close that it was practically invisible, so in my face that it was hidden in plain sight—robbing the supposedly enlightened and critically inflected far order in a scornful act of Fanonian revenge.[14] That afternoon my critical faculties were mimicked and mocked by the pickpocket magician.[15]

Distance and proximity in Delhi   39

Pickpockets in Delhi are practitioners of an everyday craft and socio-material practice that is difficult to describe without some recourse to a concept of magic. Such a characterization is not meant to reproduce the orientalist gaze that unproblematically associates India with magic and superstition (see Chapter 2 for more on this). Rather these pickpockets skillfully use proximity and distance to produce illusions and hidden realities in everyday life. These everyday, tactical mediations allow the magician to operate and survive in the midst of violent and precarious and always changing urban environments. Where conjurers stage their magic through clever misdirection and imperceptible sleight-of-hand, urban magicians use the very same skill and *metis* to pick the pockets of unsuspecting urban dwellers, who are often "elsewhere" and absent even when they physically cohabit the same space. But why limit such interpretive *metis* to thieves and thievery alone? Diverse urban actors perform similar types of everyday magic, such as when hawkers and street hustlers make their presence known to potential customers but remain invisible to authorities. Or at a bigger scale, when development agencies and land brokers speculate on the future of a piece of property, conjuring a future that doesn't yet exist. These urban subjects productively use the distractions, fears and desires of others, and invisibly subvert and appropriate the social forces that animate the city. They of necessity see the urban as the scholarly researcher only dreams she or he might. Thus I can only imagine the encounter from the pickpocket's eyes. He chose me because I was already distant, dressed in foreign brands, glancing profusely at my smart phone (admittedly not a smart look for an urban researcher), trying to locate via satellite map. I was an easy target. I had loose fitting pants with open pockets. Once my phone was reinserted into either one and I came into spatial proximity of the young man it wouldn't be hard for him to swipe it. He could just use a bit of misdirection, stare daggers into my eyes, and it would be over before long. He might have even taken a swig of liquor or smoked a courage-laced *bidi* before embarking on the mission. Who knows?

But before he could execute his plan, there was one final obstacle to overcome. The target, this apparent visitor who was carelessly brandishing an expensive phone in a busy open-air market, was not alone. Someone else (my brother) accompanied him as he was walking through the neighborhood. How to distract the both of them? Just like any self-respecting magician, the pickpocket had an assistant. My brother and I only realized this fact later that evening, as we recalled the incident to some friends. Just as my brother noticed that I was embroiled in some sort of confrontation, a small boy—no more than 8–10 years old—ran up to him and asked, *Bhaya, time kya hai?* What time is it? This was why my brother was turned toward the nearby shopkeeper as my encounter with the young man was unfolding. He was asking the shopkeeper for the time. My brother too was distracted, just like I was by the raised hand above me that seemed ready to come down as a swift blow to my face. But the potential slap was just a diversion. It was designed to make me look up as the pickpocket quickly traced his other hand—the one that began the encounter by grabbing my shirt and yanking me backwards—down toward my pocket,

40 *Distance and proximity in Delhi*

subtly—nay, invisibly—slipping his fingers inside and pulling the rabbit out of the hat. The young man and the kid were a team, and both creatively employed deception and misdirection to produce the sensorial effects they required to pull off their heist.

But again, it is not just street hustlers and their sidekicks who cunningly use *metis* and misdirection to socially survive and negotiate the modern city. As we will see in the chapters ahead, powerful and distant institutions like state development agencies, real estate lobbies, wealthy landlords and speculators, each in their own ways, misdirect someone in order to make a (temporal) space for something to happen: clearing the way for a property deal or a slum re-development project, or even conjuring a "world-class" city from scratch. As I show in the chapters that follow, postcolonial urbanism unfolds unevenly at the interstices of historically distant near and far orders. The city opens opportunities for a range of possible actions within an urban depth of field that emerges between what is perceived as being near and far, past or present or future. These mediations of distance and proximity empower certain kinds of agency while foreclosing others, as we will see. As an image of thought the politics of the postcolonial city crystallizes at these moments of proximate distance and distant proximity, where distance and proximity must be thought of as simultaneously spatial and temporal. As the encounter with the pickpocket magician shows, the far order is powerful and abstract, distancing and objective/objectifying, but it does not unambiguously dominate the near order, for the latter subordinates the former through mediations. I learned this at my own expense that afternoon in Paharganj.

At a party later that evening hosted by a wealthy ex-pat who had lived in Delhi for the last two decades, I was surrounded by other privileged and enlightened, yet also similarly distant (mostly "native" Indian) urban dwellers. I recounted the story of the magician who had pickpocketed me earlier that day. Some wondered, perhaps recalling the horrors of the recent gang rape, why didn't I call the police afterward? Why didn't I report the incident? It was not good to let pickpockets and other criminals go unpunished, they argued. I replied with something vague and unsatisfactory, something to the effect of: I got what I deserved. The young man outsmarted me. I conceded defeat. In the encounter between the pickpocket and me, the former had handily won. In any case, I could always acquire another phone to replace the one I had lost. I came, after all, from the far order. Besides, even if I did report the crime, I wanted to tell these empathetic elites at this party, even if I informed the far order and enlisted the disciplinary apparatus of the police state, what were the chances of anyone actually finding the young man with the bloodshot eyes? He was practically invisible to the state. That was a condition of his very existence. There were hundreds or thousands of people just like him in the undifferentiated mass of the near order. Far order types like us would never see those same eyes again. Not in any recognizable form.

I wanted to tell them this but I realized that even this explanation was unsatisfactory. Like me these people at the party were privileged and temporally distant from the likes of the pickpocket magician and his young assistant. But unlike me they still all had to co-exist in their everyday lives in the city, when they

Distance and proximity in Delhi 41

commuted to work, went out to eat or bought something from the market, or at home when they interacted with their domestic servants or gardeners or care takers. Perhaps my explanation was inadequate because it assumed a key condition of possibility for "urban" knowledge production on my part: that I could always leave this near order and return to my far order, far away from those bloodshot eyes and the violence of the postcolonial city, and write this.

Notes

1 The scholar of Indian philosophy and religion Lee Siegel is quoted in Vivek Gupta, "Interview: New film documents removal of Kathputli Artists' Colony in New Delhi." *Asia Society*, June 20, 2012, accessed February 8, 2013, http://asiasociety.org/blog/asia/interview-new-film-documents-removal-kathputli-artists-colony-new-delhi.
2 Paharganj is positioned just west of Ajmeri Gate, which connects this four-century-old neighborhood to Old Delhi, or Shahjahanabad. Historically a major wholesale market for grains and later cloth and other merchandise, today it comprises a heady mix of small-scale industrial, criminal, hippie, low-end tourist and other sundry elements. Perhaps more than any other neighborhood in Delhi, Paharganj contains an inordinate amount of bars, restaurants, hotels and underground establishments.
3 Google Maps is a web mapping service developed by Google. It offers satellite imagery, street maps, 360 degree panoramic views of streets, real-time traffic conditions and route planning for traveling by foot, car, bicycle or public transportation.
4 *Letter to the City Yet to Come* (Nonetheless Productions, 2015) can be viewed here, https://vimeo.com/123004044 (password: cytc). The film was directed and produced by Gorav Kalyan and Rohan Kalyan and was shot in New Delhi from December 2012 to January 2013.
5 The time-image is a wide-ranging term developed by Gilles Deleuze in his *Cinema 2: The Time-Image* (Minneapolis, MN: University of Minnesota Press, 1989). I develop the concept in the context of Delhi in the Introduction and the four substantive chapters ahead.
6 For more on this case, including its gruesome details, see, accessed December 24, 2015, https://en.wikipedia.org/wiki/2012_Delhi_gang_rape.
7 See the introductory essay entitled "The alchemy of an unloved city" (pp. 15–25) in the volume co-edited by Emma Tarlo, Veronique Dupont and Denis Vidal entitled *Delhi: Urban Space and Human Destinies* (Delhi: Manohar Publications, 2000).
8 See Brian Massumi, *Parables for the Virtual: Movement, Affect, Sensation* (Durham, NC: Duke University Press, 2002), 58–61.
9 See Alain Badiou in his *Rhapsody for the Theater* (New York: Verso Books, 2013) for more on the relationship between fear, courage and subjectivity.
10 For those interested in learning about Hawaii's colonial history, https://vimeo.com/130719245.
11 In Chapter 2 I develop this idea of *metis* in Delhi in more detail.
12 See Johannes Fabian's *Time and the Other: How Anthropology Makes its Object* (New York: Columbia University Press, 1983).
13 Lefebvre develops a theory and praxis of rhythmanalysis in his book *Rhythmanalysis: Space, Time and Everyday Life* (New York: Bloomsbury Publishing, 2013). For Lefebvre, "everywhere where there is interaction between a place, a time, and an expenditure of energy, there is rhythm" (p. 15). For a final auto-cinemagraphic reference, see my experimental music video, *Delhi in Movement* (2010), which maps the city's heterogeneous vectors of mobility and motility through an audio-visual rhythmanalysis of different modes of transportation in disparate parts of the city. It can be viewed here, https://vimeo.com/16778056.

42 *Distance and proximity in Delhi*

14 Frantz Fanon, *The Wretched of the Earth* (New York: Grove Press, 1963).
15 Homi Bhabha, "Of mimicry and man: The ambivalence of colonial discourse." *October* 28 (1984), 125–133.

Bibliography

Badiou, Alain. *Rhapsody for the Theater*. New York: Verso Books, 2013.

Bhabha, Homi. "Of mimicry and man: The ambivalence of colonial discourse." *October* 28 (1984): 125–133.

Deleuze, Gilles. *Cinema 2: The Time-Image*. Minneapolis, MN: University of Minnesota Press, 1989.

Fabian, Johannes. *Time and the Other: How Anthropology Makes its Object*. New York: Columbia University Press, 1983.

Fanon, Frantz. *The Wretched of the Earth*. New York: Grove Press, 1963.

Gupta, Vivek. "Interview: New film documents removal of Kathputli Artists' Colony in New Delhi." *Asia Society*, June 20, 2012, accessed February 8, 2013, http://asiasociety.org/blog/asia/interview-new-film-documents-removal-kathputli-artists-colony-new-delhi.

Lefebvre, Henri. *Rhythmanalysis: Space, Time and Everyday Life*. New York: Bloomsbury Publishing, 2013.

Massumi, Brian. *Parables for the Virtual: Movement, Affect, Sensation*. Durham, NC: Duke University Press, 2002.

Tarlo, Emma, Veronique Dupont and Denis Vidal. *Delhi: Urban Space and Human Destinies*. Delhi: Manohar Publications, 2000.

1   The urban

> This dual significance of desire—that it can arise only at a distance from objects, a distance that it attempts to overcome, and yet that it presupposes a closeness between the objects and ourselves in order that the distance should be experienced at all.
>
> Georg Simmel, *The Philosophy of Money*

The Commonwealth Games

In November 2003, New Delhi beat out Hamilton, Canada to host the 2010 Commonwealth Games (CWG), an international sporting competition involving the various fragments of the former British Empire.[1] At the Commonwealth Federation General Assembly meeting held in Montego Bay, Jamaica, India won forty-six votes to Canada's twenty-two in a secret ballot cast by delegations from member nations. The Indian capital became just the second Asian city to get the opportunity to host the event in its seventy-year history. "The people felt it was high time India got the Games," Indian Olympic Association president Suresh Kalmadi, who led the Indian delegation, told reporters following the announcement.[2]

Like other large world cities in recent decades New Delhi's local state and national governments approached hosting the CWG as an opportune time to re-brand the capital as a "global city" with "world class" infrastructure.[3] This came on the heels of two decisive "turns" in Indian national policy and political culture over the preceding quarter century. First, there was the economic turn toward "neoliberal" reform, broadly designed to optimize the "private sector" and government institutions at different scales to compete for capital investment. Such foreign and private capital was needed, the neoliberals argued, in order to boost economic development and growth.[4] Second, accompanying this "turn" toward economic reform, beginning haltingly in the mid-1980s and incrementally thereafter, was a corresponding "urban turn."[5] Beginning in the 1990s, almost directly after the federal government's announcement of "big bang" economic reforms that introduced privatization, de-centralization and de-regulation as structuring principles for the "liberalized" Indian economy, cities were correspondingly seen by the state, big business and civil society alike as alluring destination points for capital investment.

44   *Distance and proximity in Delhi*

While the official "turns" toward economic and urban reform were by no means unique to India in the final decades of the twentieth century, what is notable about the Indian context is the extent to which the turns represented a larger shift in the role of private capital within the domestic economy. The economic reforms of the 1990s and 2000s reversed decades of official skepticism toward the power of private business and outward reliance on international capital to finance centrally coordinated economic development. This state-led ideological distancing from especially "foreign" private capital informed the Nehruvian-era policy of import-substitution industrialization and state-led economic planning within the political economy of the 1950s and 1960s. This was quasi-socialism, since there was also space for private capital to exist and in some instances thrive in the state-led developmentalist machine. Thus private capital's class-based interests were often times subordinated to those of the hegemonic developmentalist state, but they were never wholly absent.[6]

Similarly, the state's urban turn revised its historical diffidence toward large cities as potential sites of targeted economic development. From the early decades of independence until the 1990s, India's largest cities were nearly invisible in central planning discourses, as rural development garnered a much larger portion of the state's ideological attention.[7] But following India's urban turn its cities were seen as vital "bridges" between the domestic economy and the global economy which needed to be strengthened. Cities were to attract the capital that would fuel the economic growth of the country.

A series of national-level political interventions orchestrated this urban *qua* economic "turn," including two key constitutional amendments (the Ninety-Third and the Ninety-Fourth Amendments), a new national urban policy aimed at incentivizing private investment in infrastructure, and new laws passed in the mid-2000s that opened up industries like real estate and construction to foreign investment and "global" competition.[8] This new policy infrastructure was designed to push cities to compete with each other nationally and internationally, to become more entrepreneurial, innovative and dynamic. In this new dispensation, cities and their urban spaces were poised to *mediate* between domestic and global economies, translating each into the idiom of the other. My interest is not so much in the policy debates and inter-institutional politics that informed these laws and national level urban reforms, nor is it to explore more specifically the political economy of policy mobilities in transnational cities like *Neo* Delhi, although such an undertaking would be informative and worth the effort. Rather, I take such shifts for granted and note the rapid increase in foreign direct investment coming after the 2005 loosening of restrictions on foreign capital in certain sectors of the economy (Table 1.1). The reason this is noteworthy for this study is that many of the sectors that experienced "market liberalization" in 2005 were directly tied to urbanization, including construction and real estate industries.

The 2010 CWG in Delhi provided an opportunity to showcase the results of this decisive urban *qua* economic *qua* global turn in India's frenetic capital city, which itself had been the site of dramatic spatial transformations in the run-up to

Table 1.1 Foreign direct investment: financial year-wise equity inflows between April 2000 and February 2011

Year	Equity inflow (in billion U.S.$)
2000–2001	2.3
2001–2002	3.9
2002–2003	2.6
2003–2004	2.2
2004–2005	3.3
2005–2006	5.5
2006–2007	15.6
2007–2008	24.6
2008–2009	27.3
2009–2010	25.6
2010–2011	18.4

Source: Data is from Department of Industrial Policy & Promotion, Ministry of Commerce & Industry, Government of India: http://dipp.nic.in/fdi_statistics/india_fdiiindex.htm (accessed June 22, 2016).

the 1982 Asian Games, and was poised to repeat the latter's supposed success. Hosting the Games was a chance not just to bring civic and national pride to Delhi and "shine a global spotlight" on India more generally, as some fairly prominent commentators noted, but simultaneously a chance to "fast track" and accelerate infrastructure development throughout the National Capital Region.[9] These improvements would help further cement Delhi's status as the post-colonial state's prime mediator between national and global economies.

In the wake of the public announcement at Montego Bay, dozens of major infrastructure projects were proposed for completion in time for the 2010 Games. These included the construction of modern stadia and sports facilities, extension of the mass-transit Metro rail system, a modernized International Terminal at the Indira Gandhi International Airport, widened arterial roadways, expressways and flyovers for car transport and the construction of a new Athletes' Village on the banks of the Yamuna River.[10] Accompanying this physical infrastructure would be new spaces for touristic and elite urban consumption, including hotels, convention centers, cultural venues, restaurants and retail spaces.[11]

But hosting the CWG did not merely entail revamping the existing city and building new infrastructure. It also meant doing "imaginal" battle with dominant perceptions of Delhi and Indian cities more generally as "chaotic" and "dirty," "unplanned" and "over-populated."[12] Hosting the CWG in Delhi thus comported with both the state and national governments' official goals of re-making the capital as "a global metropolis and a world-class city" by 2021.[13] Representing the state government (Union Territory) of Delhi, Chief Minister Sheila Dixit said in a 2006 speech that the "Holding of Commonwealth Games 2010 in Delhi is a matter of pride for us.... Government of Delhi has already worked out its schedule for timely completion of all identified projects relating to Commonwealth Games 2010."[14]

46 *Distance and proximity in Delhi*

Figure 1.1 Official slogan of 2010 Delhi Commonwealth Games: "Come Out and Play."
Source: Photo by author.

Although the Delhi Games were initially announced to the public in 2003, the actual commencing of projects linked to the Games was initially slow to get off the ground. By September 2008, the beginning of my first year as a researcher in Delhi, various news media outlets consistently reported delays for completion of key games infrastructure and venues, some even alleging that the postponements were putting the event itself "at grave risk of collapse."[15] These stories began to pick up steam in the subsequent weeks and months. Cable news programs sent investigative journalists into CWG-related projects in order to report on the works in progress, with headlines like "Shame Games." At the newly "finished" swimming pool complex, for instance, one program showed shoddy construction and seemingly incomplete work. These TV reports were matched by newspaper headlines like the following: "Games shocker: New stadiums falling apart," which reported of several missed deadlines for major stadia due to "slow pace" of construction. There were also numerous reports of horrific work-related accidents suffered by construction workers, public health scares at several games venues and allegations of corruption between Games organizers and private corporate developers. These were all perhaps subplots compared to the mounting commentary on the huge cost overruns that were pushing the overall budget for the Games to heights that far surpassed initial estimates. As one TV report sensationalized it, "High on price, low on quality."[16]

By late September 2010, just weeks before the opening ceremonies were to commence, a photographic exposé of the highly touted Commonwealth Games Athletes' Village on the eastern banks of the Yamuna River appeared in news media. Participating athletes and trainers from the various competing countries were to stay in the village, which was supposed to feature "state-of-the-art" architectural design and "world-class" amenities in apartment-style accommodations. The construction was contracted out to the Dubai-based real estate developer Emaar MGF Properties. But in the exposé there were images of unfinished work and shoddy construction. One picture showed animal paw prints on a white bedspread. Another depicted large puddles of gray stagnant water in a hallway. The images quickly went viral.[17] Athletes and foreign delegations from participating countries raised the possibility of withdrawing their participation from the Delhi Games on account of the apparently substandard infrastructure and unsafe environment. Games officials in Delhi were under intense pressure to somehow explain these conditions to an increasingly anxious public.[18]

It was in the midst of this tense media-saturated environment that on September 26, 2010 Lalit Bhanot, Secretary General of the OC, stepped up to a press podium and delivered the following response to the current conditions at the Athletes' Village: "You see everyone has a different standard of cleanliness. The rooms are clean according to you and me, but these people [the foreign delegations] have a different standard of cleanliness."[19]

Bhanot's words generated near unanimous condemnation in the media. "As an Indian, I feel embarrassed by that statement," one corporate executive told NDTV, apparently echoing a broadly shared public sentiment.[20] According to an online *Times of India* survey published a few days after, no fewer than 97 percent of respondents said the Games organizers had "tarnished India's image in the world."[21] The U.S.-based investment ratings agency Moody's chimed in as well, warning that "India's reputation as a tourist and investment destination could be damaged" by the Secretary General's statement.[22] In other words, Bhanot's statement, combined with the larger debacle that was the Delhi government's preparations for the Commonwealth Games, galvanized a broad public response that resounded particularly loudly from middle-class and elite quarters of Delhi. These voices were amplified by the English-language corporate media, where a recurring theme was that the Games had "tarred India's image" in the world.[23]

How did Bhanot's comments move so swiftly from being about a few dirty hotel rooms in East Delhi to "shaming the country" as a whole, as it was reported in far-off Calcutta's newspaper of record the *Telegraph*?[24] Through what discursive and spatial processes did the "Commonwealth Games debacle" in Delhi as a whole come to be interpreted through the frames of national identity and global recognition? Finally, what was it about Bhanot's distinction between "Indian" and "foreign" standards of hygiene that triggered this decidedly elite and privileged segment of the population?

Before we can address these questions, perhaps we need to raise some more basic ones. For instance, why were the preparations for the Games in Delhi so

48 *Distance and proximity in Delhi*

delayed in the first place? Why was the undertaking so lackadaisical at first, then chaotic and frenzied toward the end? If Delhi was supposed to be showcased as the "world-class" capital city of an economically resurgent India, why did it appear to be haunted by the familiar ghosts of India's "under-developed" past and apparently still "developing" present? In what ways did the answers to these questions manifest in the image of Lalit Bhanot's untimely appearance on the international news media?

This chapter is specifically about Delhi's contemporary *discursive* transformation from a "developing" to a "globalizing" urban space. As we will see, this transformation has both symbolic and material aspects, and it is fraught with multiple, contradictory trajectories, such that to speak of a singular or all-encompassing transition at the urban or regional scale is problematic to say the least. This is why approaching such a transformation at a discursive level, that is, at the level of discursive mediations, is crucial to the argument I want to make.[25] Far from a one-way transition from "developmental" to "global" city status, *Neo* Delhi is caught in-between countervailing temporalities of being and becoming, temporalities that often contradict and confound one another, forcing us to reconsider what exactly it is we mean by "development" and "globality" in the first place.

Thus this chapter develops a central concept in this book: urban mediation. I turn to a relatively obscure essay written in the 1960s by Henri Lefebvre, entitled "The specificity of the city." Lefebvre's argument is that the specificity of the modern capitalist city lies in open-ended processes of mediation. The city is "mediation among mediations," Lefebvre poetically argues. More than merely socially constructed, and far from an objective reality, cities are inter-subjectively mediated between far orders (see Introduction) and near orders, between past and present, present and future, between linear and non-linear histories, intended and unintended transformations. These mediations are sites of ideological projection and representational politics for powerful states and corporate institutions, while alternatively serving as sites of social survival and existential resistance among urban subalterns and proletariats.

My approach in this chapter is not divorced from material concerns about processes of capital accumulation, class conflict and growing socio-economic inequality in cities like Delhi. But it is also interested in what mediates between the material and symbolic life of cities. It is thus necessary to ask: what do the adjectives "global" or "globalizing," "developing" or "developed" mean when they are attached to a postcolonial city like Delhi? What work do they do? In what ways do such attachments produce the very material effects they purportedly seek to merely describe, though often in confusing and unexpected ways?[26]

In this chapter I argue that Delhi does not "globalize" without first creating an imaginary distance between its "globalizing" present and its "developmental" past. This distance produces an inter-subjective context in which a privileged and mobilized elite paradoxically experiences the city as simultaneously synchronic and diachronic. That is, globality is experienced synchronically across

The urban   49

disparate coeval spaces—home, work, consumption, mobility, exchange. But in postcolonial cities like *Neo* Delhi synchronic urban space is simultaneously experienced as succession, that is, as a temporal move away from the past of the postcolonial city and its (post)colonial ghosts. This past, as we will see, in turn gets coded as "developmental." As such the latter remains stuck in the so-called "waiting room" of history, i.e., non-contemporaneous with the synchronic seductions of the global present. The global present is synchronic in its temporal structure, connecting "here" and "now" with distant "elsewheres" through virtually instantaneous vectors of communication and transportation. Development, in contrast, is diachronically structured around a time of deferment and delay ("not yet"), the classically postcolonial prerogative of "catching up" with the modern world after centuries of colonial (and now postcolonial) under-development.[27] How do temporal imaginations of diachronic and synchronic time mediate relationships of distance and proximity across a range of scales and subjectivities in urban life? That is, if everyday life in *Neo* Delhi is structurally divided by the conflicting temporalities of development and globality, how are we to imagine and engage the politics of changing urban life? In the absence of a coherent response, this conflict only serves to legitimate the ongoing processes of urban mediation that are increasingly the post-reform state's *raison d'être*: mediating between development and globality.

Urban mediation

As Georg Simmel argued in his *Philosophy of Money*, written in 1900, distance is usually posited in order that it can be overcome, if not in actuality then at least conceptually.[28] In his terse, dense and at times poetic essay entitled "The specificity of the city,"[29] Lefebvre suggested that the modern city's specificity resided in the ongoing mediations it hosted between distances of a slightly different modality. In particular, the city and its urban spaces mediated between a "far order" and a "near order," two separate orders of everyday urban reality that were often entangled and intimately related, but could at times coexist in a relation marked by distant proximity or proximate distance. The far order was projected by the modern state and embodied in long-term urban processes of development and growth. The near order was differently composed of the open-ended assemblages of everyday urban life, where socially heterogeneous urban dwellers and objects negotiate spatial and social relationships in the process of reproduction. For Lefebvre, the far order was "that of society, regulated by large and powerful institutions (Church and State)."[30] The near order was comprised of "relations of individuals in groups of variable size, more or less organized and structured, and the relations of these groups among themselves." The far order was "abstract, formal, supra-sensible and transcending in appearances." It projected itself into the near order, into "the practico-material reality" of everyday life. The far order became "visible by writing itself within this reality," that is, within the near order.[31] According to Lefebvre the far order regulated and shaped, but could never completely determine the near order. For even though

50 *Distance and proximity in Delhi*

"the *far order* projects itself in/on the *near order* ... the *near order* does not *reflect* transparently the *far order*. The latter subordinates the immediate through mediations."[32]

This complex dialectic between near and far orders in the city relates to how "immediate," material life is always already "mediated," that is, structured and thus transformed, by distant orders represented by powerful institutions and their abstract governing logics. In the context of cities, these far orders influenced how urban subjects conducted themselves in their everyday lives. The far order expressed itself through urban master plans, building codes and zoning regulations, government initiatives for developing and "renewing" neighborhoods and districts, or more mundane things like public parks and monuments, street names, government buildings and institutional spaces. These "immediate" yet unmistakably "mediated" (that is, distant *qua* governmental) spaces both projected and actualized a virtual order onto the everyday lives of urban inhabitants that used these spaces. They thus interacted indirectly with the far order, that is, through mediations that took place in the near order of their daily lives. But these mediations were open-ended, so that within the near order subjects could potentially appropriate the representational space of the city and create counter-mediations, counter-rhythms and counter-discourses.

Consider the graffiti that inevitably comes up to deface "public" monuments dedicated to state power and official memory. Or the squatters and hawkers who occupy and use city parks and sidewalks in order to work in ways that blatantly contradict the projected economic logic of the master plan. These counter-mediations and unintended logics potentially disrupt, even if only temporarily, the becoming-hegemonic discourse of the far order of the modern state.

My argument is that the concept of the postcolonial city helps give us a better appreciation of the vast distances that can open up between near and far orders in the context of rapid socio-spatial change. Urban mediation becomes the site of political struggle in a postcolonial city-state that seeks to project a hegemonic far order onto heterogeneous and "untimely" urban spaces. For historical reasons, as we will see, the postcolonial state's authority and legitimacy, as embodied and performed in its urban far orders, is structurally challenged in ways that complicate and transform the "distance" that it attempts to project into the near order. In "modern" cities, I suggest the abstract distance of the state is seen as necessary in order for the state to project its presence in and through space as impersonal and impartial, legitimate and authoritative and thus also (more cunningly) normative. In contrast, in postcolonial city-states like *Neo* Delhi, the unbridled distance that opens up between near and far orders potentially generates "non-normative" or "haphazard" logics that are heterogeneous with respect to the desires of the state and its normative community of sense, requiring ongoing mediation. These forms and processes of mediation belong to a complex, partially planned and partially unintended logic of postcolonial urbanism.

I take mediation to be an inter-subjective process that distributes meaning and value across different communities of sense.[33] Mediation is neither a fully

The urban   51

subjective phenomenon nor is it merely objective, rather it belongs to something in-between. The inter-subjective/inter-objective process of mediation informs how cities can be read and interpreted in multiple ways, through studying encounters between dominant and subaltern discourses and urban rhythms, noticing certain repetitions and differences, and paying attention to how subjects negotiate the familiar and the strange, the distant and the close, in everyday life. Changing urban life, I argue, is mediated in multiple ways and at different levels.

"Urban mediation" is about the value and intelligibility of the built environment in the context of continual, multi-layered and inter-temporal change. As we will see in the chapters that follow, differential rates of change, say, between public and private modes of land development, and qualities of life, between elite, subaltern and middle-class populations, for example, are present in a virtual city like *Neo* Delhi. Given the radical geohistorical differences that are productive of changing urban life, mediation is what effectively sutures together—however contingently, partially or violently, as we will see—a dominant image or idea of the city as a coherent spatial construct: an intelligible "place" or "thing."

Thus mediation describes a process that is both place *and* process, material (constituted) and symbolic (nominal). Mediation describes the way in which symbolic constructions of the urban are reinforced by material processes and vice versa. This dialectic of urban mediation is expressed in the performativity of the urban, as witnessed in the CWG debacle/spectacle described above, for instance (ironically through its failure). That is, mediation is open to multiple narratives and trajectories that can quickly spin out of control, revealing contested interpretations and conflicting valuations of changing urban life. In this chapter I foreground one dominant way of ordering and valuing the present and various counter-narratives that come to challenge its dominance. This decidedly "middle-class" narrative, which I argue is actually sociologically and demographically "elite," is roughly coeval with India's urban *qua* economic *qua* global turn. As we will see, this narrative is interested in unilaterally coding the dialectical process of urban mediation as one of a linear transition away from the time of "development" and toward that of "globality," imagining "middle-class" subjects as the normative stars of the story of spatio-economic transformation. The interpretive concept of mediation renders visible that which haunts this "global" transition in postcolonial cities like Delhi, so that the idea is that "development" is not a time that belongs to the city's past, but rather comes to structure the experience of globality from within. Urban mediation is about this complex hauntology and split temporality in the postcolonial city.[34]

The colonial city

Lefebvre's approach to urban mediation must be modified to take into account the distances and proximities uniquely productive of colonial and postcolonial urban life. Consider, for starters, the anti-colonial writer Frantz Fanon's barbed description of colonial space at the beginning of *The Wretched of the Earth*:

Distance and proximity in Delhi

> The colonized world is a world divided in two. The dividing line, the border, is represented by the barracks and the police stations. In the colonies, the official, legitimate agent, the spokesperson for the colonizer and the regime of oppression, is the police officer or the soldier. In *capitalist societies*, education, whether secular or religious, the teaching of moral reflexes handed down from father to son, the exemplary integrity of workers decorated after fifty years of loyal and faithful service, the fostering of love for harmony and wisdom, *those aesthetic forms of respect for the status quo*, instill in the exploited a mood of submission and inhibition which considerably eases the task of the agents of law and order. In capitalist countries a multitude of sermonizers, counselors, and "confusion mongers" intervene between the exploited and the authorities. In colonial regions, however, the proximity and frequent, direct intervention by the police and the military ensure the colonized are kept under close scrutiny, and contained by rifle butts and napalm.[35]

Significant here is the way in which Fanon specifically foregrounds perceptions of distance and proximity at the level of everyday life. In effect, Fanon underlines two very different modes of spatial mediation that function in "capitalist society," on the one hand, and "colonial regions," on the other. Both worlds are violent and exploitative. But in European cities (i.e., "capitalist society") there exist a multitude of social agents and public institutions that ideologically mediate between the state and civil society. In the colonies, however, these socio-political mediators are largely absent. They are replaced with the direct and immediate violence of the colonial state, or the threat thereof. This constitutes a historically different form of mediation between the colonial state and its colonized subjects, producing a different articulation of distance and proximity in everyday life.

We can bring Fanon's insights to bear on the history of colonial India, where the colonial far order in the city, rather than projecting institutional proximity from a geographic or abstract distance, instead often reinforced the colonial state's fundamental distance *and* difference from its colonized subjects. Writing about public life in colonial Bengal in the late nineteenth and early twentieth centuries, Partha Chatterjee juxtaposes the spread of contractual forms of "responsible" and "impersonal" governance in post-Enlightenment Europe with their colonial mutation, which operated according to what he calls the "rule of colonial difference."[36] This was "a modern regime of power destined never to fulfill its normalizing mission because the premise of its power was the preservation of the alienness of the ruling group."[37] The rule of colonial difference was structurally ambivalent: rhetorically it trumpeted "universal" principles of progress and liberty for humanity, yet in practice the colonial state continually deferred recognition of equality between Europeans and non-Europeans. This temporal deferral was actualized in the hierarchical racial-spatial order in the colonial city.

Gyan Prakash's description of Victorian Bombay in the late nineteenth century further enhances our crystallizing image of colonial urban mediation.

The urban 53

Like Chatterjee, Prakash too emphasizes the alienating racial-spatial divisions of the colonial city, but he also foregrounds something else that is crucial: the futurist temporality of development, which, as we will see, comes to mediate these relations of proximity and distance in the postcolonial city.

> The enchantment of the city was in its very material form; its physical, political, and social geography formed the "natural" landscape for a new mythic world. The spatial order laid out by the British imagined the city according to the ideals of European civilization and civic consciousness.... There was never any doubt that entry into this urban world was conditional on the acceptance of colonial authority, that alien power and culture underpinned the public space of avenues, parks, educational institutions and learned societies. There was also little likelihood that the poor could live the ideal of colonial urbanism, but then this ideal was staged as the pedagogical model that the natives were expected to learn from and emulate.[38]

That the colonial far order was perceived as "enchanting," yet undeniably "alien" underscored that native subjects did not belong to the colonial city. They did not belong to its *present* even if they were geographically proximate to it. This exclusion at proximity was mediated through the futurist temporality of colonial urban space. After the passage of historical time, it was presumed,

Figure 1.2 Presidential complex in New Delhi.
Source: Photo by author.

54 *Distance and proximity in Delhi*

natives might eventually learn to take possession of the city. Yet this future could be endlessly deferred—"not yet." This was a colonial far order, but its ambivalent temporality lingers in the postcolonial urban present.

The developmental city

In the middle decades of the twentieth century close to seventy former colonies in Africa and Asia achieved formal independence from their European rulers. The divided colonial city described by Fanon and Prakash above transformed quite suddenly into the postcolonial city, still divided, albeit with altered class/ethnic hierarchies replacing and inheriting the racial-spatial order of the colonial city. Thus

> the major metropolis in almost every newly-industrialized country is not a single unified city, but in fact, two quite different cities, physically juxtaposed but architecturally and socially distinct.... These dual cities have usually been a legacy from the colonial past.[39]

It was the collective overcoming of this divided city that was ideologically the imperative of the postcolonial developmental city. The implicit temporal imagination of the developmental city was diachronic in its orientation. In accordance with modernization theory the divided colonial city was interpreted as an instance of "incomplete modernization," thus requiring developmentalist intervention. Postcolonial India's first concerted attempt at urban master planning came with the advent of the 1962 Master Plan for Delhi (1962 MPD), which took as one of its chief targets the spatial difference between pre-colonial Old Delhi and colonial New Delhi. Here modernist urban planning and utopian projections of a rational spatial order converged with the goal of rehabilitating the Old Delhi and disciplining haphazard outgrowths around New Delhi.[40] If successful in the nation's capital Delhi's Master Plan was to subsequently provide a model for urban planning in other Indian cities.

In some ways, the image of the developmental city that was implicit in the 1962 MPD was a clear reflection of then Prime Minister Jawaharlal Nehru's ideological embrace of developmentalism and modernism as a panacea for the social epidemics of poverty, disease, overpopulation and haphazard growth. These problems were seen as plaguing urban India as a whole. Such an explicit embrace of modernism and developmentalism often entailed a resolute rejection of India's "past" and "tradition," which were seen as holding the country back in its quest to join the modern world. Within this dominant Nehruvian worldview the urban was thus synonymous with the modern and was imagined as a blank screen for projecting the nation's developed future that was still yet to come.[41]

But the diachronic image of time implicit in the MPD's embrace of development was also a continuation of colonial urban policies of town "improvement" and village "uplift." Thirty years before the 1962 MPD was published the Delhi Improvement Trust (DIT) was established by the British to execute the re-building of Shahjahanabad. The medieval walled city had faced a steep decline in the aftermath of the 1857 rebellion, which was centered and brutally crushed in Shahjahanabad. The DIT renamed the latter "Old Delhi" and officially classified it a "notified slum," targeting it for its congested spaces and crumbling neighborhoods, unkempt streets and dark alleyways, all of which constituted a threat to public health and colonial order.[42]

New Delhi, built by the British from 1911 to 1932, was conceived by its planners to be the polar opposite of the crowded and congested Mughal capital. The former's broad streets, allayed in geometric patterns and lined with large shade-giving trees and brick pavements, its spacious bungalows and landscaped roundabouts, its open parks and green spaces, together constituted an architectural performance of sorts, projecting an imperial mastery over domestic Indian space. Although there were significant local citations in the monumental architecture of New Delhi, such as the use of locally mined red sandstone and ornamentations borrowed directly from Mughal architecture, the overtly neo-classical facades and grandiose scale of the capital complex as a whole left no doubt as to the city's symbolic purpose: to identity the British as the undisputed rulers of India.[43]

After New Delhi's construction was completed in 1932, the DIT came into being as the apex colonial authority for executing urban re-development in the old city, focusing on reducing urban densities and rebuilding crumbling infrastructure in the latter's neighborhoods. The DIT effectively transformed into the Delhi Development Authority (DDA) after the DDA Act of 1957.[44] Like the DIT, the DDA approached Delhi as a split city requiring developmental intervention and "improvement" in order to reduce urban densities, especially in the Old City, to acceptable levels. Its goal was also to rationalize land use for re-development and urban expansions beyond Old and New Delhis. The DDA inherited the colonial state's disposition toward Shahjahanabad, describing it as "full of the dust and fragrance of the past and pulsating with life" but also "a planners' nightmare with its multiplicity of conflicting uses and its millions of problems created by acute congestion, insanitary conditions and dilapidated structures."[45]

It was the DDA that produced and implemented the 1962 MPD, which aimed to achieve the "rational growth of Delhi" in the face of "uncontrolled" development in the metropolitan region. Delhi's population had nearly doubled in the decade surrounding India's independence, when the partition of British India sent hundreds of thousands of Hindus and Sikhs from Pakistan to the neighborhoods of Delhi, sometimes into the very homes that Muslim families had just abandoned.[46] To service the surplus of people coming in, however, speculators and private developers hastily built new apartment housing across the city. The DDA saw such developments as "haphazard," and in 1957 froze all speculative building by non-state developers, monopolizing this role for itself in order to rationalize land use and plan for future urban development. The DDA's goal was to leverage the land market in Delhi (which it effectively controlled) to finance housing for high-income, middle-income and low-income groups (LIGs), with

56 *Distance and proximity in Delhi*

specific emphasis on the latter two. This housing was to be dispersed across the metropolitan region of Delhi, or what became the NCR, including "the Union Territory of Delhi and the Ring Towns of Loni and Ghaziabad in [Uttar Pradesh], Faridabad, Ballabhgarh, Bahadugarh and Gurgaon in Punjab [today Haryana] and Narela in Delhi territory."[47] It was necessary, the MPD argued, to conceive of Delhi's metropolitan region "as a composite unit and have an integrated and balanced overall programme of development." Commenting on the 1962 MPD, urban theorist Ravi Sundaram writes that the Plan "emerged as the postcolonial elite's answer to colonial inequalities, a rational model of management that would ideally combine both claims for social justice and a technological dream-world of the future."[48] This was to be the ideological blueprint for the developmental city.

To put this in Lefebvre's terms: the developmental city was a form of urban mediation that projected a far order of rationality, justice and progress that was temporally distanced from the present, but presumably on arrival. Simultaneously, India's "pre-modern" past, embodied in Shahjahanabad, was also distanced. The city was imagined as a "work in progress," heralding the nation's larger transition from pre-modernity to modernity. Development was a status that was not "here" and "now" in the postcolonial city's present, rather it was projected as being "elsewhere" but "coming soon." It did not take long, however, to notice the many discrepancies between the state's temporal projections and the uneven actualizations that resulted in Delhi following the implementation of the 1962 MPD.

Unintended developments

The 1962 MPD was a single-shot exercise in long-range planning for twenty years of projected growth. After this time it would be critically appraised by both the state and civil society in Delhi. In an assessment of the MPD two decades after its implementation, professors Abhijit Datta and Gangadhar Jha sought to "comprehend the achievements as well as the failures of the plan implementation."[49] On the achievement side, the two authors found, the impact of the plan could be seen in the "wholesome environment" that was evident in many parts of the city. These parts of Delhi look "clean, green with widened roads, and a chain of local, district and regional parks."[50] They also noted that around one million "of the squatter population has been relocated in 43 planned resettlement colonies," mostly on the periphery of the existing city. The old city of Shahjahanabad had been decongested to an extent, and new townships had been created with the intention of spreading the population of Delhi in an outward direction. For instance, Rohini in the west of Delhi's Union Territory had already become home to nearly a million new residents by 1983.

But in the plan there were also innumerable shortcomings that were plainly visible two decades after implementation. First, the plan did not account for the "unabated flow of immigrants" which "overwhelmed the plan proposals."[51] From 1941 to 1951, Delhi's population (within the NCT) had climbed from 918,000 to

1.74 million, reflecting the large influx of post-Partition refugees. Over the next two decades this number more than doubled, topping four million by 1971 and 6.2 million by 1981. However, the 1962 plan projected Delhi's population at just 4.6 million by 1981, more than one-and-a-half million less than actual figures.[52] The resulting "surplus" population was excessive not just with respect to the MPD's low demographic projections but also the DDA's construction efforts to house Delhi's inhabitants. In addition to writing and implementing the Master Plan, the DDA was also tasked with acquiring and developing land for residential, industrial and commercial purposes as designated by the MPD. But the DDA fell far short of its intended targets. For example, while the MPD projected the acquisition and development of 30,000 acres for the construction of residential housing, actual development amounted to just 13,412 acres. This significant shortfall and "the slow pace of development and disposal of acquired land ... led to coming up of unauthorized colonies on a large scale."[53] I will treat these unauthorized colonies in more detail later. But for whatever residential units that the DDA did manage to develop, a disproportionate share of these units went to high-income groups. Low-income groups especially were given the short shrift when it came to DDA housing. This was due to the "revolving fund strategy" through which the DDA financed its speculative land development, where the DDA was "dependent upon maximizing the return on acquired land" so as to recover its costs and enable further land acquisition and development. As Datta and Jha concluded, "urban development for the poor in this context becomes the first casualty."[54]

On the balance the 1962 Master Plan was critiqued for its perceived failings more than for its apparent successes. The techno-social utopia it dreamed up seemed as distant from present reality twenty years after implementation as when it was first drafted. As Datta and Jha found, "the explosive demographic growth, swift physical sprawl and the pressure for civic services generated by it completely overwhelmed the static frame of the Master Plan."[55]

Critics also blamed the plan's failure on the naïve adoption of "Western" planning norms that seemed unfit for the requirements and existing conditions of Delhi. The plan itself was the product of a joint collaboration between Indian planners and the United States Ford Foundation. Neither side appeared to take an active interest in studying the historical specificities of Delhi's extant built environment, parts of which dated back to centuries of continued habitation and use.[56] The planners instead imported theories and practices largely in tact from the U.S., including strict zoning laws that segregated residential, commercial and industrial spaces, as in the burgeoning American suburbs of the 1950s and 1960s. But Delhi was a city that was historically defined by mixed uses of land and dense pedestrian-based cohabitation.[57] Much of the working class lived close to where they worked by necessity. Yet the Master Plan brazenly separated residential and occupational spaces into different zones, requiring use of public or private transportation on a daily basis for people that were too poor to afford such costs. In the spatio-temporal imaginary of the 1962 Master Plan it was assumed that modernity traveled from "West" to "East," and that "universal"

58 *Distance and proximity in Delhi*

lessons gleaned in the former could be effectively translated into the latter. For Delhi's modernist planners there was nothing of intrinsic value to learn from Delhi's existing built forms, its spatial histories and the indigenous urbanisms that had evolved there.[58] Over time, it was assumed, Delhi's residents would learn to act like the deracinated modern subjects that the Master Plan already assumed them to be, separating public (work) and private (home) life, for instance, and thus reproducing the spatial logic of the plan. This was the diachronic imagination at its most projective: the past of the Western city was projected onto the future of Delhi. The present was a space and time of historical transition, of development.

But perhaps the most glaring failure of the 1962 MPD was the underestimation of demographic growth that was to take place in cities like Delhi following independence. As a result of this tremendous shortfall in housing, migrants turned to the "unintended city," as urbanist Jai Sen provocatively named it in 1976.[59] This was the city of largely poor rural migrants who were not included in the futurist imagination of the Master Plan's developmental city but, as Ashis Nandy suggested, were always implicit in it.[60] In the absence of affordable public housing, postcolonial Delhi bore witness to the steady proliferation of "informal" housing colonies on "public" lands, including not just slums and shanties for the poor but unauthorized middle-class colonies and "farm" estates for the elite in areas zoned for non-residential purposes. Even lands that were zoned for protection as part of Delhi's "green belt" were eventually developed, first by the DDA and later by private developers operating without legal permits. In 1962, the year in which the Master Plan was published, there were 110 such unauthorized colonies already existing in Delhi. By 1977 this number had reached 471.[61]

If the developmental imagination of the Delhi government and the Ford Foundation envisioned a planned city with modern citizen-subjects moving efficiently between industrial, residential, commercial and leisure spaces, postcolonial cities like Delhi were soon inundated with diverse migrants whose experiences confounded developmentalist teleologies and normative zoning rationalities. This newly urbanized population experienced forms of exclusion and marginalization that were often times homologous with or even worse than those experienced under colonialism, including brutal slum demolitions, police intimidation and harassment, deprivations of basic urban services like clean water and toilets, and above all, slave wages in exploitative work environments. But as historian Partha Chatterjee has argued, the urban poor also formed part of an emergent political matrix in which their urban existence and survival could be negotiated and re-negotiated in an endlessly prolonged present or a continually deferred future. The unauthorized colonies and informal businesses of the poor could be forcibly removed at any time, though many managed to persist in a precarious existence by striking deals with local politicians and power-brokers. The latter emerged, along with landowners and landlords, as powerful patrons in the informal economy of housing, employment and legality, exchanging "authorized" tenure in particular slum neighborhoods for electoral votes or other forms of allegiance and loyalty. The developmental city thus gave space to the tireless dealings and improvisations of what Chatterjee has called "political society," where subaltern groups became both the target of statist development and a politicized community that could take to civil society and local politics in order to make concrete demands for life improvement or urban recognition.[62] Such demands were far from met for most in political society.

One way of reading the unintended city is as the abject failure of urban mediation in the form of the developmental city. Indeed, as we will see, this was a common interpretation by many urban elites and middle classes, but also by urban scholars that came to see the proliferation of slums and "low-grade" settlements as evidence of a lack of foresight on the part of planning institutions. But it is important to recognize as well that the "informal" urban poor provided the cheap labor and services that made the intended and planned city possible, even as the poor were themselves denied the urban services that middle-class citizens took for granted, such as piped water, electrical connections, education and healthcare. The normative subject of the developmental city could only constitute herself as such through the informal economies and arrangements that supported and effectively subsidized the "planned" city. This was not just a question of the exigencies of capital accumulation overwhelming state planning guidelines and regulations, which happens in modern cities everywhere. Rather, it is about the various mediations that allow "normative" and "non-normative" spaces to co-exist and become simultaneously proximate and distant in the developmental city. Part of this city's ideological durability is in its very flexibility in weaving together heterogeneous social groups into an uneven and frayed urban fabric. For all its visible failures in building a recognizably modern urban environment, the developmental city allowed recent rural migrants with few resources to improvise a livelihood, however precarious and wanting. This was not so much a failure of urban mediation, but rather evidence of a spatial morphology that had moved well beyond the experience of the Western city that served as the implicit model for the modern developmental city.

In postcolonial Delhi, the rational and progressive legal order projected as the developmental city, what Lefebvre would call its "far order," was paradoxical. On the one hand, the far order was too provincial, too Western, too detached from local building practices and everyday livelihoods. This was particularly the case in places like Old Delhi or in the proliferating urban slums that emerged within the gap between a distant far order and a radically heterogeneous near order. On the other hand, this postcolonial far order was in some ways not distant enough. The Master Plan's land-use guidelines, its zoning laws and building regulations were constantly changing, written and re-written by the state, often in half-veiled collusion with property speculators and influential real estate developers.[63] Meanwhile, politicians and bureaucrats used their positions of power to negotiate with lower-income groups in slums and informal settlements, holding out the carrot stick of a legally sanctioned life in exchange for votes. The Master Plan was thus "unable to detach itself from the existing

60   Distance and proximity in Delhi

social order, so as to re-order it."[64] Reliance on powerful local leaders in order to acquire land zoned for urban development in the city often led to outright graft and corruption, undermining in practice the progressivist ethos of the MPD and the developmental city it projected. In their uneven actualizations within the near order of the postcolonial city, the multiple, complex mediations of distance and proximity muddied the idealistic spatio-temporal projections of the developmental city.

But this does not imply that the developmental city is simply "ungoverned," "ungovernable," nor even an outright "failure." For the political endurance of development both as a ruling state ideology and as a strategy for urban mediation in a postcolonial city like Delhi is witnessed in the fact that "development" continues to be the dominant motif used for mediating the political present in India.[65] Conceptualized through the notions of far and near orders, the urban mediation of the 1962 Delhi Master Plan (its projection of a distant "elsewhere" that was ostensibly "coming soon" through rational planning and legalistic regulation) effectively entailed its distance and alienation from the everyday lived realities, or the near order, of a vast segment of the urban population. Most who were the plan's intended targets interfaced with a state represented not in the concrete abstractions of rationally planned streets, meticulously ordered spaces and accountable public institutions, but rather with unscrupulous local politicians and a labyrinthine bureaucracy, thug-like police, dysfunctional schools and hospitals, vicious slumlords and unsympathetic courts. The temporality of the developmental city was one of continued postponement and deferral. For the poor it was waiting for "regularization" from the state as legally recognized inhabitants and workers of the city. For the wealthy it was less about existential recognition and more about global recognition, that is, waiting for a recognizably modern city to materialize in the present. But in both cases, the developmental city seemed unable to overcome the vast distances in space and time it set out to master and enclose through modernization, planning and, of course, development.

Over time, many urban elites and the middle class, empowered by economic liberalization both in Delhi and in other Indian cities, began to see themselves as "formal" tax-paying citizens drowning in a sea of "informality" and postcolonial under-development.[66] Their critique was not so much that development had failed the very people it was supposed to target, namely the rural poor that were languishing in villages and increasingly migrating to cities, moving into slums and other precarious settlements. Rather, the elite felt that whatever else it could produce, postcolonial development could not deliver the cosmopolitan modernity that elites saw elsewhere in the world and desired at home. In the midst of the developmental city's perceived failures, postcolonial urban elites began to conjure a new dream-world in collaboration with increasingly business-friendly governments and global investors hungry to feed off India's post-liberalization economic growth. The "global city" as projected in India was not just an implicit critique of the developmental city and its unintended outgrowths but a privatized escape from both.

Between development and globality

As capital of an economically "vibrant" India, mediating between India's "renewed" national image and the demands of the global economy, *Neo* Delhi is in part projected by ruling institutions in order to conjure away the ghosts of colonial and postcolonial under-development. Such conjuring tricks are often performed through urban spectacles like hosting sporting mega-events, or building hyper-modern skyscrapers and glamorous shopping malls (as we will see in the next chapter). These spectacles are meant to distract from the underlying violence of the postcolonial city, the vast systems of internal displacement and spatio-temporal marginalization that defined the everyday relations between sub-alterns, elites and the middle class. The Commonwealth Games was Delhi's vain attempt to project India's economic confidence on a global stage through a confidence trick. Its attempt was to distance India's "globalizing" present from its developmentalist past, so that the Games were seen by mainstream elite/middle-class society as "vital to India's status as an emerging power,"[67] and a "sure way of shooting the host city into the limelight, resulting in an 'economic windfall.' "[68] In concluding this chapter, I return to the 2010 Delhi Games, and seek to analyze the various specters that interfered with the spectacle of the mega-event, revealing a politicized postcolonial urbanism that confounded the global dreams of the postcolonial nation-state.

Evidence of widely shared benefits through the hosting of large-scale urban events like the CWG is meager.[69] For "developing" cities like Delhi in particular, the costs of hosting seem to far outweigh the benefits. These cities often have to begin from scratch, building basic urban infrastructures like roads, electrical grids, sewage systems and the like before even getting to the stadiums and sports facilities required for competition. For instance, whereas the United States spent less than $30 million renovating existing stadiums for the 1994 World Cup, South Korea spent more than $2 billion to host the same event in 2002, building brand new stadiums, hotels and more. And for the 2008 Olympic Games in Beijing, the Chinese government spent a record $20 billion in constructing not just new stadiums and games venues but building entirely new urban infrastructure in previously undeveloped areas.[70]

Seen in this light, the 2010 CWG in Delhi fit a familiar mold. While the initial budget approved for the Games by the Indian government was $766 million in 2005, by the time the Games began, "it was estimated to have cost upward of $8.5 billion."[71] Much of this went to basic infrastructure. But such costs, according to critics, had to be measured not merely in terms of money *spent on* the Games but also in terms of money *not spent on* basic services for a country that was already ranked amongst the lowest of the low when it came to per capita spending on things like public health and education.[72]

There were also more direct human costs involved in hosting the Games. These came in the form of mass displacement of the poor across Delhi. Many slums, small businesses, factories and other "low-grade" settlements were forcibly removed by the Delhi government in the years leading up to 2010, often

62   *Distance and proximity in Delhi*

without prior warning or subsequent compensation given to the displaced. A report published by the Housing and Land Rights Network (HLRN) in 2011 estimated that in the half-decade prior to the CWG, "at least 200,000 people in Delhi [were] forcibly evicted ... [with] many more demolitions and evictions in the run-up to the Commonwealth Games."[73] This process was marked by state suppression in the form of police intimidation, sudden and random demolitions performed by bulldozers and trucks, and the damage or loss of personal property.[74] HLRN's report found that only a small proportion of those dislocated received any resettlement compensation, and those who were resettled did "not have access to basic services such as water, sanitation, electricity, adequate transport, schools, and healthcare."[75] Even more striking, but perhaps not surprising, was the utter lack of mainstream media attention given to this mass displacement and violent spatial re-structuring in the capital.[76] As the report observed, mainstream media in the months ahead of the Games focused disproportionately on government ineptitude and bureaucratic slowness in delivering "world class" infrastructure, missing out entirely on the government's well-practiced prowess in evicting those who were already living on the margins of "globalizing" Delhi.

In the midst of all this spatial violence and "creative destruction" there were the ghosts of the 1982 Asian Games, also held in Delhi. The Asiad bore witness to an eerily similar series of events, though there were significant and meaningful differences. Like the 2010 CWG, the 1982 Asian Games were touted as "an announcement to the world that India had arrived."[77] But here too, construction was lethargic during the early years of preparations, and then frantic at the finish line, with the majority of the development work taking place over the last two years. Like the CWG, the Asiad involved not just the building of sporting infrastructure, but also the thickening of the city's urban fabric through the construction of flyovers and widened roads, particularly in southern Delhi. The Asian Games also left in its wake new hotels, convention halls and the Asiad Village, which after servicing the Games' athletes and coaches were turned over to senior government bureaucrats for full-time residence.

But the connections between these two urban spectacles do not end there. Because of the heightened construction in Delhi for the event, the 1982 Asian Games brought tens of thousands of workers into the city. According to some estimates as many as 150,000 people came during this time and most stayed in the city long after.[78] Many were paid below government-mandated minimum wages and thus lived in temporary shacks close to their work sites. Some never managed to move out of these "temporary" spaces and so incrementally built them into more sturdy settlements and neighborhoods. Yet their "temporary" status was never resolved, as these slums remained subject to future removal at the behest of an opportunistic and predatory postcolonial state. The urban sociologist Amita Baviskar interviewed slum dwellers in 2011 that were evicted from the banks of the Yamuna River in 2004 across from the eventual site of the infamous CWG Athletes' Village. Most of the displaced first settled in this area in the early 1980s, including many who came during the building boom for the

1982 Asiad. In subsequent years the residents of Yamuna Pushta, as the slum neighborhood was called, struck deals with "populist governments at the centre [who] were willing to allow the migrants some recognition, albeit of a limited nature."[79] In this way the residents incrementally built the area up, as "hundreds of brick and cement dwellings came to line the streets." But the limited nature of recognition in Yamuna Pushta was savagely revealed in 2004, when "150,000 people were displaced over the course of one week in June."[80] The government claimed that the slum occupied land that fell under environmental protection codes. Yet just two years later the same type of land on the opposite bank of the river was auctioned to private developers to build the notorious CWG Athletes' Village.

The fate of Yamuna Pushta's residents marked a profound contrast between Delhi in the first decade of the twenty-first century and the Delhi of the penultimate decade of the twentieth century. The frenzy of creative destruction and state violence in 2010, according to Baviskar,

> was reflective of a new hardening of attitudes towards the city's working class, an antipathy towards "informal" livelihoods and spaces on the part of an urban elite that had become disproportionately empowered by the liberalization policies adopted in the 1990s.[81]

This antipathy was not necessarily new. The postcolonial government of Delhi was historically negligent if not needlessly cruel to lower-class slum dwellers in favor of the middle and upper classes, as we will see in the next chapter. And yet in the 1980s the presence of slum dwellers "was tolerated and even encouraged by local politicians who secured for them water taps and ration cards," helping "informal" residents find partial inclusion into the city.[82] While the concern of politicians "did not extend to the provision of low-cost housing or most civic amenities, it did give workers a temporary reprieve in the battle to create homes around their places of work."[83] Thus for all its imperfections, Baviskar suggests, the previous era allowed the poor at least some room to socially survive in the city, to create a collective life in the slums.

Compare the virtual invisibility of the demolition of Yamuna Pushta in 2004 with the hyper-visibility of the CWG debacle itself. The latter reached its pinnacle in 2010 with Lalit Bhanot's comments on the Athletes' Village, which stood close to the same ground where Yamuna Pushta once existed. Why was Bhanot's apparition in 2010 so publicized and decried in mainstream media when the disappearance of Yamuna Pushta (and many other neighborhoods) was basically ignored? Why were the unfiltered remarks of an inept state bureaucrat so reviled when the everyday struggle faced by millions of poor in the capital was routinely ignored? What did this tell us about the process of urban mediation in a city like *Neo* Delhi, a city that, for an empowered urban elite, remains perpetually stuck between "development" and "globality"?

One mainstream media outlet explained the uproar over Secretary General Lalit Bhanot's controversial remarks in the following way: "Mr. Bhanot's

64 *Distance and proximity in Delhi*

comments hit a raw nerve because many middle class Indians make a distinction between public and private standards. If public bathrooms in government buildings are usually dirty, private houses are usually immaculate."[84] In this curious but instructive interpretation, the implication is that Bhanot's comments offended not because he was wrong about urban India's supposed filth; rather he was wrong about where this filth could be countenanced. Low standards of hygiene might have been acceptable in the "public" spaces of the city, which, from a middle-class or elite perspective, were perhaps already seen as plagued by governmental inefficiencies and bureaucratic ineptitude. But within new privately developed spaces like the CWG Athletes' Village, built by highly coveted and supposedly synchronic foreign capital, such an acceptance of inferiority was not to be tolerated. For such spaces projected Delhi's new and unconditional "globality," so that nothing less than "world-class" standards would do. In this ideological construction, "public" urban space was coded as "local" and "under-developed," and therefore still stuck in the time of "development." New privately constructed spaces, boasting the latest in architectural design and building materials, and financed by multi-national capital, on the other hand, signified the difference that constituted "globality" in Delhi's urban landscape. In other words, it was precisely globality's difference and distance from the space–time of development that marked its intelligibility as such. For urban elites in cities like Delhi, the more these ambiguously mediated "global" spaces were seen as synchronic with their own everyday lives, the more distant the everyday reality of developmental spaces like Yamuna Pushta appeared to be. Yet developmental spaces never fully disappeared from the "globalizing" temporality of the Indian city. How could they? They would in fact "reappear" unexpectedly, for instance, in Lalit Bhanot's humiliating statements in the international media. Bhanot's apparition was a rude reminder that, for all its pretentions of globality, Delhi was still very much stuck in the time of development.

Distance and proximity in the postcolonial city

Mainstream urban scholars and policy makers see India's urban *qua* global *qua* economic turn as key to sparking capital accumulation and development in its largest cities.[85] More critical voices have written about how policies of privatization, de-regulation and de-centralization associated with this turn have created conditions of virtual economic "secession" for urban elites.[86] Gayatri Chakravorty Spivak, for instance, has described the Indian megacity as a space where "electronic capitalism" selectively engages with the domestic economy by constructing a limited infrastructure suited to its needs and little else.[87] This new "global" urban apparatus connects particular segments and subjects of the city (or a satellite city), namely India's English-speaking elite and middle classes, while "bypassing the squalor."[88] Thus neoliberal economic *qua* urban development leaves vast segments of urban society on the outside looking in. New "globalized" precincts like corporate campuses for MNCs, office buildings and shopping malls, multiplexes and resorts, gated communities and high-rise

The urban 65

apartment towers, all negotiated by means of private automobile, allow these mobilized elites to live *amongst* but not *with* the heterogeneous social groups that surround them.

Yet what has received far less attention by scholars is the way in which such "secessionist" spaces and infrastructures, fueled by capital investment and consumerist mobility, are dependent upon the projection of a stable and intelligible image of "globality." Without this image India's cities would never be seen as safe and profitable sites of investment in the first place.[89] In this sense "globalizing" cities like Delhi seek to distance their visible and haptic urban environments from the developmentalist spaces that are ubiquitous, in order to project a new temporal intelligibility in the urban present. During the CWG the state hired workers to erect bamboo walls to hide slums and dumping grounds from the line of sight of international visitors. In a typically poetic and tragic postcolonial irony, the workers themselves were from slums located elsewhere in the city.[90] Such visual-spatial schemes seek not only to place the poor "out of sight/out of mind," but to relegate the historical era of colonial and postcolonial underdevelopment to a different time altogether. Thus, elites in large and economically vibrant cities like Delhi (but also Mumbai, Bangalore, Chennai, Hyderabad and others) do not just encounter and bypass differential urban spaces; in doing so, they mediate different urban temporalities in their everyday lives. Through their spatial and temporal movements, investments and attachments, they attempt to mediate a city whose globality is contingent upon this "forgetting" of urban India's geohistorical difference.[91] As a result, elites are often repulsed by the "unexpected" appearance or re-appearance of the developmental city and its "unintended" urban outgrowths. They are especially perturbed when signs of lingering under-development crystallize within the hyper-sanitized precincts of the global city. For such untimely traces challenge the very structures of intelligibility that elites in Indian cities internalize to inoculate themselves and their normative status as "middle-class" citizen-subjects. Writing from this haunted middle-class perspective, Ashis Nandy writes

> In this century, we too have mastered the art of looking at large sections of humanity as obsolete and redundant. These sections seem to us to be anachronistically sleepwalking through our times, when they should be safely ensconced in the pages of history. Such communities should not trouble us morally, we believe, by pretending to be a part of the contemporary world and relevant to human futures.[92]

Nandy calls this form of everyday urban mediation "popular economics," an increasingly common sense discourse that views abstract economic ideas such as corporate rationality, market efficiency and "middle classness" as spelling the solution to India's age-old problems of poverty and destitution. For Nandy, this mediating discourse is a form of collective ego defense on the part of India's psychologically fragile urban elite and its postcolonial state. Both use this discourse to avoid having to confront the realities of India's neoliberal present: that

66 *Distance and proximity in Delhi*

they have in large part abandoned idealistic discourses of postcolonial development and social progress in favor of increasingly privatized-lives barricaded behind secured gates and high walls, inside exclusive and secure consumerist enclaves and protected sites of privileged enjoyment, consuming a split modernity inside an ocean of postcolonial urban destitution.[93]

In the end, the 2010 Commonwealth Games in Delhi went off without a major hitch in the program. India won the most medals it had ever garnered in the Games, and the second highest gold medal count of all competing countries.[94] And for all the anxiety over incomplete or inadequate infrastructure for the Games, most of the venues were ready on time.[95] Yet by the closing ceremonies of the 2010 Games, it seemed that the damage had already been done. Delhi's government had aspirations of using the CWG as a springboard to hosting the 2014 World Cup and perhaps even the 2016 Summer Olympics. After the 2010 CWG no one seriously harbored such dreams. In the next state elections, Sheila Dixit's Congress Party lost badly at the polls, relinquishing control of the Union Territory to the anti-corruption Aam Aadmi (Common Man) Party. The latter capitalized on the resentment felt by many not only toward the embarrassing inefficiencies of government bureaucrats like Bhanot and others, but of the large scale corruption between the ruling government and private contractors that threatened India's "global" image as a safe and profitable business environment.[96]

But my concern is not with New Delhi or India's "global" reputation as such. That is, I am not interested in taking adjectives like "global" or "developmental" as objective descriptions of urban reality. Nor am I interested in explaining why exactly the CWG preparations were such a disaster in Delhi, on whom we should place the blame, or why India's government did not plan better for this event. For one thing, it is not obvious that the government's performance was not in some ways a perverse "success." As noted above, not only was most of the infrastructure completed in time for the event, but in the process Delhi got several new stadiums and athletics facilities, nearly 1200 luxury apartments in the form of the CWG Village, new flyovers and hotels, shopping malls and perhaps most notably, an extensive Delhi Metro Rail Transit System that inaugurated a new mode of trans-local mobility within the NCR. Although not all of these projects were directly linked to the event, it was the impending arrival of the CWG in 2010 that added the necessary impetus to fast-track developments that otherwise could have taken decades longer to deliver.[97]

Yet in each of these urban "achievements," a more pessimistic interpretation is also possible. For instance, since the 2010 Games, the new stadiums built across Delhi have been largely under-utilized, with some already in a state of disrepair. The new luxury apartments at the Games Village were hastily built on the Yamuna River's flood zone, a piece of seasonal land that was to be environmentally protected as per the MPD.[98] In fact this was the major justification given by the Delhi government for clearing out the Yamuna Pushta slums in 2004, which as Baviskar notes, were far less polluting to the beleaguered river than the air-conditioned luxury apartments that subsequently came up.

Most troubling, however, were the additional flyovers and expressways for more "efficient" car transport. These were not only blatantly targeted at elites who had access to automobility and thus access to this new transportation infrastructure, but it only served to cement Delhi's long-term trajectory toward a landscape dominated by cars and private vehicles.[99] At a time of increasingly ominous signs of ongoing climate change fed by the burning of fossil fuels, critics of "automobility" (including not just cars but their spatio-temporal infrastructures) have argued that this kind of "development" constitutes a one-way ticket to catastrophic planetary change.[100] Moreover the increasing turn toward private vehicular transport negates any "public" benefit brought about by the construction of the Delhi Metro.

These calamitous "global" developments in *Neo* Delhi seemingly undermine the modern future that the postcolonial city so obsessively projects through its spatio-temporal mediations. In this sense, as Jennifer Robinson notes, "the aim to be a 'global' city in the formulaic sense may well be the ruin of most cities."[101]

What is especially baleful in this regard is the spatial violence that attends the urban spectacle of the mega-event. But we witness spatial violence in other urban spectacles as well, such as in the pursuit of high-profile slum redevelopment projects that go under the name "urban renewal" (the next chapter), or the regional expansion of urban agglomerations out into the peripheries of the existing city, resulting in the construction of new "global" spaces from scratch (Part II of this book). In each case the spectacular image of "globality" that is conjured is one that effectively splits the temporality of the postcolonial city into two, separating parts that look "global" from those parts that are left "behind," that no longer seem to be relevant to the larger fate of the city, or at least to the fate of the elite city. My argument has been that far from transitioning in a linear fashion from "development" to "globality," however, postcolonial cities like Delhi seem to remain perpetually caught between two forms of mediation that are not merely ideological projections, but ways of negotiating relationships of distance and proximity in everyday urban life. Thus globality haunts development and development haunts globality from a space of intimate distance and a time of familiarized estrangement.

Globality synchronically projects geohistorically distant "elsewheres" that materialize in the "here" and "now" of the urban present. They are manifest in spectacular developments such as new world-class infrastructures, high-profile slum re-development schemes, or elite expansions into the urban-rural periphery. Globality is a far order that is spatially distanced from the near order of the developmental city, which continues to diachronically project a time that is "coming soon" but that is not yet here. The fact that these projections of development and globality so often seem to "fail" to fully and finally materialize only means that further mediations are required. The city, to return once more to Lefebvre, is "a mediation among mediations."[102] This is doubly the case in the postcolonial city, where the distance between near and far orders stretches out not merely in terms of space, but also in terms of time.

Notes

1 The Commonwealth Games are held every four years and feature track and field and sporting competition amongst countries that are part of the British Commonwealth Nations (i.e., the UK and its former colonies). The Delhi Commonwealth Games took place October 3–14, 2010.
2 "New Delhi to host 2010 Commonwealth Games." *The Age*, November 14, 2003, accessed October 28, 2014, www.theage.com.au/articles/2003/11/14/106867436816 7.html?from=storyrhs.
3 For more on sporting mega-events as urban spectacles see Kevin Fox Gotham, "Theorizing urban spectacles." *City* 9.2 (2005), 225–246.
4 Himadeep Muppidi, *The Politics of the Global* (Minneapolis, MN: University of Minnesota Press, 2004), 24–41.
5 Gyan Prakash, "The urban turn." *Sarai Reader* 2.7 (2002), 2–7.
6 Atul Kohli, "Politics of economic growth in India, 1980–2005: Part I: The 1980s." *Economic and Political Weekly* 41.3 (2006), 1251–1259.
7 Annapurna Shaw, "Urban policy in post-independent India: An appraisal." *Economic and Political Weekly*, 31.4 (1996), 224–228. For more on the postcolonial state's role of mediation between modernity and pre-modernity, see Muppidi, *The Politics of the Global*.
8 Anant Maringanti, "Urban renewal, fiscal deficit and the politics of decentralization: The case of the Jawaharlal Nehru Urban Renewal Mission in India." *Space and Policy* 16.1 (2012), 93–109.
9 Vinayak Uppal, "The impact of the Commonwealth Games 2010 on urban development of Delhi." *Theoretical and Empirical Researches in Urban Management* 10 (2009), 18.
10 See, for example: "Commonwealth Games construction under labour spotlight." *Guardian*, September 17, 2010, accessed October 28, 2014, www.theguardian.com/world/gallery/2010/feb/02/child-labour-commonwealth-games-india.
11 For more on the idea of "inhabited infrastructure" in the "global city" see Saskia Sassen, "Why cities matter." *Catalogue of the 10th International Architecture Exhibition, Venice Biennale* (2006), 26–51.
12 Delhi fits into a broader pattern regarding Indian cities and their stereotypical urban "dysfunction." For recent writing on Delhi's ongoing public battle with dominant perceptions of an "unloved city," see Emma Tarlo, Veronique Dupont and Denis Vidal (eds), *Delhi: Urban Space and Human Destiny* (New Delhi: Manohar Publishing, 2000). For a more general take on perceptions of Indian cities as chaotic and disorderly, see Ananya Roy, "Why India cannot plan its cities: Informality, insurgence and the idiom of urbanization." *Planning Theory* 8.1 (2009), 76–87. For more on the "imaginal," see Chiara Bottici, *Imaginal Politics: Images beyond Imagination and the Imaginary* (New York: Columbia University Press, 2014).
13 V. K. Puri, *Master Plan of Delhi 2021* (Delhi: JBA Publishers, 2007), 1.
14 Sheila Dixit, "Government of National Capital Territory of Delhi Speech to National Development Council Meeting, 9th December 2006, New Delhi," accessed October 29, 2014, http://planningcommission.nic.in/plans/planrel/52ndc/delhi.pdf.
15 Dean Nelson, "New Delhi to hide slums with bamboo 'curtains' during 2010 Commonwealth Games." *Telegraph*, August 17, 2009, accessed October 29, 2014, www.telegraph.co.uk/sport/othersports/commonwealthgames/6043719/New-Delhi-to-hide-slums-with-bamboo-curtains-during-2010-Commonwealth-Games.html.
16 Based on my field notes as a media anthropologist in Delhi from September 2008 to August 2009, my first stint as an interdisciplinary urban researcher in *Neo* Delhi. For some archival examples of this mounting discourse of skepticism and building anxiety accompanying and even mediated by the urban media spectacle, see "Commonwealth Games a comedy of errors." *Christian Science Monitor*, September

The urban 69

22, 2010, accessed October 29, 2014, www.csmonitor.com/World/GlobalNews/2010/0922/Commonwealth-Games-a-comedy-of-errors-for-India.

17 "Games of squalor." *DailyMail.com*, September 24, 2010, accessed October 29, 2014, www.dailymail.co.uk/news/article-1314514/Commonwealth-Games-2010-Filthy-rooms-await-athletes-Delhi.html.

18 For a good introduction to the uniquely social media phenomenon of going "viral," see A. J. Mills, "Virality in social media: The SPIN framework." *Journal of Public Affairs* 12 (2012), 162–169.

19 "Games village world class: Lalit Bhanot." *NDTV.com*, September 21, 2010, accessed October 29, 2014, www.ndtv.com/article/commonwealth-games/games-village-world-class-lalit-bhanot-53784.

20 Jim Yardley (NYT News Service), "Lalit Bhanot angers nation with hygiene comment." *NDTV.com*, September 25, 2010, accessed October 29, 2014, www.ndtv.com/article/commonwealth-games/lalit-bhanot-angers-nation-with-hygiene-comment-54660.

21 "Chaotic CWG run-up hitting India's global image." *Times of India*, September 25, 2010, accessed October 29, 2014, http://timesofindia.indiatimes.com/news/Chaotic-CWG-run-up-hitting-Indias-global-image-Moodys/articleshow/6622899.cms?

22 Ibid.

23 Although the dynamics of class are increasingly fluid (in both an upward and downward direction) in a space like *Neo* Delhi, knowledge of English in general connotes some level of privilege and mobility. English is spoken by roughly 10–15 percent of India's total population, but the expected percentage would be much higher in a "middle-class" city like Delhi. Yet even in relatively wealthy cities like Delhi this "middle class" is a small minority. This segment is almost exclusively urban or urbanized (i.e., access to increasingly distant far orders), as access to English-medium schools is uncommon outside of cities and towns. The English-language media thus reflects an elite bias and serves as a good proxy for middle-class and elite perceptions of the city. For more on this class-linguistic bias, see David Faust and Richa Nagar, "Politics of development in postcolonial India: English-medium education and social fracturing." *Economic and Political Weekly* 36.30 (2001), 2878–2883.

24 "Lalit shames the country." *Telegraph* (Calcutta, India), September 22, 2010, accessed October 29, 2014, www.telegraphindia.com/1100922/jsp/sports/story_12966666.jsp.

25 Cornelius Castoriadis, "Democracy as procedure and democracy as regime." *Constellations* 4.1 (1997), 1–18.

26 For more on how certain discourses produce the very effects they purportedly merely "describe," see Judith Butler, *Bodies that Matter: On the Discursive Limits of "Sex"* (London: Routledge, 1993).

27 Partha Chatterjee, *The Nation and its Fragments: Colonial and Postcolonial Histories* (Princeton, NJ: Princeton University Press, 1993).

28 Georg Simmel, *The Philosophy of Money* (London: Routledge, 1978), 79.

29 Henri Lefebvre, "The specificity of the city," in *Writings on Cities* (Oxford: Blackwell, 1996), 100–103. This essay, perhaps because of its enigmatic theoretical language, has received little attention despite the increasing attention Lefebvre's work has received within critical urban theory. Two exceptions are Christian Schmid, "Patterns and pathways of global urbanization: Towards comparative analysis," in Neil Brenner (ed.) *Implosions/Explosions: Towards a Study of Planetary Urbanization* (Copenhagen: Jovis Verlag, 2014), 203–217 and Neal Patel, "If these walls could talk: The mental life of the built environment." *Ethnographic Praxis in Industry Conference Proceedings*, 2012:1 (Oxford: Blackwell Publishing, 2012), 74–87.

30 Henri Lefebvre, "The specificity of the city."

31 Ibid., 101.

70   *Distance and proximity in Delhi*

32 Ibid.
33 I elaborate on the concept of communities of sense in the Conclusion of the book.
34 For more on the hauntology of postcolonial cities, through a specifically Benjaminian reading (to accompany and perhaps complicate my decidedly Derridean reading), see Rajeev S. Patke, "Benjamin's Arcades Project and the postcolonial city." *diacritics* 30.4 (2000), 2–14.
35 Fanon, Frantz, *The Wretched of the Earth* (New York: Grove Press, 2004), 3, emphases mine.
36 Partha Chatterjee, *The Nation and its Fragments*.
37 Ibid., 18.
38 Gyan Prakash, "Mumbai: The modern city in ruins," in Andreas Huyssen (ed.) *Other Cities, Other Worlds: Urban Imaginaries in a Globalizing Age* (Durham, NC: Duke University Press, 2008), 187.
39 Janet Abu-Lughod, "Tale of two cities: The origins of modern Cairo." *Comparative Studies in Society and History* 7.4 (1965), 429.
40 Ravi Sundaram, *Pirate Modernity: Delhi's Media Urbanism* (London: Routledge, 2009).
41 Prakash, "The urban turn." See also Srirupa Roy, *Beyond Belief: India and the Politics of Postcolonial Nationalism* (Durham, NC: Duke University Press, 2006).
42 Stephen Legg, *Spaces of Colonialism: Delhi's Urban Governmentalities* (London: John Wiley & Sons, 2008), and Awadhendra Sharan, *In the City, Out of Place: Nuisance, Pollution, and Dwelling in Delhi* (Oxford: Oxford University Press, 2015).
43 Suneetha Dasappa Kacker, "The DDA and the idea of Delhi," in Romi Khosla (ed.) *The Idea of Delhi* (Mumbai: Marg, 2005), 68–77.
44 Ibid.
45 MPD quoted in Biswajit Banerjee, "Shahjahanabad and the Master Plan for Delhi: A critical appraisal." *Economic and Political Weekly* 10:46 (1975), 1781.
46 Urvashi Butalia, *The Other Side of Silence: Voices from the Partition* (Durham, NC: Duke University Press, 2000).
47 1962 MPD, 1.
48 Sundaram, *Pirate Modernity*, 37.
49 Abhijit Datta and Gangadhar Jha, "Delhi: Two decades of plan implementation." *Habitat International* 7.1–2 (1983), 37.
50 Ibid., 40.
51 Ibid.
52 Ibid., 39.
53 Ibid., 41.
54 Ibid., 41.
55 Ibid., 43.
56 Sundaram, *Pirate Modernity*, 56.
57 Banerjee, "Shahjahanabad and the Master Plan for Delhi."
58 Sundaram, *Pirate Modernity*, 56.
59 Jai Sen, *The Unintended City: An Essay on the City of the Poor* (Calcutta: Cathedral Relief and Social Services, 1975).
60 Ashis Nandy, "The death of an empire." *Sarai Reader* 2.7 (2002), 14–21.
61 Kacker, "The DDA and the idea of Delhi," 76.
62 Partha Chatterjee, *The Politics of the Governed: Reflections on Popular Politics in Most of the World* (New York: Columbia University Press, 2004).
63 Amulya Gopalakrishnan, "A house in disorder." *Frontline* 20:10 (2003), accessed February 25, 2015, www.frontline.in/static/html/fl2010/stories/20030523002104500.htm.
64 Kacker, "The DDA and the idea of Delhi," 74.
65 Narendra Modi's populist appeal to make development a "mass movement" speaks to the lasting ideological seduction of development as a mediation of India's still

"under-developed" present, accessed February 24, 2015, www.narendramodi.in/gu/development-should-be-a-mass-movement-we-need-to-integrate-the-people-and-make-it-a-mass-movement-shri-narendra-modi-in-delhi-6022.

66 For general commentary on Indian middle class historically see Pavan Varma, *The Great Indian Middle Class* (Delhi: Penguin Books India, 1998). For "new" middle class in post-reform context, see Leela Fernandes, *India's New Middle Class* (Minneapolis, MN: University of Minnesota Press, 2008). For middle-class and elite politics in Delhi, see Amita Baviskar, "Between violence and desire: Space, power and identity in the making of metropolitan Delhi." *International Social Science Journal* 55.175 (2003), 89–98.

67 Ronojoy Sen, "The perils of playing games." *India in Transition*, November 11, 2010.

68 Uppal, "The impact of the Commonwealth Games 2010," 8.

69 Sen, "Perils of playing games."

70 Uppal, "The impact of the Commonwealth Games 2010," 11.

71 Sen, "Perils of playing games."

72 "India: Human Development Indicators." *UNDP.org*, accessed February 28, 2015, http://hdr.undp.org/en/countries/profiles/IND.

73 *Planned Dispossession: Forced Evictions and the 2010 Commonwealth Games*, Housing and Land Rights Network, Fact-finding Mission Report 14 (New Delhi: Housing and Land Rights Network, 2011), iii.

74 Ibid., iv.

75 Ibid., v.

76 Ibid.

77 Uppal," The impact of the Commonwealth Games 2010," 13.

78 Amita Baviskar, "What the eye does not see: The Yamuna in the imagination of Delhi." *Economic and Political Weekly*, 46.50 (2011), 45–53.

79 Ibid., 48.

80 Ibid., 49.

81 Ibid., 50.

82 This was in part due also to the aftermath of the Emergency, from 1975 to 1977 when then-Prime Minister Indira Gandhi suspended constitutional rule and civil liberties, and imposed authoritarian rule on the country. The period was especially brutal for residents in Old Delhi, who experienced violent dislocation when their slums were destroyed by the Delhi government. After the end of the Emergency, Gandhi and her Congress Party were voted out of office and in the years after a more lax attitude toward slums and informal settlements ensued in Delhi. See Emma Tarlo, *Unsettling Memories: Narratives of the Emergency in Delhi* (Berkeley, CA: University of California Press, 2003).

83 Baviskar, "What the eye does not see," 48.

84 Jim Yardley (NYT News Service), "Lalit Bhanot angers nation with hygiene comment." *NDTV.com*, September 25, 2010, accessed October 29, 2014, www.ndtv.com/article/commonwealth-games/lalit-bhanot-angers-nation-with-hygiene-comment-54660.

85 This mainstream approach is critiqued by Eric Sheppard, Helga Leitner and Anant Maringanti in "Provincializing global urbanism: A manifesto." *Urban Geography* 34.7 (2013), 893–900, and described in the Introduction.

86 Maringanti, "Urban renewal, fiscal deficit and the politics of decentralisation."

87 Gayatri Chakravorty Spivak, "Megacity." *Grey Room* 1 (2000), 8–25.

88 Rajesh Bhattacharya and Kalyan Sanyal, "Bypassing the squalor: New towns, immaterial labour and exclusion in postcolonial urbanization." *Economic and Political Weekly* 46.31 (2011), 41–48.

89 This is particularly true in an era of entrepreneurial urbanism and a global economy of appearances. See David Harvey, "From managerialism to entrepreneurialism: The

72 *Distance and proximity in Delhi*

transformation in urban governance in late capitalism." *Geografiska Annaler. Series B. Human Geography* 71:1 (1989), 3–17, and Anna Tsing, "Inside the economy of appearances." *Public Culture* 12.1 (2000), 115–144.

90 Nelson, "New Delhi to hide slums with bamboo 'curtains' during 2010 Commonwealth Games."

91 One of the more striking examples of this geohistorical "forgetting" I came across during the course of my research was in Aravind Adiga's *The White Tiger* (New York: New Press, 2008). As I argue in an upcoming essay on everyday movement and urban esthetics in India, the middle-class/elite reception of Adiga's work following its publication in Delhi, where much of the story takes place, revealed some of the deep psycho-geographic and ontological investments that privileged urban elites make in this forgetting. Adiga's novel examines the violent temporalities and geohistorical differences that haunt and thus structure elite movements and everyday experiences in contemporary Delhi, revealing a politics of secession through mediation that did not sit well with many middle-class Indian audiences.

92 Ashis Nandy, "The beautiful, expanding future of poverty: Popular economics as a psychological defense." *International Studies Review* 4.2 (2002), 117.

93 Ibid.

94 "Awakening of a giant: From one to 101 medals for India in 76 years." Commonwealth Games Federation website, October 15, 2010, accessed February 25, 2014, http://d2010.thecgf.com/news/awakening_giant_one_101_medals_india_76_years.

95 Boria Majumdar, "Commonwealth Games 2010: The index of a "new" India?" *Social Research: An International Quarterly* 78.1 (2011), 231–254.

96 Sahana Udupa, "Aam Aadmi: Decoding the media logics." *Economic & Political Weekly* 49:7 (2014), 13–15.

97 Uppal, "The impact of the Commonwealth Games, 2010."

98 Baviskar, "What the eye does not see," 47.

99 John Urry, "The 'system' of automobility." *Theory, Culture & Society* 21.4–5 (2004), 25–39.

100 John Urry, "Climate change, travel and complex futures." *The British Journal of Sociology* 59.2 (2008), 261–279.

101 Jennifer Robinson, "Global and world cities: A view from off the map." *International Journal of Urban and Regional Research* 26.3 (2002), 545.

102 Lefebvre, "The specificity of the city," 103.

Bibliography

Abu-Lughod, Janet. "Tale of two cities: The origins of modern Cairo." *Comparative Studies in Society and History* 7.4 (1965): 429–457.

Banerjee, Biswajit. "Shahjahanabad and the Master Plan for Delhi: A critical appraisal." *Economic and Political Weekly* 10:46 (1975): 1779–1784.

Baviskar, Amita. "Between violence and desire: Space, power and identity in the making of metropolitan Delhi." *International Social Science Journal* 55.175 (2003): 89–98.

Baviskar, Amita. "What the eye does not see: The Yamuna in the imagination of Delhi." *Economic and Political Weekly* 46.50 (2011): 45–53.

Bhattacharya, Rajesh and Kalyan Sanyal. "Bypassing the squalor: New towns, immaterial labour and exclusion in postcolonial urbanization." *Economic and Political Weekly* 46.31 (2011): 41–48.

Bottici, Chiara. *Imaginal Politics: Images beyond Imagination and the Imaginary* (New York: Columbia University Press, 2014).

Butalia, Urvashi. *The Other Side of Silence: Voices from the Partition.* Durham, NC: Duke University Press, 2000.

The urban 73

Butler, Judith. *Bodies that Matter: On the Discursive Limits of "Sex."* London: Routledge, 1993.

Castoriadis, Cornelius. "Democracy as procedure and democracy as regime." *Constellations* 4.1 (1997): 1–18.

"Chaotic CWG run-up hitting India's global image." *Times of India*, September 25, 2010, accessed October 29, 2014, http://timesofindia.indiatimes.com/news/Chaotic-CWG-run-up-hitting-Indias-global-image-Moodys/articleshow/6622899.cms?.

Chatterjee, Partha. *The Nation and its Fragments: Colonial and Postcolonial Histories.* Princeton, NJ: Princeton University Press, 1993.

Chatterjee, Partha. *The Politics of the Governed: Reflections on Popular Politics in Most of the World.* New York: Columbia University Press, 2004.

"Commonwealth Games a comedy of errors." *Christian Science Monitor*, September 22, 2010, accessed October 29, 2014, www.csmonitor.com/World/GlobalNews/2010/0922/Commonwealth-Games-a-comedy-of-errors-for-India.

Datta, Abhijit and Gangadhar Jha. "Delhi: Two decades of plan implementation." *Habitat International* 7.1–2 (1983): 37–45.

de Certeau, Michel. *Practice of Everyday Life.* Berkeley, CA: University of California Press, 1988.

Dixit, Sheila. "Government of National Capital Territory of Delhi Speech to National Development Council Meeting, 9th December 2006, New Delhi," accessed October 29, 2014, http://planningcommission.nic.in/plans/planrel/52ndc/delhi.pdf.

Fanon, Frantz. *The Wretched of the Earth.* New York: Grove Press, 2004.

Faust, David and Richa Nagar. "Politics of development in postcolonial India: English-medium education and social fracturing." *Economic and Political Weekly* 36.30 (2001): 2878–2883.

Fernandes, Leela. *India's New Middle Class.* Minneapolis, MN: University of Minnesota Press, 2008.

"Games of squalor." *DailyMail.com*, September 24, 2010, accessed October 29, 2014, www.dailymail.co.uk/news/article-1314514/Commonwealth-Games-2010-Filthy-rooms-await-athletes-Delhi.html.

"Games village world class: Lalit Bhanot." *NDTV.com*, September 21, 2010, accessed October 29, 2014, www.ndtv.com/article/commonwealth-games/games-village-world-class-lalit-bhanot-53784.

Gopalakrishnan, Amulya. "A house in disorder." *Frontline* 20:10 (2003), accessed February 25, 2015, www.frontline.in/static/html/fl2010/stories/20030523002104500.htm.

Gotham, Kevin Fox. "Theorizing urban spectacles." *City* 9.2 (2005): 225–246.

Harvey, David. "From managerialism to entrepreneurialism: The transformation in urban governance in late capitalism." *Geografiska Annaler. Series B. Human Geography* 71:1 (1989): 3–17.

Housing and Land Rights Network. *Planned Dispossession: Forced Evictions and the 2010 Commonwealth Games*, Housing and Land Rights Network, Fact-finding Mission Report 14 (New Delhi: Housing and Land Rights Network, 2011).

Kacker, Suneetha Dasappa. "The DDA and the idea of Delhi," in Romi Khosla (ed.) *The Idea of Delhi.* Mumbai: Marg, 2005: 68–77.

Kohli, Atul. "Politics of economic growth in India, 1980–2005: Part I: The 1980s." *Economic and Political Weekly* 41.3 (2006): 1251–1259.

Lefebvre, Henri. "The specificity of the city," in *Writings on Cities.* Oxford: Blackwell, 1996: 100–103.

Legg, Stephen. *Spaces of Colonialism: Delhi's Urban Governmentalities.* London: John Wiley & Sons, 2008.

74   Distance and proximity in Delhi

Majumdar, Boria. "Commonwealth Games 2010: The index of a "new" India?" *Social Research: An International Quarterly* 78.1 (2011): 231–254.

Maringanti, Anant. "Urban renewal, fiscal deficit and the politics of decentralization: The case of Jawaharlal Nehru Urban Renewal Mission in India." *Space and Policy* 16.1 (2012): 93–109.

Mills, A. J. "Virality in social media: The SPIN framework." *Journal of Public Affairs* 12 (2012): 162–169.

Modi, Narendra. "Development should be a mass movement." *NarendraModi.in*, February 17, 2014, accessed February 24, 2015, www.narendramodi.in/gu/development-should-be-a-mass-movement-we-need-to-integrate-the-people-and-make-it-a-mass-movement-shri-narendra-modi-in-delhi-6022.

Muppidi, Himadeep. *The Politics of the Global*. Minneapolis, MN: University of Minnesota Press, 2004.

Nandy, Ashis. "The beautiful, expanding future of poverty: Popular economics as a psychological defense." *International Studies Review* 4.2 (2002): 107–121.

Nandy, Ashis. "The death of an empire." *Sarai Reader* 2.7 (2002): 14–21.

Nelson, Dean. "New Delhi to hide slums with bamboo 'curtains' during 2010 Commonwealth Games." *Telegraph*, August 17, 2009, accessed October 29, 2014, www.telegraph.co.uk/sport/othersports/commonwealthgames/6043719/New-Delhi-to-hide-slums-with-bamboo-curtains-during-2010-Commonwealth-Games.html.

"New Delhi to host 2010 Commonwealth Games." *The Age*, November 14, 2003, accessed October 28, 2014, www.theage.com.au/articles/2003/11/14/1068674368167.

Patel, Neal H. "If these walls could talk: The mental life of the built environment." *Ethnographic Praxis in Industry Conference Proceedings*. Oxford: Blackwell Publishing, 2012.

Patke, Rajeev S. "Benjamin's Arcades Project and the postcolonial city." *diacritics* 30.4 (2000): 2–14.

Prakash, Gyan. "The urban turn." *Sarai Reader* 2.7 (2002): 2–7.

Prakash, Gyan. "Mumbai: The modern city in ruins," in Andreas Huyssen (ed.) *Other Cities, Other Worlds: Urban Imaginaries in a Globalizing Age*. Durham, NC: Duke University Press, 2008: 181–204.

Puri, V. K. *Master Plan of Delhi 2021*. Delhi: JBA Publishers, 2007.

Robinson, Jennifer. "Global and world cities: A view from off the map." *International Journal of Urban and Regional Research* 26.3 (2002): 531–554.

Roy, Ananya. "Why India cannot plan its cities: Informality, insurgence and the idiom of urbanization." *Planning Theory* 8.1 (2009): 76–87.

Roy, Srirupa. *Beyond Belief: India and the Politics of Postcolonial Nationalism*. Durham, NC: Duke University Press, 2006.

Sassen, Saskia. "Why cities matter." *Catalogue of the 10th International Architecture Exhibition, Venice Biennale* (2006): 26–51.

Schmid, Christian. "Patterns and pathways of global urbanization: Towards comparative analysis," in Neil Brenner (ed.) *Implosions/Explosions: Towards a Study of Planetary Urbanization*. Copenhagen: Jovis Verlag, 2014: 203–217.

Sen, Jai. *The Unintended City: An Essay on the City of the Poor*. Calcutta: Cathedral Relief and Social Services, 1975.

Sen, Ronojoy. "The perils of playing games." *India in Transition*, November 11, 2010.

Sharan, Awadhendra. *In the City, Out of Place: Nuisance, Pollution, and Dwelling in Delhi*. Oxford: Oxford University Press, 2015.

Shaw, Annapurna. "Urban policy in post-independent India: An appraisal." *Economic and Political Weekly* 31.4 (1996): 224–228.

Sheppard, Eric, Helga Leitner and Anant Maringanti, "Provincializing global urbanism: A manifesto." *Urban Geography* 34.7 (2013): 893–900.

Simmel, Georg. *The Philosophy of Money*. London: Routledge, 1978.

Spivak, Gayatri Chakravorty. "Megacity." *Grey Room* 1 (2000): 8–25.

Sundaram, Ravi. *Pirate Modernity: Delhi's Media Urbanism*. London: Routledge, 2009.

Tarlo, Emma. *Unsettling Memories: Narratives of the Emergency in Delhi*. Berkeley, CA: University of California Press, 2003.

Tarlo, Emma, Veronique Dupont and Denis Vidal (eds). *Delhi: Urban Space and Human Destiny*. New Delhi: Manohar Publishing, 2000.

Tsing, Anna. "Inside the economy of appearances." *Public Culture* 12.1 (2000): 115–144.

Udupa, Sahana. "Aam Aadmi: Decoding the media logics." *Economic & Political Weekly* 49:7 (2014): 13–15.

United Nations. "India: Human Development Indicators," *UNDP.org*, accessed February 28, 2015, http://hdr.undp.org/en/countries/profiles/IND.

Uppal, Vinayak. "The impact of the Commonwealth Games 2010 on urban development of Delhi." *Theoretical and Empirical Researches in Urban Management* 10 (2009): 7–29.

Urry, John. "The 'system' of automobility." *Theory, Culture & Society* 21.4–5 (2004): 25–39.

Urry, John. "Climate change, travel and complex futures." *The British Journal of Sociology* 59.2 (2008): 261–279.

Varma, Pavan. *The Great Indian Middle Class*. Delhi: Penguin Books India, 1998.

Yardley, Jim. "Lalit Bhanot angers nation with hygiene comment." *NDTV.com*, September 25, 2010, accessed October 29, 2014, www.ndtv.com/article/commonwealth-games/lalit-bhanot-angers-nation-with-hygiene-comment-54660.

2 The neighborhood

Magical economics

> Our ancestors were well respected artists who performed for kings and queens.
>
> Puran Bhat

In March 2012, the London-based newspaper *The Economist* ran a front page story on India's recent economic troubles entitled "India's economy: Losing its magic." The editorial drily asserted that after displaying impressive economic growth following two decades of liberal reform, India's bureaucratic state, "still huge and crazy after all these years," threatened this growth with sluggish democratic and populist politics.[1] The ruling party in the center had proven reluctant to push controversial reforms through Parliament (in particular regarding labor laws and regulations on foreign direct investment) lest they pay the price in the upcoming elections. Meanwhile, increasing acts of protest and unrest on the part of farmers, small-scale merchants and industrial workers around the country were proving these fears well founded. "India is a place that has fallen out of love with reform," the editorial opined, "It needs to get the magic back."

Why would an influential international news magazine that prides itself on "objectivity" and "a reverence for facts" rely on imagery of magic to explain India's need for economic reform?[2] What imaginative work was *magic* doing here?

At one level, recourse to magic here is deliberately metaphorical and colloquial, and is perhaps too obvious to even merit attention. Not wanting to appear like they were disparaging the open-ended nature of democratic politics in India altogether, the paper nevertheless wanted to establish that popular politics was precisely what had gotten in the way of further economic reforms that would surely boost India's economic growth. "Magic" was thus needed to perform the seemingly impossible: reconciling *contingent* democratic political outcomes with the *necessity* of economic reform. For anyone familiar with its output, this kind of rhetorical trick was rather unremarkable for *The Economist*, which has long argued for neoliberal economic reform in India and other "developing" countries.

More darkly, the British magazine's rhetorical use of magic also quite clearly summons orientalist imagery from the mid-nineteenth-century, when the Victorian

The neighborhood 77

fascination with Indian conjurers led to a strong association between India and "black magic." Magicians, jugglers and snake charmers "came to be presented as one of the greatest sights of India ... almost a trademark of Hindustan."[3] The magazine's cover of a cartoon Indian snake charmer (complete with turban), literally trying to hypnotize the line of a graph representing India's economy in the direction of higher growth, makes the adoption of the colonial stereotype obvious. Here, imagery of Indian magic suggests a continued fascination with—and perhaps a corresponding anxiety over—the Orient as an inscrutable object of both knowledge and desire in Anglo-capitalist discourses.

There is also a third connotation, this one more implicit than the others. Here, the association of economics with "magic" comports with recent turns in neo-classical economics that have had to reckon with the irrational forces at work in social and individual behavior. Economics has had to reconcile the unpredictable "animal spirits" of capitalism and the frequent "irrational exuberance" of the market with the otherwise rational assumptions of modern economic theory, which sees humans as primarily self-interested optimizing actors.[4] As recent academic work on the history of the discipline has shown, the birth of modern economics was coterminous with the rise of "natural" sciences such as modern physics. Economics imported several of the key concepts of the latter, assuming that metaphors of equilibrium, elasticity, inflation and interaction at the molecular scale translated unproblematically onto the human and social scale.[5] But neoclassical economic theory has had a particularly difficult time translating those moments when ostensibly rational economic actors behaved in ways that contradict their utility-maximizing preference curve, leading to market disequilibria and systemic crisis.[6]

The Economist's curious recourse to Indian "magic" perhaps betrays a larger "tragicomic romance with science" on the part of the discipline of neoclassical economics.[7] This theoretical discourse, which prizes efficiency, rationality, and predictability remains haunted by what it structurally excludes: the unpredictable "human" and "social" element. Thus, even as neoclassical economics disenchants the world with modern techno-science and instrumental rationality, human reality itself remains obstinately elusive and illusionary, magically resistant to these rationalist designs.

There are two different kinds of magic at work here, both productive of the theoretical discourse of neoclassical economics and the neoliberal worldview of *The Economist*. Both enact a becoming-global ideological discourse that plays a significant role in mediating changing urban life in cities like *Neo* Delhi, as I will show in this chapter. First, magic represents the "constitutive outside" of modernity, excluded as a pre-modern remnant yet subtly shaping it and even haunting it from without.[8] Magic is the unknown that comes to structure "the known." In this case it is the arbitrary boundary line that "fixes the economy," as it were, into an object or an abstract space of representation (separate from the non-economic). Late liberal states attempt to manage and manipulate this partially constructed, partially representational assemblage called "the economy" in the direction of never-ending accumulation and growth. In this view, magic is what

78 *Distance and proximity in Delhi*

must appear as unintelligible (or non-economic because it contradicts this singular fixation on growth) in order for the economy to gain intelligibility as a rationally managed space for the engineering of such "growth." But to successfully perform this kind of meta-discursive magic, another, everyday kind of magic is required: the privileging of the economic over the political in everyday spatial negotiations and movements.[9] This "post-political" discourse emerges through an appeal to a higher economic rationality on par with "science," that is, the very negation of "magic." Both of these tricks come together in producing the apparition on the cover of the March 2012 issue.

But in some ways, the cover is apt for describing the global economy as it is imagined and projected in neoliberal India. In cities like *Neo* Delhi especially, the global is spatialized through a similar practice of performative interpretation that "transforms the very thing it interprets."[10] With respect to such cities and their urban economies, the global can be understood as functioning within an "economy of appearances," where wealth and value must first be conjured in the abstract as an appealing/profitable interpretation of the future before it can ever be actualized as such.[11] But in order to realize this potential accumulation, these cities must produce imitative "world-class" architecture and infrastructure in order to convince investors that their environment is sufficiently safe, that is, "business friendly," or profitable. Thus, through "entrepreneurial urbanism," cities re-brand themselves as competitive and forward-looking, as stable and safe destinations for investors and tourists alike.[12] In some cases, the drive on the part of cities to brand themselves as already "global" or "globalizing" can become something of a self-fulfilling prophecy. In an economy of appearances global capital often creates the world in its own image. But just as often, it seems, postcolonial cities produce untimely images that falsify their own appearance and create the possibility for an alternative apprehension of the urban present.

Here the place of the slum in the "globalizing" postcolonial city serves as an instructive challenge both to the inherently elitist narrative of magical economics, on the one hand, and to more critical narratives that foreground the spread of finance capitalism on a global scale, on the other. The image of the slum, as both a metaphor and a metonym for what Jai Sen once called "the unintended city," comes into untimely encounter with new initiatives that "re-brand" the city for the sake of global investment and projection.[13]

This chapter looks at a slum re-development scheme in contemporary Delhi in order to argue that slums are both part of this synchronic capitalist world but form a boundary line of intelligibility where economic appearances become altered and change in interesting and unexpected ways. *Neo* Delhi is a postcolonial city that is trying desperately to "globalize" its image, yet its "globality" might be better understood within the dialectic of appearance and disappearance that structures and haunts it.

I examine the peculiar yet instructive case of Kathputli Colony, a fifty-year old "slum" inhabited by magicians and other performance artists who realize, paradoxically, that there is no such thing as magic when it comes to urban or economic development.[14] That is, they fully understand that for a "global" image of Delhi to appear something else will have to disappear, namely themselves. In the drive to re-brand Delhi as a "slum-free" city as per its 2021 Master Plan, the DDA seeks to perform the very kind of magic called for by *The Economist*, that is, producing neoliberal urban spaces available to financial capital. Its self-imposed task is to move slums and other "urban blight" to outside of the "globalizing" precincts. Moving slums into spaces of invisibility, I argue, is one way in which cities like Delhi seek to "get their economic magic back."

Moving slums

> In our family we remove fear from the child's mind at a very young age.
>
> Maya Pawar

Kathputli Colony is a decidedly magical place.[15] It is populated with performance artists whose trade involves artistry and charisma, illusion and deception, pathos and drama. Kathputli Colony (herein KC) also makes a brief but significant appearance in Salman Rushdie's celebrated novel *Midnight's Children*. But KC is a real place. It is a densely built and well-known slum community set within the Shadipur neighborhood of west central Delhi. Puppeteers, dancers, musicians, fire-breathers, jugglers, drummers, acrobats and myriad conjurers of everyday spectacle constitute the diverse groups that reside in one of the larger slum clusters in the city. These artists live in tightly-packed one or two room homes made out of brick, cement or sheets of corrugated iron and metal. These homes were arranged in clusters divided by narrow alleys and lanes. Nearly invisible from the main road outside the slum itself, once one walked into the neighborhood one crossed paths with artists practicing their crafts and routines, carving puppets and making other props for their performances. Kathputli Colony's streets were filled with music, dancing and creativity, giving the space a frenetic buzz that was difficult not to notice for a first-time visitor.

The person who took me into Kathputli Colony for the first time was Kailash Bhatt. Kailash took visitors (mostly from the West) into the slum to tour its streets and to enjoy an exclusive performance by his own troupe in the neighborhood itself.[16] Kailash was himself a puppeteer, a musician, a dancer, and also ran a French-funded NGO whose mission was preserving traditional Rajasthani arts. His ancestors had been traveling between Rajasthan and Delhi for the past 100 years, performing both for Delhi's aristocratic elite and for the public on the streets. Kailash himself was born and raised in the slum. He was proud of this fact. His father Mohan was one of the first to move into the area in the late 1960s, when the nascent community was first formed out of collections of tents on an empty field on the outskirts of Delhi. In settling the area known as Shadipur, their family helped inaugurate a stable but ever-evolving space for artists and performers in the city. In this way the slum managed to endure for more than five decades, gaining increasing fame through literary representations such as that of Rushdie's *Midnight's Children*, or through the nationally recognized talents of some of its artists, as we will see.

80 *Distance and proximity in Delhi*

Meanwhile the capital city grew and expanded around Kathputli Colony. Today the slum is surrounded by postcolonial Delhi's sprawling settlements for miles in every direction.[17] And while the city grew around it, other slum settlements came up in and around Shadipur, as the slum neighborhood itself grew manifold. Today it is estimated that anywhere from 2100 to 3300 families live in the Shadipur slums, as migrants from all over India moved into the place incrementally over the past half-century, forming dense clusters and neighborhoods adjacent to and surrounding Kathputli Colony.[18]

One day in the midst of field work here in December 2012, Kailash took me to the roof of a tall, narrow, brick building in the middle of the slum. From three stories above the surrounding slum clusters, the "informal" expanse of Shadipur was visible; it was a bustling mini-city in the midst of a larger and expanding metropolis. The Delhi Metro's elevated Blue Line, connecting central New Delhi and the western suburbs, prominently formed the northern boundary line in the horizon. In the foreground the machicolated roofs had alternating concrete, brick and metal surfaces, unevenly and irregularly distributed. They were set at different slopes and heights; some dwellings had second or third floors added to them while others made do with more rudimentary arrangements. The homes formed a dense cluster of heterogeneous exteriors that nonetheless had a kind of spatial coherence by virtue of their proximity and the stark juxtaposition of this "informal" settlement with the Delhi Metro tracks and surrounding commercial spaces behind it.

Just recently, Kailash informed me, the Delhi government had decided to sell all of Shadipur's land to a private real estate developer. The Delhi Development Authority (DDA) claimed that Kathputli Colony and its adjacent slums were on "public" land that the government owned. Back in 1957 the DDA declared that it held monopoly control over all unenclosed lands in the NCT, although it selectively used these monopoly rights to develop much of this land thereafter. "Now the government wants to get rid of us," Kailash said. "They will build a skyscraper right here in Shadipur, one that will be taller than the Eiffel Tower!"[19]

The reference to Paris was deliberate. Kailash and his troupe had been to that city several times. They had also been to Europe and North America, places that seemed a world away from their tight quarters in Shadipur. In Delhi they struggled to make ends meet month-to-month, increasingly finding it difficult to perform their acts in public streets and pavements without getting intimidated by the police and forced to pay bribes.[20] Yet folk artists like Kailash and his family had been commissioned by the Ministry of Culture to showcase their talents at diplomatic and cultural events both in India and abroad. The ministry would produce special passports that enabled them to travel to various foreign countries. Some in their community had been awarded national recognition, shaking hands with presidents and government ministers, so that at international meetings and gala receptions in foreign consulates and palaces, the artists of Kathputli Colony represented India's rich cultural "authenticity" abroad, even as they were facing imminent eviction in their own neighborhood.

As mentioned in passing above, the slums of Shadipur also make a brief but significant appearance in the novel *Midnight's Children* by Salman Rushdie. A classic within the genre of magical realism and Anglo-Indian fiction, *Midnight's Children* allegorically tells the story of India's journey from colony to postcolony, focusing especially on the three decades following independence (roughly 1947–1980). The story is told through the life of Saleem Sinai, who serves as the narrator and protagonist of the novel. Sinai's movements, perceptions and memories come to embody the history of the nation itself, so that he also becomes the novel's central metaphor. Through the use of magical realism as a narrative technique, where the fantastic and the ordinary exist side-by-side, Rushdie's novel artfully renders the dialectic between changing national life and its symbolic metaphors. Towards the end of the story, however, the plot becomes specifically urban. Sinai's adventures lead him to Delhi, where he comes to stay in a slum full of magicians, jugglers, acrobats and other artists in the Old City. The timing of this transition is significant, for it comes shortly before then-Prime Minister Indira Gandhi declares National Emergency under Article 352 of the Indian Constitution, suspending elections and civil liberties. During this time, in a campaign to "beautify" the city, slum demolitions ramp up. The "magicians' ghetto" that houses Sinai and others gets targeted by the state and the bulldozers and police show up to carry out the removal. But as is "normal" in Rushdie's magical realist retelling, something unexplainable (that is, by secular and rational means) happens when the demolition crew arrives at the slum. It disappears and manages somehow to evade the state for the duration of Gandhi's twenty-one months of authoritarian rule. The "moving slum," as it soon becomes known, eventually ends up in Shadipur, becoming visible once again, once the Emergency is declared over. This is where Kathputli Colony resides today, facing eviction by the postcolonial state in Delhi.

We will return to Rushdie's novel later in the chapter, particularly its untimely conjunction with the present-day fate of Kathputli Colony. But before further exploring these connections, it is necessary to frame Shadipur's slums within the larger history of slums in Delhi, including the frequent and violent demolition of slums carried out by the state, in particular the DDA. This spatial violence abated after the brutalities of the Emergency became publicized and were condemned in the immediate aftermath, but have picked up with perhaps even more force and urgency in an era of neoliberal urbanism.

Slum demolitions in Delhi

> When they move us, no one will come here wondering where all the artists went.
>
> Puran Bhat

The social psychologist Ashis Nandy has described the urban slum in India as "a living critique of the political economy of the city. By virtue of its existence, it is a comment on the failure of a political economy to provide certain kinds of lifestyle to its people."[21] The proliferation of urban slums in postcolonial cities is

82 *Distance and proximity in Delhi*

often seen as evidence of "state failure" in development literature, namely a failure to provide safe and adequate housing to urban residents.[22] But the persistence of slums can also be read as a perverse sign of governmental "success" in the midst of high rates of rural to urban migration in the midst of economic deregulation. Though they are often characterized as "unplanned," "haphazard" and "ungoverned" spaces, the very existence and growth of slums and non-legal squatter settlements in postcolonial cities presupposes a range of ongoing political and economic negotiations among diverse urban institutions and populations that is part of what Partha Chatterjee calls "political society" in India.[23] In large cities in particular, the unequal relationships of dependency, access and mobility amongst these urban actors greatly shapes how political society works. Thus, populist politicians often compete for influence and patronage in slums, while slum dwellers too strategically use their limited economic means and electoral votes to negotiate and survive in unstable non-legal habitats.[24] While many neighborhoods are suddenly and remorselessly removed without warning (as we saw in Chapter 1 in the case of the Commonwealth Games in Delhi in 2010), many other slums manage to survive in a precarious urban temporality, like Kathputli Colony. Yet demolition and displacement hovers as a lingering possibility among the improvised domiciles and communities of slum dwellers. Slums and their "informal" urban residents are in this way entangled with "formal" structures of citizenship and governance, which "exclude subjects from the political order, only to include them more completely in politics by their outcast state."[25]

In the city of Delhi, with over 3000 officially recognized and non-recognized slums housing upwards of three million residents,[26] state practices of slum demolition go back to the British period, when colonial governments depicted slums as a threat to both public health and security.[27] The unorganized and precarious settlements of the "native population" in the city were to be cleared out so that the state could discipline and re-order their "unhygienic" and "chaotic" environments. Such representations of space were particularly prevalent in and around the Old City of Shahjahanabad, where slum neighborhoods, or *bastis*, were more common.[28] But slum demolitions continued even after independence. Under the 1956 Slum Areas (Improvement and Clearance) Act, the postcolonial state began categorizing unauthorized squatter settlements on "public" land as "notified slums," which "the Delhi government could use as an instrument for slum clearance as and when required."[29] The Jhuggi Jhonpri Removal Scheme of 1958 was then devised by the Delhi government to "remove squatters from government land," with the promise of re-settling them on the periphery of the city at a subsidized rate.[30] These promises were often left unfulfilled, however, leaving the evicted to fend for themselves and create new "informal" settlements elsewhere within the city. Forced evictions of notified slums continued into the 1960s but their numbers rose dramatically during the Emergency period of autocratic rule between 1975 and 1977. Many settlements of the urban poor in Delhi were demolished during this time and the poor were forcefully relocated to the peripheries of the city.

The neighborhood 83

After the Emergency was declared over and Indira Gandhi's Congress Party was voted out of government, the practice of forcibly removing slums was temporarily curtailed, with "no major evictions taking place after 1977 until 1997–98."[31] Meanwhile, in the 1980s and 1990s, due to high levels of migration into the city, a profusion of new non-legal or "informal" settlements surrounded and penetrated the "intended," or formally planned city.[32] Today, 30 percent or more of Delhi's urban population resides in slums, many without publicly serviced infrastructure, including potable water and working toilets.[33] In the absence of these basic urban services, residents rely instead on pirated infrastructure and improvised service networks.[34]

Most slum dwellers are daily wage earners, laborers, guards, domestic workers, small shopkeepers and petty traders. They constitute a key site of surplus extraction as "informal" workers in Delhi's urban economy, a seemingly never-ending supply of flexible, contingent and unprotected workers that effectively subsidize the economic growth of Delhi.[35] It is the abundance of labor that keeps wages down, middle-class lives affordable and postcolonial cities competitive. Yet, while slums are central to the functioning of the city's urban economy, their residents exist in a quasi-legitimate "notified" status, "which gave the [Delhi Development Authority] the authority to destroy [slums] even before the internal Emergency of the 1970s, although it was the Emergency conditions that enabled them to exercise that right."[36] As noted above, after the notable decline in number of demolitions from the late-1970s to the early 2000s, slum demolitions orchestrated by the state in Delhi were once again on the rise.[37] This increase corresponded with the 2021 Master Plan of Delhi's officially stated desire to re-invent the capital as a "slum-free" city. Between 1990 and 2003, one report found, "51,461 houses were demolished in Delhi under 'slum clearance' schemes. Between 2004 and 2007, however, at least 45,000 homes were demolished."[38]

The increase in slum demolitions has reintroduced a precarious temporality into spaces of quasi-legal or non-legal recognition. As a recent humanitarian report on slum demolitions in Delhi explains,

> Most squatters feel it is not worth investing their meager incomes in their immediate environment when their homes might be destroyed by the authorities at any moment. On the other hand, that moment might string out for several years, if not decades owing to the political games of local leaders and politicians who patronize squatter settlements. In the meantime, the inhabitants of such areas carry on living in what are often deplorable conditions.[39]

Ironically, this occurs even in so-called "re-settlement" colonies, where erstwhile residents of demolished slums are often relocated. Over time these "re-settlement" colonies endure and expand and often become notified slums in their own right, facing the imminent possibility of demolition sometime down the road. This is precisely what is happening today in Kathputli Colony.

Urban renewal or removal?

> Since the day I came here, everyone has told me, "Tomorrow your home will be demolished. A bulldozer will come today...." It hasn't been demolished yet.
>
> Because this isn't a normal colony.
>
> Rehman Shah

Rumors of Kathputli Colony's demolition have persisted throughout the duration of Kathputli Colony's existence. In the past, aligning with the right elected leaders or influential NGOs sufficed to ensure that the bulldozers and wreckers stayed away from Shadipur. As one resident of Kathputli Colony told a journalist in 2009, just as talk of the slum's demolition was beginning once again: "We know our very existence here would become a problem if we do not vote. Just because we vote we are allowed to stay here, otherwise we would be thrown out from this place."[40]

Yet the current talk of impending demolition rings differently than before. It is being articulated now as part of a novel and potentially lucrative urban renewal strategy whose rationale is outlined in the 2021 Master Plan for Delhi (2021 MPD). The idea is to "re-habilitate" old urban neighborhoods, while self-financing the provision of housing for the urban poor by "using land as a resource for private sector participation."[41] The strategy is consistent with the 2021 MPD and new national urban policy, which focuses on "optimizing" land use in the city and facilitating public–private partnerships as much as possible in order to transform Delhi and other Indian cities as "world-class" cities.[42] Among other things, the Master Plan seeks to put a "humanitarian face" on the process of slum demolitions in the city. Rather than forcibly evicting current residents and moving them to the urban peripheries, which had long been the practice (indeed, Shadipur itself was once on the western periphery of the city), the new strategy includes "in-situ rehabilitation," in which "in-site up-gradation of the land pockets of slum and JJ Clusters, which are not required for public priority use, is the first option for provision of affordable housing for rehabilitation of squatters."[43] Under this scheme those current slum dwellers able to furnish proof of tenure in a notified slum colony would be able to secure a future flat within the "re-habilitated" site. The DDA claims that up to 40 percent of Delhi's housing could be satisfied through such in-site rehabilitation or up-gradation of existing areas.

Shadipur's slums were slated to be among the first of these so-called "in-situ rehabilitations." The DDA had been pushing for re-development in the area since 1986, when it "proposed the resettlement of Kathputli residents in the South Delhi region of Vasant Kunj." Later efforts in 1990 and 1996 also attempted to relocate the residents of KC, yet "all of these proposals were rejected on the grounds that neither location was as centrally located as their current Shadipur settlement."[44] The new in-situ strategy was adopted by the DDA after 2007 in consultation with planning professionals from both government and the private sector. According to the DDA's plan, the current residents of the slum would be temporarily relocated to a transit camp (in a site to be decided later) for the duration of the construction period. Through a public–private partnership, the DDA would work with Raheja Developers Ltd., an Indian firm, to build 2800 flats for slum families free of charge. Each flat would be a minimum of 30.5 square meters, including one room of nine square meters and one multipurpose room of 6.5 square meters, with a small bathroom and kitchen. The re-development site would also include a primary and secondary school, a community hall, a police station, a ration store and dairy. Reiterating the DDA's goal of transforming Delhi into a "world-class city," the developer's website characterizes this project as "a move to provide better living conditions for the urban poor, the development work at Kathputli Colony project would act as a pilot project in Delhi to make Delhi a slum-free State."[45]

But what makes this particular plan for "re-habilitating" the Shadipur slum clusters different from past demolitions is not simply this "in-situ" aspect. In addition to the subsidized flats to re-settle the slum's current residents within the re-developed site, the scheme also contains an appeal to self interest and property market speculation in *Neo* Delhi: the Raheja "Phoenix"—Delhi's first "official" skyscraper. Raheja would partner with a multi-national firm, Dubai-based Arabtec Construction LLC, which famously built what is currently the world's tallest building, the half-a-mile-high Burj Khalifa in Dubai. The result of this transnational collaboration was to be a spectacle of grand proportions in New Delhi: the Phoenix would feature a fifty-four-floor tower with a "skyclub" and helipad with 170 premium apartments at more than 1000 square feet each. The buildings for the displaced residents of Kathputli Colony would ostensibly lie adjacent to these high-end luxury dwellings.

Yet for all the appeal of luxury skyscrapers and retail space coupled with subsidized housing for the poor, all in close proximity to the newly completed Delhi Metro Blue Line, the so-called "rehabilitation plans" for Kathputli Colony have hit a prolonged impasse. As of August 2016, construction still had not started for Raheja's Phoenix project, making it more than six years behind schedule. The biggest problem for the developers is the refusal on the part of many current residents in Kathputli Colony and Shadipur to give up their homes, many of which have been inhabited for forty or more years. Many residents are skeptical about Raheja's timeline for the construction for the resettlement housing and eventual return to Shadipur after shifting to the transition housing. Although in the contract between the DDA and Raheja the social housing for Kathputli residents was to be delivered within two years of the "clearing out" date, many current Kathputli residents remain skeptical about the likelihood of such a timetable. There is also controversy regarding who exactly will be included in the re-development plans. Proof of sufficient tenure in KC must be established through forms of government identification like ration cards and the like. The cut-off date for sufficient tenure in Kathputli Colony has been "vague," according to one assessment of the DDA's "in-situ" plan, with "continuity of residence" varying from 1998 all the way back to 1990, thus excluding potentially large numbers of families whose arrival to KC came in between these dates.[46] There

86 *Distance and proximity in Delhi*

were also contrasting figures for the exact population of Delhi. A 2010 DDA survey indicated that the colony contained 3100 identified single-family *jhuggis* but many in Kathputli Colony claim the actual number is much higher.[47]

Many residents are wary of being moved into transitional housing, only for this supposedly "temporary" transition to lead to their permanent removal from Shadipur. Rumors circulated constantly, Kailash informed me. Kailash's younger brother Samir emphasized the lack of storage space for their costumes, puppets and other artistic tools in the transition housing. "Where will we keep our drums and poles?" Samir exclaimed?[48] Skepticism about the move was common amongst many of those with whom I interacted in Kathputli Colony in the winter of 2012 and 2013. Many recited instances of trickery and misdirection on the part of the Delhi government in the past. "As soon as we leave," Samir predicted, "they will build their skyscraper and never let us come back."

Adding credibility to the skepticism expressed by Kailash, Samir and others is the fact that each of the sites proposed thus far for the so-called "temporary" relocation of the evicted slum dwellers has ignited stern resistance from locals who also question the "temporariness" of these sites. Many fear that hosting a relocation camp in their neighborhood would also attract others to squat on the land. As Navin Raheja, chairman of the re-development firm has bluntly stated, "No one wants poor people to be their neighbor."[49]

Meanwhile, Raheja Developers, still eager to speculate on the land underneath Kathputli Colony, is instead frustrated by what has become an increasingly familiar impasse in urban "renewal" and "development" projects across India.[50] A spectacular image of future profitable real estate development promises to replace one kind of spectacle (the everyday practice of magicians) with another (the spectacle of "city-branding" through high-end urbanism). Yet the magicians, wary of past tricks and deceptions, refuse to leave without written assurance that they will be able to return. Thus far, the Delhi government has refrained from using force to evict the slum dwellers of Kathputli Colony, perhaps fearing the repercussions of such a move against the famous community of performance artists. As a *Wall Street Journal* article recently reported,

> Mr. Raheja says he can't begin work until the residents have been moved into transit camps that he is supposed to build, and for which the DDA has yet to provide him sufficient land. Kathputli colony residents say they won't move until the DDA provides them a list of all the families who are eligible for free flats and promises in writing to return all of them to this site once construction is completed ... as many as 63 real estate projects around Delhi that were supposed to supply 40,000 units of housing are four years behind schedule for reasons that range from lack of capital to "socio-political reasons."[51]

Reading divergent spatial morphologies

> The builders are very sly. Everyone just wants their own profit.
>
> Maya Pawar

The neighborhood   87

If one is to take the Delhi government at its word, then its policy of squatter evictions and slum demolitions achieves two ostensibly laudable goals, "simultaneously decongesting the urban center and providing better amenities to the poor."[52] In the state's urbanist discourse, moving squatters from slums to "re-settlement" colonies "is a marker of progress in people's lives."[53] But in order to generate consent among the soon-to-be evicted, the government must conjure an appealing image of the future: promising slum dwellers secure and comfortable lives in "formal" housing, with "adequate access to electricity, water, health, education and other basic services." In the context of postcolonial Delhi, however, many of these projections turn out to be mere deception and trickery.

For the artists of Kathputli Colony, re-location to the urban periphery (even if only temporary) is doubly threatening to their livelihood possibilities, as their central location in Shadipur has become a well-known place for patrons of their arts to find and book them for entertainment, either in the city or abroad. These artists are thus apprehensive about being removed from the vibrant, informal commercial habitat that makes their livelihood possible. In fact, the habitat, such as it is, would be completely destroyed and transformed by the Phoenix project.

At a small *chai* shop in Shadipur, Kailash told me in a voice that was both earnest and optimistic: "If we were able to collect 10,000 rupees from every family in the slum, we could come up with enough money to buy the land from the developers." He had already done the math, and seemed quite confident that, with some effort, he could mobilize the residents and necessary resources. But as soon as optimism made its fleeting appearance, his disposition returned to its ordinary pessimism. "Of course, the government would still build it [the Phoenix]. They look for any excuse to remove us from Delhi. Today it is the skyscraper. Tomorrow it will be something else."

As conjurers of everyday spectacle and illusion themselves, the puppeteers and magicians of Kathputli Colony seem fully aware of the government's own callous methods of misdirection and deceit when it comes to its rhetoric and practices of slum clearance and "re-settlement." The narratives of slum dwellers like Kailash and those all over postcolonial cities like Delhi are informed by the hard lessons learned in the art of urban survival.

In her ethnographic work on narratives of slum demolition and "resettlement" in Delhi during the Emergency, Emma Tarlo writes that, "From the accounts of the resettled, it is possible to make an alternative reading of the distribution of space" in postcolonial cities.[54] Re-settlement camps and colonies, often far away from urban centers, are spaces that are built upon acts of erasure, "each one recalling something which no longer exists."[55] Tarlo's perceptive reading allows us to understand re-settlement camps in their inter-temporal context, so that these camps, which are usually located on the periphery of the city, "cannot be seen independently of the re-development of different sites within the city." As Tarlo's temporally sensitive analysis reveals in the context of post-Emergency Delhi, "In the spaces left behind by these acts of erasure new parks, trees and public buildings sprouted all over the city whilst a ring of poverty accumulated and thickened around its edges."[56]

88 *Distance and proximity in Delhi*

Moving slums like Shadipur might not literally move as a unified object does continuously across physical space, but the dis-located lives of slum dwellers gives the effect of movement "not only through the memories of the displaced but also through the bricks and materials that arrived with them. Initially [the evicted slum dwellers] built their homes in the re-settlement camp out of the rubble of the previous slum."[57] The concept of moving slum thus provides an interpretive lens, a time-image of demolition and reconstruction in the post-colonial city that connects diachronic times across synchronic spaces.[58]

Time-images of moving slums are particularly effective for rendering the alterity of inter-temporal space, for tracking divergent spatial narratives. Recounting a passage from the autobiography of Jagmohan, the notorious vice-chairman of the DDA during the Emergency and mastermind of many of the most violent slum demolitions, Tarlo juxtaposes the state's urbanist narrative of spatial transformation with the narratives of those who were themselves evicted. Jagmohan describes a particular slum demolition at the Jamuna Bridge with remarkable economy, emphasizing change, continuity and closure in a pithy description: "In about three days the clearance and simultaneous resettlement was completed."[59] In contrast, based on the narratives of those who actually experienced the clearance, Tarlo brings a radically divergent sense of time into deep focus: "For the people of Jamuna Bridge there had been no simple continuity between their experience of demolition and their experience of resettlement."[60] Instead, many had to wait months if not years to secure a new settlement with a semblance of stability and security. Such a juxtaposition not only demonstrates the radical divergence in experience between a high-level bureaucrat and victims who were displaced by state policies, it underlines the more profound insight that in many ways, slum "re-settlement" is never "completed," it is never "final." Rather, as Tarlo writes, "the development of squatter colonies is a never ending process."[61] In these narrative disjunctures, a time-image of the moving slum crystallizes on an urban depth of field, bringing into the same frame the haunting co-existence of "past" environments re-constructed on the margins of the city and new speculative environments in the urban center.

What also stands out in the testimonies of displacement that Tarlo collects from the Emergency is the practical wisdom gained through surviving and narrating the experience of slum "re-settlement." Such experiential wisdom emerges as a kind of tired cynicism, similar to the attitude of many of the current residents of the Shadipur slums. In Tarlo's account, this cynicism is expressed in the sarcastic use of phrases such as "of course" when narrating traumatic events like slum evictions. For instance, a tea stall owner who was displaced from Jamuna Bazaar in 1967 talks of one local slum leader "who assured us that he would force the government to give us land at Jamuna Bazaar itself. But *of course* that never happened."[62] This person goes on to describe the bulldozers coming in and forcing them to move to a re-settlement camp shortly after. Another resident of Jamuna Bazaar, a sweeper, refers to a meeting that was organized by the DDA to inform the residents that they would be moved to a new place:

The neighborhood   89

Of course nobody believed them because this kind of talk had been going on for years. But a few days later the police came and told us to remove our belongings because the whole area was going to be cleared.[63]

The sarcastic tone used in these narratives suggests a kind of skeptical realism among the urban poor with respect to the discourse of urban "renewal" by the state, a counter-narrative whose condition of possibility is the collective memory of spatial violence. In this dislocated and disjunctive context, the body of the slum dweller and the materiality of the slum itself takes on a new role as "the developer of time, it shows time through its tiredness and waitings."[64]

These time-images complicate our understanding of displaced peoples as merely the victims of urban development. For victims are also positioned, albeit ambiguously, as agents who make decisions according to their experiential knowledge and the practical narratives they employ in order to situate themselves in space and time—to make some sense out of the disjointed, fractured, alienating present of the postcolonial city. For her part, Tarlo looks into the active and often unwitting role "victims" of the Emergency played in helping to actualize the state's exploitative land and sterilization policies. In concluding this chapter, I want to bring this insight on the ambiguous agency and experiential knowledge of slum dwellers into conversation with the present-day slum demolition and "re-settlement" plans that are being proposed for Kathputli Colony in Shadipur.

Magical urbanism and urban *metis*

When you don't know the words to a song, sing louder so others join in.

Puran Bhat

As noted above, Kathputli Colony is located in the very same Shadipur that appears briefly in Salman Rushdie's magical realist novel *Midnight's Children*. But the connection with Rushdie's novel does not end there. For in the story the slum in Shadipur is a magical "moving slum" that perpetually outmaneuvers the state's slum demolition department. The slum of magicians and conjurers is itself endowed with a kind of magic that is consistent with the larger literary universe of Rushdie's *Midnight's Children*, where magic often animates the narrative texture of everyday life within the story. Just as Saleem has the magical ability to telepathically communicate with other people born at the same moment as he (the very moment of India's independence from Britain), the magicians' ghetto is a magical moving slum, and manages to escape the Emergency State by somehow disappearing whenever the authorities would come to demolish its buildings and evict its residents.

[T]he day after the bulldozing of the magicians' ghetto, a new slum was reported in the heart of the city, hard by the New Delhi railway station. Bulldozers were rushed to the scene of the reported hovels; they found

90 *Distance and proximity in Delhi*

nothing. After that the existence of the moving slum of the escaped illusionists became a fact known to all the inhabitants of the city, but the wreckers never found it.[65]

As Saleem informs us, "Only after the end of the Emergency did the moving slum come to standstill."[66] It settles into a concrete location, "hard by the New Delhi railway station," as Saleem tells us: "Shadipur bus depot on the western outskirts of the city."[67]

If we read Rushdie's novel as a political allegory for post-independence India, a literary invention like a "moving slum" represents subaltern resistance to the Emergency State's demolition machine, which targeted the urban poor in particular for not only geographical re-location to the periphery of the city, but also for temporal displacement through forced sterilizations intended to limit the reproductive potential of the urban poor. The fact that this slum magically disappears when the demolition machines show up and reappears elsewhere in the city represents the resilience and perseverance of slums, which despite the intentions and desires of urban planners and destructive political elites, continue to exist and resist the abstract far order of the postcolonial state.

It is interesting to note, however, that in the midst of all the magical events that animate Rushdie's novel, the magicians in the moving slum emerge as skeptics regarding the very possibility of magic in real life. In *Midnight's Children*, Rushdie explicitly underlines this cynical realism on the part of the illusionists and performance artists in the magicians' ghetto: "the magicians were people whose hold on reality was absolute; they gripped it so powerfully that they could bend it every which way in the service of their arts, but they never forgot what it was."[68] I would argue that such skepticism is potentially illuminating in the narratives of those still living in Kathputli Colony.

In his innovative ethnographic and textual study of magic in India in the late-1980s (a study that in many ways inspired this one), Sanskrit scholar Lee Siegel asks Naseeb, a skilled illusionist who lived in Shadipur, a direct question: "Is there real magic?" Naseeb's response comports with, and deeply enriches, Rushdie's depiction of the cynical magicians above:

> No, but I shouldn't ever say it. I earn a living only if people believe these things, only if they believe in the possibility of miracles. But there are no real miracles, and all the holy men and god-men, Sai Baba and Jesus and other men like them, are just doing tricks, tricks that I can do, that I can teach you to do, tricks that all the street magicians can do.[69]

Urban *metis* is a term that Michael J. Shapiro develops to conceptualize the practical knowledge that "diverse social types employ to flourish or survive in the face of procedures and structures of surveillance and control."[70] Urban *metis* is a kind of everyday pragmatics that in turn illuminates the city's micropolitics: "the forces shaping its sensorium, its partitions, its social issues, tensions, and factions."[71] Writing about *metis* more generally, James Scott describes it as a form

The neighborhood 91

of socially produced knowledge that "resists simplification into deductive principles which can successfully be transmitted through book learning, because the environments in which it is exercised are so complex and non-repeatable that formal procedures of rational decision making are impossible to apply."[72]

Many residents of Kathputli Colony, in voicing skepticism and resisting the in-situ rehabilitation scheme in Shadipur, display a rugged urban *metis* based on collective memories of displacement in Delhi. Next, I examine a recent documentary film shot in Kathputli Colony that foregrounds the *metis* and entrenched skepticism on the part of slum dwellers regarding their possible relocation to state subsidized social housing. The film documents a range of subjectivities that mediate between expectations and what happens to meet them in the anxious and precarious urban present of Kathputli Colony.

Economies of disappearance

> When we were children, we thought we would be children forever.
> But now I've grown up. And I can see how fast this world moves.
> I wish I could stop the world for just a moment.
>
> Rehman Shah

Tomorrow We Disappear (*TWD*) is a film that documents changing urban life from the perspective of three residents of Kathputli Colony on the eve of its impending demolition.[73] The first is Puran Bhat, a puppeteer. He is also a middle-aged father and husband with profound emotional attachment to KC. In the film he is frequently depicted trying to organize his neighbors, friends and family in order to collectively act and stop the demolition of their homes. He comes across as charismatic, smart and optimistic, even against the onslaught of Geohistory 1 and the impending demolition of KC. His words frame the film's general orientation at the beginning of the story:

> I want to have a video made of my house. That way, after they have torn all this down, I'll still have a memory of it. I want you to shoot every room, where we sleep, eat, drink and enjoy life together. So in the future we can watch it and say this is how we used to live.[74]

Maya Pawar stands in stark contrast to Puran. She is a young woman, perhaps sixteen or seventeen years old. She is an acrobat and devoted to her art. But Maya is shown as willing and even desiring to move out of KC and enter into a "normalized" urban life, into a proper building with a proper address, into Geohistory 1.

> Up to now we've been living on land that is not ours. We know that this land is not ours; it's government land. But our people think they've built solid, finished homes, so it's theirs now. They think that they own it. They don't realize it can be torn down at any moment. That it can all crumble.

92 *Distance and proximity in Delhi*

While she shows an appreciation for the tradition of performance art she has inherited, she is also attempting to integrate this "tradition" with a more "modern" lifestyle.

> It'll be sad when we leave here. I spent my whole childhood here. But we all need to move forward and not look back [her mother is positioned directly behind Maya, who is in the foreground facing the camera]. The world is moving fast but we need to keep up with it.

In seeking to balance her art with the goal of getting an education, a job and perhaps a degree of independence as a young woman in the city, Maya is shown as wanting something more normative and upwardly mobile.

Finally, Rehman Shah is a magician, and is positioned somewhere between Puran and Maya in terms of his attachments to KC and to his artistic craft itself. He is the same age as Puran and grew up with the latter. At times he is wildly nostalgic about the childhood he experienced in KC, desiring an impossible return to the past and to the certitudes and fantasies of that time. But he is also traumatized (more visibly than Puran and Maya) by the vicissitudes of modern economic life in a megacity like Delhi. More specifically he is faced with the increasing difficulty of making ends meet for his family through the performance of street magic. After the camera shows one particular scene in which the police abruptly close down a public performance, he asks the camera despondently: "What will my family eat? I have no money." The camera later shows Puran lending money to Rehman to smooth over the hard times.

But *TWD*'s critical strength does not so much lie in its ability to document the "real life" of these slum residents as ethnographic subjects. In fact, the film is at its strongest when it is filming performances that are delivered as if for the camera, whether as intentional artistic performances or as filmed interactions with the camera/cameraman, whose presence becomes recognized through these interactions. This immediately challenges the traditional role of the ethnographic documentary films as producing "visual evidence" of pre-existing and "authentic" cultural realities. For the question of performativity forces us to ask to what extent ethnographic films, including the camera, the filmmaker, the editor and the audience, "construct" the very cultural realities they seek to merely "represent." As I have written elsewhere, this ambivalence regarding documentary film and cultural representation goes back to the oldest such films, beginning with the infamous *Nanook of the North* in 1922.[75] But *TWD* is at its most creative and critical when it departs from the practice of "traditional" documentary filmmaking (i.e., filming actualities) and explores more critical images of thought (filming virtualities while virtualizing memories).[76]

Rather than inquiring into the authenticity of its ethnographic subjects, I argue that a more fruitful avenue of inquiry involves looking at *TWD*'s central three subjects as "aesthetic subjects." Drawing on the work of Deleuze and other post-Kantian thinkers, Shapiro argues that the esthetic subject is a "conceptual personae" whose appearance in certain artistic works articulates a non-representational mode of thinking. Aesthetic subjects are "characters in texts whose movements and actions (both purposive and non-purposive) map and often alter experiential, politically relevant terrains."[77] Shapiro juxtaposes esthetic subjects with "psychological subjects" that predominate in the intellectual *doxa* of the modern social sciences, particularly in post-war America. After the so-called "behavioral turn" in the 1960s, for instance, the study of individual behavior in disciplines like economics, political science and sociology was increasingly framed in terms of "psychological attributes such as attitudes and beliefs ... [that] have value for both policy-makers and social scientists."[78] To know what motivated and shaped attitudes and beliefs of psychological subjects thus became the purview of the modern social sciences, producing knowledge for states that were interested in knowing individuals and collectivities in order to better rule over them, to "conduct the conduct" of citizen-subjects.[79] Rather than the interiorized subjectivity of psychological subjects, or the structural formation of ethnographic subjects, esthetic subjects are exteriorized in that their movements, perceptions and experiences articulate centrifugally with the experiential life-worlds these subjects inhabit and move through everyday. What esthetic subjects reveal are the lines of division in "common sense" perception and inter-subjective experience that shape how individuals and collectivities experience changing life. In revealing these lines of division, which separate the visible from that which is hidden in plain sight, the audible from that which is heard as "merely" noise, esthetic subjects can supply a critical "uncommon" sense that helps us think the present anew.

Shapiro cites the work of Leo Bersani and Ulysse Dutoit to demonstrate the creative potential of esthetic subjects in critically engaging everyday spatial politics. Bersani and Dutoit analyze Jean-Luc Godard's 1963 film *Contempt*, a film in which a couple becomes estranged as the wife, Camile, has her feelings for her husband, Paul, turned from love to contempt. But what is notable about the film for Bersani and Dutoit is that

> Goddard's focus is not on the "psychic origins of contempt" but on "its effects on the world." In the context of cinema, that shift in focus is conveyed by "what contempt does to cinematic space ... how it affect[s] the visual field within which Godard works, and especially the range and kinds of movement allowed for in that space".[80]

Contempt *between* Camile and Paul is not something that belongs to the "interior" lives of the two. Rather it is the result of mediation, that is, of interaction and friction *between* the two that affects both subjects in different ways, and thus affects the inter-subjective space they share. As the film deftly shows, contempt brings Camile and Paul together as much as it splits them apart, producing a relational space that is both intimate and estranged, proximate and distant. Thus Godard's Camille and Paul are best understood, for Shapiro, "as aesthetic rather than psychological subjects. Their movements and dispositions are less significant in terms of what is revealed about their inner lives than what they tell us about the world to which they belong."[81]

94 *Distance and proximity in Delhi*

If we extract this image of thought and project it into *TWD* we can begin to look at individuals like Puran, Maya and Rehman not as psychological or even ethnographic subjects, but rather as esthetic subjects. Such a move, I argue, helps us appreciate the multiplicity of changing urban life even in the midst of impending demolition and reconstruction. Moreover, it teaches us esthetically how these multiplicities, and the spatio-temporal distance and proximity between them, get mediated (but not resolved) in everyday life. Puran Bhat is featured the most throughout the film, and in some ways is the film's central esthetic subject. The camera follows him as he negotiates local and trans-local spaces, meeting with family members, community leaders and the representatives of Raheja. Puran's subtle changes in comportment across these various scenes reveal the different space-power relations that he must negotiate in his everyday life.

About mid-way through the film, during a particularly heated public meeting between community leaders and Raheja representatives, the latter attempt to convince the former that the move out of KC is both inevitable and "progressive." The residents will get a more stable life for themselves and their next of kin. The community responds with incredulity, questioning the veracity of the re-settlement plans, doubting the timeline for transition and transformation provided by the company. The Raheja people in turn advise the residents to think about the future: "It's not just about you. It also has to do with future generations. Your time has passed already. Look, your children.... If you get some property, it's not for you, its for the future."

After the meeting Puran retreats to his home, visibly disgusted both by the behavior of his neighbors, who argue and bicker with each other during the meeting, as well as with the developers, who come across as smug and patronizing. Puran is alienated, that is, from both his near order and his far order. In the midst of failed mediation, he seeks a line of escape. The camera follows him into the back room of his home, which is more built up and larger than the homes of other residents in KC. Puran shows us an old puppet his uncle made and gave to him. With the camera tightly trained on Puran, he brings the old painted wooden blocks to life. Puran performs his emotional response to KC's uncertain predicament, unable to vocalize his feelings in words and otherwise mediate his disjunctive near and far orders. In a depth of field shot that starts off from an alienated space of disappointment and disenchantment but then becomes increasingly salvational in its own terms, Puran's majestic art is performed in the dramatic movements of the puppet whose strings *he* controls. The camera zooms in on the emotive puppet. We see it wipe tears away from its face in stylized and choreographed movements. There is no music but we can imagine a somber siren of inevitability sounding off in the background. Through the treatment of the camera that captures this impromptu performance from a space of proximity and intimacy, Puran's puppetry is given a virtual charge, becoming perhaps even more dramatic on screen than in "real life." The camera's esthetic and stylized treatment of the performance opens up a virtual urban *qua* cinematic space in which to appreciate the temporality of the cultural traditions that artists like Puran inherit, embody and seek to elongate. In a city that is seemingly moving

The neighborhood 95

away from "tradition" and embracing urban "modernity" wholesale, this performative "magic" on the part of Puran—conjuring to life an old, dusty, forgotten puppet from the back of his storage room—emerges as radically Other with respect to the temporality of "magical economics" discussed earlier in this chapter. For both Geohistory 1 and Geohistory 2 are magic acts. The discourse of Geohistory 1, I have argued, conjures the space of KC not as one of artistic production and creative temporality but as universally translatable exchange value, that is, into the cold, abstract logic of market valuation. From this view, KC is temporalized hegemonically as unrealized exchange value. Puran, as the slum's biggest defender in the film, also comes to signify the gap or depth of field that opens up between exchange value (Geohistory 1) and use value (Geohistory 2). When it comes to the removal of slums in cities like Delhi, this deep focus opens up an untimely space from which to watch and mourn the artistry and artistic life of Puran and others like him.

In a contrasting depth of field shot, one that privileges not GH2 but GH1, Maya becomes an esthetic subject in her own right. In this scene Maya is sitting on the floor facing the camera. She is in the foreground; her mother is in the background, out of focus and in the shadows but still exerting a significant presence, as if hovering over her daughter. As stated before, Maya has her eyes on something more than just performance as an acrobat. In this scene she tells us about her dreams of going to school and studying to get a job as a schoolteacher or a computer programer. But her mother interrupts her and tells us about a debilitating accident Maya suffered as a small child. After spending months in the hospital the mishap left Maya unable to bear children for the rest of her life. As her mother is sharing this tragic memory and its implications for Maya's present and future, we see Maya in the foreground, smiling embarrassingly at first before tears start trickling down her cheeks. She quickly wipes the tears away and looks off camera. In the depth of field between Maya in the foreground and her mother in the back, the latter's presence becomes a reminder of Maya's place in the world, as a daughter and as a woman, but also as "damaged." Maya's far order is not just Raheja or the DDA or the accelerated "developmental" time of the "globalizing" city, but also the patriarchal time of the household and the family, which is much more constraining and problematic for her than it would be for someone like Puran, who is not only a man but relatively privileged and established in KC, and thus reluctant to move from his current station. For Maya, in contrast, moving out of the slums might also signify a movement from gendered confinement within the temporality of family to a more open-ended temporality of the city and possibly more flexible gender norms.[82] The mother's presence in the background is thus spatially distant but temporally present, even dominant, marking a depth of field that opens up Maya's vexed attachments inside and outside of the slum.

Finally, in Rehman's character, we witness an esthetic subjectivity that is more untimely with respect to the current issues facing KC than Puran and Maya. But it is not so much that Rehman has an anachronistic attachment to the artistic traditions he has inherited. Rather, Rehman seems to inhabit a world of

96   *Distance and proximity in Delhi*

existential distance that is nevertheless haunted by the exigencies of modern economic life. Simultaneously, he attempts to mediate the ambiguous tradition of the artist, whose inheritance is both a gift and a curse. The scenes that best capture Rehman's esthetic subjectivity are those in which he is shown playing with his children, two young boys, with simultaneous voice-over narration describing feelings of displacement in the present, and a desire to return to the certitudes of childhood.

> If I could tell my son one thing, it would be this. Son, you aren't anyone's slave. Do this work and eat. This art is a gift from our elders. It will give you opportunities and poverty, it will give you the good and the bad.... And if you don't want to do it one day, then don't.

Corresponding with other residents of KC discussed earlier in this chapter, each of the subjects at different times displays a certain informed skepticism, or urban *metis*, regarding their impending removal from Shadipur. This *metis* is hard earned through life experience. Because he is in some ways the most optimistic and proactive in the beginning of the film, Puran's skepticism toward the end hits home the hardest. But it also comports with *TWD*'s larger expression of cynical realism—a sort of cinematic urban *metis*—which is expressed in its very title. The film is an attempt to virtually preserve a presence that will no longer be actual. In the face of the "magical urbanism" of slum re-development in *Neo Delhi*, one form of spectacle must die in order to bring a different one to life.[83]

Towards the end of the film, Puran visits the National Heritage Exposition in New Delhi, which displays the cultural diversity of India preserved in museum-like models of village dwellings, costumes and artisanal crafts. In an "authentic" Rajasthani village dwelling, built of mud and clay but ornately decorated and beautiful in its austerity, the whimsical Puran allows himself to get carried away by the representational space and transported into his past. "It reminds me of my house!" He praises the artistry and creativity of his culture, pointing to the artistic inscriptions on the door:

> Look. Are you seeing this art? These are small things but they're from the heart. Every man works from his heart. It's just a door but whatever his thoughts were, he put them into this work. He worked hard, he made it. Every tile has its own story. They'd look so beautiful on our walls. I used to apply mud to our walls every year. We mixed cow dung and mud, then applied it. It used to shine like gold. Like gold. And its smell was like ... ahh. Really it was amazing.

In a way this is the very material culture and cultural materiality that is being erased in Kathputli Colony, replaced with its virtual Other in a high-rise, commodified, but governable space. There is an enigmatic connection between built environment and cultural identity that is at risk in the artists' impending removal from KC. It is this idea that is most obscured by the discourse of the developmental/globalizing city. "How are we supposed to know what to do," Puran asks at one point in the film, "if we don't even know who we are? What are we? Are we artists or poor people? We have no idea."

In some ways Puran's statement underlines something that hasn't been brought up yet, and is perhaps mentioned only too late, namely, the privileged position a famous place like Kathputli Colony enjoys compared with most slums in Delhi. Most do not have the benefit of housing nationally recognized artists or being featured in a Booker Prize-winning novel. But KC's privilege might also serve to better point out the limits of "magical economics" as a dominant political discourse in *Neo* Delhi. To return to Ashis Nandy's idea of "popular economics," introduced in Chapter 1, mainstream pro-growth and pro-developmental discourses use images and ideas of historical progress, and the eventual elimination of poverty to help mediate the messiness of the postcolonial urban present.[84] Nandy continues:

> It is an important part of that belief that the idea of underdevelopment has redefined many communities as *only* collections of the poor and the oppressed. We talk of indigenous peoples, tribes or Dalits as if they had no pasts, no myths, no legends and no transmittable systems of knowledge; as if their grandparents never told them any stories, nor did their parents sing them any lullabies. We steal their pasts paradoxically to push them into the past. To speak on behalf of the poor and the oppressed has become a major ego defense against hearing their voices and taking into account their ideas about their own suffering.[85]

Popular economics in Nandy's sense thus fits within Geohistory 1, or the universalizing narrative of global capitalist development. GH1 discourses like slum redevelopment in KC seek to speak for the populations they displace, in the name of rendering them into subjects of "development." Such temporal subjectivizations come at the expense of alternative experiences of time. This point hits home for Puran in the encounter he has with the model Rajasthani village at the cultural expo. Commenting on the middle-class audience walking through the installation with him on that day, gleefully "consuming" the model village in all its virtual authenticity, Puran's *metis* is profound:

> All of these [middle-class] people who are roaming around, they live in good homes. But as they enter here, their thoughts change. They go back in time. But this will remain in models only. It will never return to real life. Slowly everything will be forgotten.

Notes

1 *The Economist*, "India's economy: Losing its magic." March 24, 2012, accessed May 5, 2012, www.economist.com/node/21551061.
2 See *The Economist*'s editorial philosophy here, accessed May 5, 2012, www.econ omistgroup.com/what_we_do/editorial_philosophy.html.

98 *Distance and proximity in Delhi*

3 Peter Lamont and Crispin Bates, "Conjuring images of India in nineteenth-century Britain." *Social History* 32.3 (2007), 310.
4 Robert J. Shiller and G. Akerlog, *Animal Spirits* (Princeton, NJ: Princeton University Press, 2010).
5 See Timothy Mitchell's "Fixing the economy." *Cultural Studies* 12.1 (1998), 82–101.
6 For a fuller critique of neoclassical economics along these lines, see Ha-Joon Chang, *23 Things They Don't Tell You about Capitalism* (New York: Bloomsbury Publishing, 2012).
7 Erik Davis, *TechGnosis: Myth, Magic, and Mysticism in the Age of Information.* (New York: North Atlantic Books, 2015), 17.
8 Gayatri Chakravorty Spivak, "Megacity." *Grey Room* 1 (2000), 8–25.
9 As Himadeep Muppidi, *The Politics of the Global* (Minneapolis, MN: University of Minnesota Press, 2004) shows, this is a common worldview among those that support the continued "liberalization" of the Indian economy (p. 31).
10 Jacques Derrida, *Specters of Marx* (London: Routledge, 1994), 51.
11 Anna Lowenhaupt Tsing, "Inside the economy of appearances." *Public Culture* 12.1 (2000), 115–144.
12 David Harvey, "From managerialism to entrepreneurialism: The transformation in urban governance in late capitalism." *Geografiska Annaler. Series B. Human Geography* 71.1 (1989), 3–17.
13 Jai Sen, *The Unintended City: An Essay on the City of the Poor* (Calcutta: Cathedral Relief and Social Services, 1975).
14 In this chapter I retain use of the word slum because that English word, or its Hindi equivalent, *jhuggi*, were used most often by my interlocutors in Kathputli Colony and Shadipur. Far from seeing it as a pejorative term residents like Kailash (see below) used the term more or less descriptively, even with some pride.
15 As *TIME* magazine reported in 2008: "You'll find magic in the Kathputli slum, if you know where to look" (quoted in Subhadra Banda, Yashas Vaidya and David Adler, *The Case of Kathputli Colony: Mapping Delhi's First In-situ Slum Rehabilitation Project*, CPR Working Paper 3 [New Delhi: Centre for Policy Research, 2013], 1).
16 Although space does not allow further exploration of this, there is a rich literature on "slum tourism" in India and other poor countries. For a good overview, see Julia Meschkank, "Investigations into slum tourism in Mumbai: Poverty tourism and the tensions between different constructions of reality." *GeoJournal* 76.1 (2011), 47–62.
17 According to the Indian census, over the life span of the slum (sixty years), Delhi's population has multiplied close to ten times, from 1.7 million in 1951 to over sixteen million in 2011. Accessed February 8, 2013, www.censusindia.gov.in/2011-prov-results/prov_data_products_delhi.html.
18 As I'll explain, population surveys in the slum have produced numbers that vary wildly from study to study.
19 All quotations and paraphrases are based upon multiple formal and informal interviews/conversations with residents in Kathputli Colony over a three week period from late December 2012 to early January 2013. I wish to thank Kailash and his family for their hospitality to me and my brother over the course of our time together. You can learn more about and help support the artists and residents of Kathputli Colony by visiting the House of Puppets page on the following website: www.facebook.com/pages/House-of-Puppet-NGO/157211307649292.
20 Kailash tells me that the police no longer allow them to perform in front of assembled crowds on public streets. Police often break up the crowds before a performance can finish, demanding bribes just in order to retain their instruments and props. For a recent media report on the mistreatment of Delhi's street performers, see "Street artists fear they're being edged out of modern India." *The International News*, May 14, 2012, accessed May 20, 2012, www.thenews.com.pk/Todays-News-1–108211-Street-artists-fear-theyre-being-edged-out-of-modern-India.

The neighborhood 99

21 Ashis Nandy, "The darkness of the city," Plenary talk given at "City One" conference at Sarai, Center for the Study of Developing Societies, New Delhi, January 9–11, 2003.
22 P. G. Dhar Chakrabarti, "Urban crisis in India: New initiatives for sustainable cities." *Development in Practice* 11.2–3 (2001), 260–272 and Hari Mohan Mathur, *Displacement and Resettlement in India: The Human Cost of Development* (London: Routledge, 2013).
23 Partha Chatterjee, *The Politics of the Governed* (Princeton, NJ: Princeton University Press, 2004).
24 Solomon Benjamin, "Occupancy urbanism: Radicalizing politics and economy beyond policy and programs." *International Journal of Urban and Regional Research* 32.3 (2008), 719–729.
25 Stephen Legg, *Spaces of Colonialism: Delhi's Urban Governmentalities* (London: John Wiley & Sons, 2007).
26 Government of India, Ministry of Housing and Urban Poverty Alleviation, accessed January 28, 2013, http://pib.nic.in/newsite/PrintRelease.aspx?relid=72280.
27 Legg, *Spaces of Colonialism*, see in particular 190–207.
28 See William Dalrymple, *The Last Mughal* (New York: Vintage, 2008) for a detailed historical account of Delhi immediately before, during and after 1857.
29 Amitabh Kundu, "Provision of tenurial security for the urban poor in Delhi: Recent trends and future perspectives." *Habitat International* 28.2 (2004), 260.
30 Emma Tarlo, *Unsettling Memories* (Berkeley, CA: University of California Press, 2000), 55.
31 Kundu, "Provision of tenurial security for the urban poor in Delhi," 262.
32 Jai Sen, *The Unintended City: An Essay on the City of the Poor* (Calcutta: Cathedral Relief and Social Services, 1975) and Ravi Sundaram, *Pirate Modernity: Delhi's Media Urbanism* (London: Routledge, 2009).
33 Gyana Ranjan Panda, and Trisha Agarwala, "Public provisioning in water and sanitation." *Economic & Political Weekly* 48.5 (2013), 25.
34 Waquar Ahmed, "Neoliberal utopia and urban realities in Delhi." *ACME: An International E-Journal for Critical Geographies* 10.2 (2011), 163–188.
35 Sugata Marjit, and Saibal Kar, *The Outsiders: Economic Reform and Informal Labour in a Developing Economy* (Oxford: Oxford University Press, 2011).
36 Tarlo, *Unsettling Memories*, 61.
37 Gautam Bhan, "'This is no longer the city I once knew': Evictions, the urban poor and the right to the city in millennial Delhi." *Environment and Urbanization* 21.1 (2009), 127–142.
38 Ibid., 127.
39 Veronique Dupont, Emma Tarlo and Denis Vidal, *Delhi: Urban Space and Human Destinies* (New Delhi: Manohar, 2000), 20.
40 "Puppets in the hands of politicians!" *Hindustan Times*, May 1, 2009, accessed May 4, 2012, www.hindustantimes.com/India-news/NewDelhi/Puppets-in-the-hands-of-politicians/Article1–406331.aspx.
41 V. K. Puri, *Master Plan for Delhi 2021* (Delhi: JBA Publishers, 2007), 1.
42 Anant Maringanti, "Urban renewal, fiscal deficit and the politics of decentralisation: The case of the Jawaharlal Nehru Urban Renewal Mission in India." *Space and Polity* 16.1 (2012), 93–109. Note: Delhi received disproportionate funding through JNNURM as per this study.
43 Puri, *Master Plan for Delhi*, 16.
44 Banda, Vaidya and Adler, *The Case of Kathputli Colony*, 4.
45 Accessed May 13, 2012, www.rahejabuilders.com/pr-phoenix.asp.
46 Banda, Vaidya and Adler, *The Case of Kathputli Colony*, 11.
47 Ibid., 10.
48 Transcribed from field notes taken during December 28, 2012 visit to Kathputli Colony.
49 Tripti Lahiri, "Delhi journal: From slum to skyscraper." *Wall Street Journal Online*,

100 *Distance and proximity in Delhi*

February 17, 2012, accessed May 4, 2012, http://blogs.wsj.com/indiarealtime/2012/02/17/delhi-journal-from-slum-to-skyscraper/.

50 Partha Chatterjee, "Democracy and economic transformation in India." *Economic and Political Weekly* 43.16 (2008), 53–62.

51 Lahiri, "Delhi journal."

52 D. Leena, and S. Chotani (eds), *A Fact-Finding Report on: The Eviction and Resettlement Process in Delhi* (New Delhi: Hazards Centre, 2007), 12.

53 Ibid., 26.

54 Tarlo, *Unsettling Memories*, 56.

55 Ibid., 58.

56 Ibid., 61.

57 Ibid., 57.

58 Deleuze's concept of the time-image and its related concept of depth of field in the context of cinema is further developed as a interpretive methodological tool for critiquing changing urban life in the Introduction and several other chapters in this book.

59 Tarlo, *Unsettling Memories*, 58.

60 Ibid., 60.

61 Ibid., 56.

62 Ibid., 57, italics added.

63 Ibid., italics added.

64 Gilles Deleuze, *Cinema 2: The Time-Image* (Minneapolis, MN: University of Minnesota Press, 1989), xi.

65 Salman Rushdie, *Midnight's Children* (New York: Penguin Books, 1991) 526.

66 Ibid., 514.

67 Ibid., 526.

68 Ibid., 476.

69 Lee Siegel, *Net of Magic: Wonders and Deceptions in India* (Chicago, IL: University of Chicago Press, 1991), 43.

70 Michael J. Shapiro, *The Time of the City: Politics, Philosophy and Genre* (New York: Routledge, 2010), 46.

71 Ibid., 46.

72 James C. Scott, *Seeing Like a State: How Certain Schemes to Improve the Human Condition Have Failed* (New Haven, CT: Yale University Press, 1998), 313.

73 The film is co-directed by Jimmy Goldblum and Adam Weber and was released in 2015.

74 All quotations from the film (including the epigraphs at the beginning of previous sections in this chapter) are from the English subtitles provided on the officially released version.

75 Rohan Kalyan, "Ghostly images, phantom discourses, and the virtuality of the global." *Globalizations* 7.4 (2010), 545–561.

76 Marcus A. Doel, and David B. Clarke, "Afterimages." *Environment and Planning D: Society and Space* 25.5 (2007), 890–910 and Jacques Ranciere, *Film Fables* (Oxford: Berg, 2006), particularly the chapter "Documentary fiction: Marker and the fiction of memory."

77 Michael J. Shapiro, *Studies in Trans-disciplinary Method: After the Aesthetic Turn* (London: Routledge, 2013), xiv.

78 Ibid., 10–11.

79 Michel Foucault, *Security, Territory, Population* (New York: Palgrave Macmillan, 2007).

80 Shapiro, *Studies in Trans-disciplinary Method*, 11.

81 Ibid., 11.

82 Such flexibility is of course not limitless, nor is it necessarily actualized, as the fate of Jyoti Singh Pandey in the Delhi gang rape case of 2012 (see the preface to Part I above) sadly reminds us.

The neighborhood 101

83 The terminology "magical urbanism" was originally used, as far as I can tell, in Mike Davis, *Magical Urbanism: Latinos Re-invent American Cities* (New York: Verso, 2001). My use of "magical" is quite different from Davis', rooted more in magical realism as narrative technique and theories of subaltern pasts whose unintelligible presence in the present haunt the postcolonial modern.

84 For my purposes, it does not so much matter whether or not economic policies generated within this discursive machine "work" or not. For whether and how and to what degree policies "work" or not at a large scale is itself not detachable from the performative/interpretive discourse of neoclassical economic theory and neoliberal economic reform. This is the crux of Derrida's argument in *Specters of Marx*.

85 Ashis Nandy, "The beautiful, expanding future of poverty: Popular economics as a psychological defense." *International Studies Review* 4.2 (2002), 117.

Bibliography

Ahmed, Waquar. "Neoliberal utopia and urban realities in Delhi." *ACME: An International E-Journal for Critical Geographies* 10.2 (2011): 163–188.

Banda, Subhadra, Yashas Vaidya and David Adler. *The Case of Kathputli Colony: Mapping Delhi's First In-situ Slum Rehabilitation Project*. CPR Working Paper 3. New Delhi: Centre for Policy Research, 2013.

Benjamin, Solomon. "Occupancy urbanism: Radicalizing politics and economy beyond policy and programs." *International Journal of Urban and Regional Research* 32.3 (2008): 719–729.

Bhan, Gautam. "'This is no longer the city I once knew': Evictions, the urban poor and the right to the city in millennial Delhi." *Environment and Urbanization* 21.1 (2009): 127–142.

Chakrabarti, P. G. Dhar. "Urban crisis in India: New initiatives for sustainable cities." *Development in Practice* 11.2–3 (2001): 260–272.

Chang, Ha-Joon. *23 Things They Don't Tell You about Capitalism*. New York: Bloomsbury Publishing, 2012.

Chatterjee, Partha. *The Politics of the Governed*. Princeton, NJ: Princeton University Press, 2004.

Chatterjee, Partha. "Democracy and economic transformation in India." *Economic and Political Weekly* 43.16 (2008): 53–62.

Dalrymple, William. *The Last Mughal*. New York: Vintage, 2008.

Davis, Erik. *TechGnosis: Myth, Magic, and Mysticism in the Age of Information*. New York: North Atlantic Books, 2015.

Davis, Mike. *Magical Urbanism: Latinos Re-invent American Cities*. New York: Verso, 2001.

Deleuze, Gilles. *Cinema 2: The Time-Image*. Minneapolis, MN: University of Minnesota Press, 1989.

Derrida, Jacques. *Specters of Marx*. London: Routledge, 1994.

Doel, Marcus A. and David B. Clarke. "Afterimages." *Environment and Planning D: Society and Space* 25.5 (2007): 890–910.

Dupont, Veronique, Emma Tarlo and Denis Vidal. *Delhi: Urban Space and Human Destinies*. New Delhi: Manohar, 2000.

The Economist, "India's economy: Losing its magic." March 24, 2012, accessed May 5, 2012, www.economist.com/node/21551061.

Foucault, Michel. *Security, Territory, Population*. New York: Palgrave Macmillan, 2007.

102 *Distance and proximity in Delhi*

Government of India, Ministry of Housing and Urban Poverty Alleviation, accessed January 28, 2013, http://pib.nic.in/newsite/PrintRelease.aspx?relid=72280.

Hacking, Ian. "Making up people," in Margaret M. Lock and Judith Farquhar (eds) *Beyond the Body Proper: Reading the Anthropology of Material Life*. Durham, NC: Duke University Press, 2007: 150–163.

Harvey, David. "From managerialism to entrepreneurialism: The transformation in urban governance in late capitalism." *Geografiska Annaler. Series B. Human Geography* 71.1 (1989): 3–17.

Kalyan, Rohan. "Ghostly images, phantom discourses, and the virtuality of the global." *Globalizations* 7.4 (2010): 545–561.

Kundu, Amitabh. "Provision of tenurial security for the urban poor in Delhi: Recent trends and future perspectives." *Habitat International* 28.2 (2004): 259–274.

Lahiri, Tripti. "Delhi journal: From slum to skyscraper." *The Wall Street Journal Online*, February 17, 2012, accessed May 4, 2012, http://blogs.wsj.com/indiarealtime/2012/02/17/delhi-journal-from-slum-to-skyscraper/.

Lamont, Peter and Crispin Bates. "Conjuring images of India in nineteenth-century Britain." *Social History* 32.3 (2007), 308–324.

Leena, D. and S. Chotani (eds). *A Fact-Finding Report on: The Eviction and Resettlement Process in Delhi*. New Delhi: Hazards Centre, 2007.

Legg, Stephen. *Spaces of Colonialism: Delhi's Urban Governmentalities*. London: John Wiley & Sons, 2007.

Maringanti, Anant. "Urban renewal, fiscal deficit and the politics of decentralisation: The case of the Jawaharlal Nehru Urban Renewal Mission in India." *Space and Polity* 16.1 (2012): 93–109.

Marjit, Sugata and Saibal Kar. *The Outsiders: Economic Reform and Informal Labour in a Developing Economy*. Oxford: Oxford University Press, 2011.

Mathur, Hari Mohan. *Displacement and Resettlement in India: The Human Cost of Development*. London: Routledge, 2013.

Meschkank, Julia. "Investigations into slum tourism in Mumbai: Poverty tourism and the tensions between different constructions of reality." *GeoJournal* 76.1 (2011): 47–62.

Mitchell, Timothy. "Fixing the economy." *Cultural Studies* 12.1 (1998): 82–101.

Muppidi, Himadeep. *The Politics of the Global*. Minneapolis, MN: University of Minnesota Press, 2004.

Nandy, Ashis. "The beautiful, expanding future of poverty: Popular economics as a psychological defense." *International Studies Review* 4.2 (2002): 117–140.

Nandy, Ashis. "The darkness of the city." Plenary talk given at "City One" conference at Sarai, Center for the Study of Developing Societies, New Delhi, January 9–11, 2003.

Panda, Gyana Ranjan and Trisha Agarwala. "Public provisioning in water and sanitation." *Economic & Political Weekly* 48.5 (2013): 24–28.

"Puppets in the hands of politicians!" *Hindustan Times*, May 1, 2009, accessed May 4, 2012, www.hindustantimes.com/India-news/NewDelhi/Puppets-in-the-hands-of-politicians/Article1–406331.aspx.

Puri, V. K. *Master Plan for Delhi 2021*. Delhi: JBA Publishers, 2007.

Ranciere, Jacques. *Film Fables*. Oxford: Berg, 2006.

Rushdie, Salman. *Midnight's Children*. New York: Penguin Books, 1991.

Scott, James C. *Seeing Like a State: How Certain Schemes to Improve the Human Condition Have Failed*. New Haven, CT: Yale University Press, 1998.

Sen, Jai. *The Unintended City: An Essay on the City of the Poor*. Calcutta: Cathedral Relief and Social Services (1975).

Shapiro, Michael J. *The Time of the City: Politics, Philosophy and Genre*. New York: Routledge, 2010.

Shapiro, Michael J. *Studies in Trans-disciplinary Method: After the Aesthetic Turn*. London: Routledge, 2013.

Shiller, Robert J. and G. Akerlog. *Animal Spirits*. Princeton, NJ: Princeton University Press, 2010.

Siegel, Lee. *Net of Magic: Wonders and Deceptions in India*. Chicago, IL: University of Chicago Press, 1991.

Spivak, Gayatri Chakravorty. "Megacity." *Grey Room* 1 (2000): 8–25.

"Street artists fear they're being edged out of modern India." *The International News*, May 14, 2012, accessed May 20, 2012: www.thenews.com.pk/Todays-News-1-108211-Street-artists-fear-theyre-being-edged-out-of-modern-India.

Sundaram, Ravi. *Pirate Modernity: Delhi's Media Urbanism*. London: Routledge, 2009.

Tarlo, Emma. *Unsettling Memories*. Berkeley, CA: University of California Press, 2000.

Tsing, Anna Lowenhaupt. "Inside the economy of appearances." *Public Culture* 12.1 (2000): 115–144.

Part II

Aura and trace in Gurgaon

Before beginning Part II: Aura and trace in Gurgaon, the reader is encouraged to watch the musical video *Delhi in Movement* (8 min). Produced by Rohan Kalyan and screened in 2010, the video juxtaposes different modes of transportation with disparate parts of Delhi, ending up in the new elite suburb of Gurgaon. To view the video, visit: www.neodelhi.net/videos/.

Arrival

I landed at Indira Gandhi International Airport on September 12, 2008 to begin research on the town of Gurgaon. Gurgaon was most prominently known then as a high-tech satellite city comprising private residential, commercial and industrial spaces developed through real estate speculation and multi-national investment. The old town of Gurgaon was about thirty kilometers from Connaught Place in New Delhi, but postcolonial urbanization had effectively connected the two spaces, bringing Gurgaon into Delhi's ever-expanding urban fabric. In fact Gurgaon had been considered part of the greater Delhi metropolitan region since at least the 1962 Master Plan of Delhi. By 2008 Gurgaon had become increasingly synchronous with the giant megacity to the north through investment in the built environment and industry that was tied to Gurgaon's proximity to Delhi, as well as through automotive connectivity on the Delhi–Gurgaon Expressway and later through the Delhi Metro rail system, which only served to bring Gurgaon and Delhi closer together, at least for some. Gurgaon was also close to Delhi's international airport, so that not only was the national far order (New Delhi) accessible form the near order of Gurgaon, but so too was the global far order of the international. In the mediations between multiple far orders and (as we will see) an unevenly developed, fragmented and fractured near order, Gurgaon became known as India's Millennium City. Part II of this book is about the troubled transformation of *Neo* Delhi's premier suburb.

Sometime in the 1990s Gurgaon began to distinguish itself from Delhi's other peripheral satellite towns, in some ways even from the sprawling megacity itself. By 2008 Gurgaon was fast becoming one of India's "global" economic and cultural landmarks, attracting foreign investment and providing high-paying jobs for India's well educated and expanding middle classes. As one prominent writer described it, Gurgaon was "famous for its sleek office towers, shopping malls, multiplexes with state-of-the-art projection systems, upscale homes and condominiums, and even a world-class golf course."[1] In popular media discourses Gurgaon's ostensible "globality" was often metonymically described as embodying the economic dynamism and emerging potential of the "new urban India": cosmopolitan and urbane, globally recognized and confident, a city/nation "on arrival" and "on the move," poised to grow.

Such amplified, if not exuberant, descriptions arose in part because of the relatively recent and rapid transformation Gurgaon had undergone over the past decade or so before 2008. Prior to this transformation Gurgaon consisted of a small municipal township surrounded by many miles of barren fields, punctuated with occasional rural villages and isolated agricultural settlements. But by the time of my first research trip to Gurgaon the place had morphed into a futuristic metropolis that betrayed many of the visual trappings of the twenty-first-century "global city."

Commonly referred to as India's "Millennium City," Gurgaon's rapid visual and spatial transformation seemingly served a distinct ideological function: it was a metonymic part (the urban) which stood for the whole (the nation), heralding a broader historical transition from the "old" India to the "new." But as I gradually discovered over subsequent years of research, in reality the ideological

Figure II.1 Unrealized Mall of India project in Gurgaon.
Source: Photo by author.

Aura and trace in Gurgaon 107

role of the postcolonial city was something more complex. Global recognition was never quite secure, even if the trappings of a certain kind of globality were materializing in cities like Gurgaon. Such recognition was complicated by countervailing intelligibilities of the city that frequently interrupted and confounded new ideological projections, resulting in something far from expected.

Synchrony and diachrony

Imagery of the so-called "new urban India" abounds in popular media and culture. Bollywood films, for instance, armed with ballooning production budgets, sell a sleek, glamorous and increasingly commodified "India" to audiences around the world.[2] It is of course easier to project this new "cosmopolitan" identity on celluloid than it is on the actual urban street. In such films the renewed nation becomes intelligible after deftly framing or editing out any uncomfortable visual signs of a "developing" country in which over half the population survives on less than two dollars a day, and less than 5 percent of the country live something comparable to a "global" middle-class lifestyle of ten dollars a day.[3]

Similarly, best-selling books on the so-called "new India" celebrate the neoliberal economic reforms that make cities like Gurgaon possible.

Figure II.2 Unrealized Mall of India project in Gurgaon.
Source: Photo by author.

108 *Aura and trace in Gurgaon*

Distributed in corporate "non-places" across the world, like airports and Barnes & Nobles, these books render a "common sense" discourse that understands the reforms as "awakening" India from its economic slumber, shaking it from the dreaded "Hindu rate of growth" that dogged the country during the Nehruvian era, when other Asian economies experienced "miraculous" growth.[4] Now India was poised to finally "catch up." It was turning to its largest and most dynamic cities to attract private investment and spark competition among different regions, hoping to generate positive feedback loops through self-organizing market mechanisms. These discourses generally celebrated the reasoning behind such reforms, if not necessarily the results. Yet they usually did not bother to connect the two, relating the process of economic liberalization and "market" reform in the city to the intensification of urban-rural and intra-urban inequality. They strategically hid from view the fact that markets always benefited first of all those that were already in advantageous positions to begin with, and perhaps a few lucky and hard-working exceptions. These discourses made invisible the profound and multi-fold effects of market exclusion.[5] In the discourse of magical economics, those that were excluded could gain an alternative intelligibility, now simply as people "below the poverty line" (BPL). Within the magical discourse of neoclassical economics and the increasingly popular neoliberal policies it informed, the lives of the poor, their social relations and complex modes of survival, were reduced to a number, namely the percentage of the total population that fell under an arbitrary poverty line.[6] As if the groups positioned just above this line were thriving in neoliberal India.

As Nandy writes, "these are not easy facts to live with; one has to spend enormous psychological resources to ensure that they do not interfere with our 'normal' life by burdening us with a crippling sense of guilt."[7] And so these uneasy urban realities require everyday mediations that are the collective ego defense of an elite urban society that has long abandoned the idea of "socialist development" for the synchronic seductions of capitalism, consumerism and global belonging. This elite ego defense is materialized in new exclusivist urban design, which has always favored the rich in Indian cities but now does so with a reckless abandon underwritten by virtual economic consensus, namely that there is simply no other alternative. One way of living in a world as violently divided and foreclosed as that of the contemporary postcolonial city is to avoid having to encounter these uneasy realities. To simply escape. This seemed to have been the intention behind Gurgaon and its enclave urbanism, to escape from Delhi's crowded and heated streets and from "India" at a more existential level. But as I was to observe over the period of my prolonged study in Gurgaon, spanning seven years and three separate research stays, traces of "India" kept returning to haunt Gurgaon's materialization as a virtual economic space, so that the synchrony of its global projections remain haunted by the diachrony of their geohistorical difference.

Neoliberal urbanism

The term neoliberalism gets thrown around a lot these days, as if capitalism *only just recently* became ruthlessly competitive, violent and destructive at a global scale. But it remains a useful concept if used cautiously. I follow the work of Foucault,[8] who defines neoliberalism as a form of governmental rationality (a continuation and intensification of a longer history of the liberal arts of government, which always privileged, albeit to differing degrees, the economic over the political); Harvey,[9] who gives neoliberalism an historical designation as the name of an era dominated by a utopian and pragmatic (if not necessarily fully intentional) class-based project that produces an uneven geography of reform and creative destruction; and Ong,[10] for whom neoliberalism is most visible in those moments of exception to "normal" economic and political governance, for instance, in special economic zones that follow their own rules and not those of the locality in which they are physically embedded. I find enough resonance among these three distinct uses of neoliberalism. A city like Gurgaon, for instance, is clearly exceptional in Ong's sense of neoliberalism. It is precisely Gurgaon's *difference* with respect to its immediate surroundings and in particular Delhi that marks its futurity, its seduction and broader intelligibility. Gurgaon is a constellation of disaggregated but spatially proximate economic spaces in a city where municipal government seems distant and ineffective, as we will see. But this distance is temporal as well as spatial. For the unevenly developed urban frontier fosters conditions ripe for neoliberalism, or the class-based project Harvey describes as unfolding on a mass geohistorical scale since the 1970s, leading to the destructive creation of spaces governed by a distinctly neoliberal economic rationality.

Neoliberalism is an apt way of describing this fractured, disjointed and dynamic present in synchronic terms. The concept, I argue, is necessary insofar as this synchronicity allows us to make visible critical trans-local linkages that give globality a problematic intelligibility. For instance, the dominance of trans-national financial institutions makes possible the process of "financialization" in urban contexts, leading to hyper-speculation and inflation in local real estate markets and increasing private debt in working-class neighborhoods, as we will see respectively in Chapters 3 and 4. This local scene of urban change (the near order) is thus entangled with global processes of neoliberalism and financialization (the far order) that shape the dominant modes of "surplus" extraction in the form of interest payments and the collection of rents.

Yet an exclusively synchronic focus on neoliberalism and its emergent technologies of accumulation has its limits. It misses out on the diachronics of the present, the differential histories and temporalities that haunt synchronic global spaces like Gurgaon. For mediation is not merely spatial, between near and far orders that are either local or global. Mediation is also deeply temporal, between past and present, between times closely recalled and those distant enough to forget. Global urbanization both transforms and reproduces existing geohistorical differences in the postcolonial city. I argue that it is in the mediation

Figure II.3 Unrealized Mall of India project in Gurgaon.
Source: Photo by author.

between global synchronicity and historical diachrony that one locates the specificity of the postcolonial city. This is a city that is perpetually yet to come, yet presumably always on arrival.

Crisis

Just a few days after my arrival in Gurgaon, on September 15, 2008 the New York-based investment bank Lehman Brothers declared bankruptcy, and the "global financial crisis," as it was soon called, quickly ensued.[11] While the event which triggered this crisis—Lehman's declaration of bankruptcy—was largely unforeseen by most, in the months prior to September 2008 it was becoming increasingly clear that the U.S. economy was teetering on the edge of an upcoming economic recession or worse. For nearly a year prior to my departure for India, economic discourses in mainstream American media were mired in claims and counter-claims regarding the status of the U.S. economy, debating whether it was heading toward a recession or not.[12] One day, you would read the views of one financial or economic expert, or even the President himself, backed up by some set of statistics and data, arguing that the U.S. economy remained strong, that a recession would be avoided. But the very next day, it seemed, you would read or hear the views of someone else coming to a very different conclusion, using a different set of data to underline the inevitability of an upcoming economic downturn. What struck one about these mainstream economic debates in the U.S. was the fundamental uncertainty regarding an object of quantitative measurement and analysis often taken to be self-evident in its coherence: the national economy.

In the schizophrenic debates that led up to Lehman Brothers' financial demise—one day optimistic, the next day pessimistic—one could glean an economic discourse that was haunted by its own epistemological uncertainty. Moreover, the role of such a discourse was precisely *performative*. Arguments on both the pessimistic and optimistic sides were performing the ideological work of economics in a time of intense uncertainty. What was this work? Conjuring a virtual image of the economy that could influence and even shape the way in which economic "agents" (investors, producers and consumers) would react to it.[13]

This was what Jacques Derrida called "performative interpretation," which he linked to a "new thinking of the ideological" within the realm of international political economy.[14] Performative interpretation was, for Derrida, a "kind of interpretation that transforms the very thing it interprets."[15] The concept resonates best when juxtaposed with Marx's well-known formulation: "Philosophers have only *interpreted* the world, in various ways; the point is to *change* it."[16] In an era of virtual globalization, however, when economic realities are inaugurated in the virtual realm of policy think tanks and academic departments, armed with abstract equations and theoretical models, and subsequently performed through digital markets that lack a tangible materiality but nevertheless produce reality *effects*, shaping the way actors and environments respond to these virtual realities, the distinction between interpretation and performance begins to blur.[17] In an "economy of appearances," non-isomorphic yet often relational flows of people, capital, technology, policy and digital media influence where, when and how much investment capital goes to particular locations. Thus, how economic actors and mobile capital interprets the world is constitutive of some of the most dramatic of the many transformations taking place across it. So often the politics of neoliberal economics concerns the discursive and imaginal battle to shape the dominant interpretation of "the market," or even the experience of "capitalism" as such. This effort on the part of economic discourses is of course the most political of them all, and its political intensity becomes especially manifest at times of growing uncertainty and panic, such as a financial crisis, particularly one that was dramatized as apocalyptically as the one that began in September 2008.[18]

In the first month of my research stay in Gurgaon, I found that similar performative and interpretive discourses were at work in Indian media, but here the schizophrenic economic debate had an important postcolonial twist, a different economy of ghosts. For India was then in the midst of an unprecedented economic expansion, thanks to economic reform and liberalization, which, according to the dominant economic narrative, freed up the long-repressed "animal spirits" of capitalism and produced robust economic growth over the past quarter-century. In India the question that was debated *ad nauseam* in the major newspapers in the weeks and months following Lehman Brothers' declaration of bankruptcy (and my nearly simultaneous arrival in the country) was whether or not India's once protected economy, now liberalized and increasingly exposed to the vicissitudes of global finance and trade, would be adversely impacted by the economic crisis that had started in "the West." While some argued that India's financial system retained a sufficient degree of protection and autonomy from the crumbling global financial architecture, thanks to stringent regulations on banking and financial exchange that dated back to pre-reform times, others argued that India would indeed pay the price for its increased immersion within the global economy.[19]

While in America, the discourse of economics was haunted by the epistemological uncertainty of "the national economy" as a key term in popular discourse,[20] in India this economic discourse was haunted by an additional, postcolonial, specter: the perceived extent to which the national economy itself was incorporated and recognized within "the global." As we will see, this degree of global incorporation and recognition is not simply an empirical matter, subject to quantitative measurement and calculation; it is a deeply *ontological* one.

Figure II.4 Unrealized Mall of India project in Gurgaon.
Source: Photo by author.

Arrested development

In the midst of tireless and heated debates regarding the question of the financial crisis and its predicted impact in India, one could surmise at least a cursory answer by merely surveying the visual landscape of Gurgaon, which had mushroomed rapidly over the past decade thanks to liberalized flows of finance and investment (both foreign and domestic) in the district. This flood of investment enabled a rate of speculative development that was unprecedented in postcolonial India.[21] When I first arrived in September, the place was busily animated with the activity of building and urban construction: ubiquitous presence of cranes, excavators and other tools for construction. These monstrous machines were clearing ground for new real estate: upcoming commercial, industrial and residential projects assembled one steel beam at a time. Where structures stood half-built, giant billboards were positioned in front of them, projecting an anticipated urban future of pristine gated communities and condominiums, lush green office parks and futuristic shopping malls.[22]

But the billboards for future real estate that were ubiquitous in Gurgaon were also noteworthy for what they left out of their visual narrations: the workers who built the city and whose absence from these simulations was a sure sign of their temporal transience and ontological insecurity within this new urban imaginary. This erasure through simulacra was starkly contradicted by the raw visuality of the present. When I first arrived in Gurgaon, each morning and evening long lines of construction workers could be seen walking to and from the sites of Gurgaon's virtual development, their yellow hardhats under their arms as they marched individually or in groups to the work site. If you talked to them they would tell you they came from states like Bihar and Bengal, Himachal or Uttar Pradesh. These workers were physically building the "new India" during the day while sleeping in nearby workers' shanties at night.[23] These temporary homes were often just off the construction site itself, and would be swiftly deconstructed as soon as the job was finished. These workers constituted a socially transient, necessarily abstract supply of labor whose temporality of impermanence in the urban landscape was both integral to, yet simultaneously excluded from, the economic imaginaries visualized on the real estate billboards. Many of these workers would be told to leave, to go back to their rural villages once one particular job finished. But many would stay anyway, determined to stick it out and survive in Gurgaon.

All these images and signs in Gurgaon's transformational urban *qua* economic landscape—ubiquitous cranes, billboards, construction workers—underlined a time of anticipation and future arrival. "Just come back in a few years, then you will really see something nice" was a common refrain in my conversations with locals. These sentiments embodied the promise and potential of building a *new* India right on top of the old, in projections of images and actualized spaces that were visually striking and spectacular in their appearance. But such resplendent imagery was also structurally unstable, haunted by a contingency that was always *virtually* there, but which only actualized after the event of the financial crisis, rendering the postcolonial city visible in a new way.

Figure II.5 Unrealized Mall of India project in Gurgaon.
Source: Photo by author.

By the winter of late 2008, the signs of newness and progress in the urbanizing terrain took on a very different affective tone. In the immediate weeks after the economic crisis began, foreign investors panicked and collectively withdrew nearly $12 billion from the country's newly opened financial markets, with much of this investment tied in to speculative real estate development.[24] As globally mobilized finance fled for ostensibly safer grounds, once well-capitalized builders found themselves suddenly and unexpectedly strapped for cash, and the hyper-development of futurist Gurgaon ground to a near complete halt. Everyone, it seemed, was hedging their once certain bets on the future by abandoning their projects in the Millennium City. A city that was still only half-built and half-projected seemed to be aborted in mid-birth. That fall and winter, when Gurgaon's hyper-development came to an abrupt stop, the cranes and excavators began gathering dust, looking frozen in time. The workers were long gone.

It was in this uncertain context that my research proceeded. The financial crisis interrupted Gurgaon's exuberant narrative of hyper-development and increasing global recognition as an "emerging market," creating an *un-timely* space from which to pause and ask questions anew. What were the stakes (both financial and ontological) involved in the metonymic project of the "new urban India"? What exactly was invested in the *virtual* reality of a city like Gurgaon, a key visual and spatial element of the assemblage I am calling *Neo* Delhi?

Is that all?

After the end of my first year of research in Gurgaon and later Delhi, I came across an issue of *Newsweek International* at Liberty International Airport in Newark, NJ.[25] This special issue was a sustained reflection on the global financial crisis, now one year removed from the initial hysteria and panic over the event. Quite tellingly, the issue was titled "Is that all?" The question was written in bold white letters across a solid black background.

In a manner befitting the performative discourse of neoliberal economics, the magazine was attempting to interpret the state of the world at a time of lingering existential uncertainty. The magazine featured articles by some of the most respected experts and public intellectuals of the capitalist world: economists, philosophers and technocrats alike performing and interpreting a virtual economic reality. Francis Fukuyama, Robert Rubin, Robert Shiller, among others, each had their contributions. Moreover, the titles of the various articles made obvious the aim of the entire ideological performance: "History is still over: How capitalism survived the crisis" was Fukuyama's contribution, while Rubin's was titled "Back on track: How to keep globalization working." Most interesting for me was an article written by the Indian diplomat and politician Shashi Tharoor, titled "No retreat: India keeps going global," which I will get to shortly.

The magazine and its articles constituted a collective effort of performative interpretation "from above" that sought to transform the very thing it interpreted (the economic state of the world post-crisis). The issue's editor, Fareed Zakaria, unwittingly stated this much in his introductory note when he pointed out that, "The return to confidence is itself a very powerful economic force."[26] Indeed, the magazine itself performed this confidence and conjured this economic force by presenting arguments and analyses that would ostensibly assure jittery investors and ontologically uncertain capitalists that all was well in the capitalist world. The magazine's circulation in transnational "public" spaces throughout the global economy (in this case, having now arrived at Indira Gandhi International Airport), and its internal distribution of discourses, images and signs within its pages, aimed to reassure readers that the global project of neoliberal globalization—and the considerable financial stakes invested in this project—was safe.

If various "Western" authors in the magazine were busy conjuring forth a stable image of the global in which capitalism still safely and confidently reigned, despite the financial turbulence and uncertainty of the previous year, Tharoor's article was characterized by a particularly postcolonial prerogative: securing the intelligibility of the postcolonial nation in front of an ostensibly global (capitalist) audience. Tharoor, a prominent Indian writer and now a national politician, explained "how India avoided turning inward" after the financial crisis, reassuring his readers that the country would continue unabated with its program of economic reform and liberalization initiated roughly two decades before. He noted that in the immediate aftermath of Lehman Brothers' bankruptcy and the turbulent shockwaves that reverberated around the world's financial markets, proponents of neoliberal reform

116 *Aura and trace in Gurgaon*

were indeed pushed on the defensive by the crisis. The Indian stock markets dropped, foreign investors pulled out, and trade fell. But the country recovered quickly. In part that's because it is much less dependent than most on global trade and capital.[27]

Tharoor highlights the relative autonomy of India's economy with respect to the global, compared to other Asian economies, and cites this as one reason that the Indian economy escaped largely unscathed from the financial crisis:

> India relies on external trade for about 20 percent of its GDP versus 75 percent in China; India's large and robust internal market accounts for the rest. Indians continued producing goods and services for other Indians, and that kept the economy humming.[28]

Notwithstanding the credit Tharoor seems to give here to India's self-sufficient internal markets and industries, which, for better or for worse, are usually associated with or blamed on the quasi-socialist policies of pre-reform India, the author paradoxically argues that India's post-crisis economic stability demonstrates that, "The cause of economic liberalization remains safe in India."[29] Given his "global" audience, Tharoor has a hard time giving too much credence to India's quasi-socialist ideology of economic self-sufficiency, whose roots trace back to a previous era with a decidedly *different* political economic imaginary at work.[30] But the self-sufficient "internal market" that kept India's economy "humming" in a time of crisis ultimately becomes unintelligible as such within Tharoor's discourse, largely because this same self-sufficient economy is usually associated with the dreaded "Hindu rate of growth" and the "economic failures" of the "old" India, that is, pre-reform India.

"India was less affected by the crisis than the rest of the world," Tharoor goes on to argue, "not because it was isolated but because its capitalist fundamentals are strong,"[31] seemingly contradicting his earlier praise for India's economic isolationism. But such contradictions are pushed to the side as Tharoor delivers a more forceful message to the world:

> India will not return to the economics of nationalism, which equated political independence with economic self-sufficiency and so relegated us to chronic poverty and mediocrity. Instead of retreating from the world, India is advancing with more *confidence* than ever.[32]

Confidence is indeed a powerful economic force, one that is performatively ideological and thus magical. To the extent that it is effective, Tharoor's discourse conjures a particular image of India as confidently advancing with the economics of globalism over nationalism. For the international audience of Tharoor's discourse, seated in airport terminals, boardrooms and offices, an image of the nation proceeding confidently toward further economic liberalization and reform potentially brings significant material benefits. In a neoliberal economy of

Aura and trace in Gurgaon 117

Figure II.6 Unrealized Mall of India project in Gurgaon.
Source: Photo by author.

appearances, marked by inter-urban competition for hyper-mobile investment capital, these confident images can assure foreign investors who are continuously interpreting Indian economic spaces for their temporal signs and indicators, and acting on these readings, with dramatic transformative effects.[33] But the relay of meaning and intelligibility communicated through images, signs and discourses, so crucial in an economy of appearances, is frequently disturbed by the appearance of "untimely" images of changing urban life. As we will see in the chapters of Part II, the dominant aura of "globality" and "self-confidence" in Gurgaon is structurally haunted by traces of alternative geohistories. These traces of coexisting urbanisms and ruralisms constitute the spatio-temporal disruptions that *Neo* Delhi seeks to actively mediate.

The Mall of India project constituted one sight of failed mediation: unactualization. But then again, postcolonial cities are filled with these. Even before the financial crisis in India, new malls in places like Gurgaon and Delhi had trouble attracting sufficient foot-traffic, or else were dealing with people who visited the mall more to enjoy the exclusive interiors than to spend any money. These malls were hermetically sealed off from the outside world, supplying cool air-conditioning and continuous electrification, thanks to back-up generators. By 2008, Gurgaon had more than two dozen such shopping malls, all air-conditioned,

118 *Aura and trace in Gurgaon*

enclosed and secured. Yet retailers renting space in these malls consistently failed to meet sales targets.[34] In the post-financial crisis environment, when investors were no longer so eager to speculate on the urban future of spaces like Gurgaon, many projects already underway had to be abandoned. The Mall of India project in Gurgaon, whose visual projections illustrate this preface, was scrapped due to declining demand for malls in the Millennium City, relocating eventually to NOIDA, another satellite town of Delhi.

Notes

1 Tarun Khanna, *Billions of Entrepreneurs: How China and India Are Reshaping their Futures and Yours* (Boston, MA: Harvard Business School Press, 2007), 76.
2 See Kazi K. Ashraf, "Raga India: Architecture in the time of euphoria." *Architectural Design* 77.6 (2007), 6–11, and Rao Shakuntala, "The globalization of Bollywood: An ethnography of non-elite audiences in India." *The Communication Review* 10.1 (2007), 57–76.
3 Sankaran Krishna, "Notes on the dramatic career of a concept: The middle class, democracy, and the anthropocene." *Alternatives: Global, Local, Political* 40.1 (2015), 3–14.
4 See Gurcharan Das, *India Unbound* (New York: Anchor Books, 2002), and Nandan Nilekani, *Imagining India: Ideas for the New Century* (London: Penguin, 2013).
5 For more on Geohistory 1 (GH1) see Introduction, "Image 6." See Eric Sheppard, Helga Leitner and Anant Maringanti. "Provincializing global urbanism: A manifesto." *Urban Geography* 34.7 (2013), 893–900. Drawing on Shepard et al.'s adaptation of Chakrabarty's concepts of History 1 and History 2, that is, capitalism's "universalizing" narrative and the historical difference it cannot fundamentally overcome, Geohistory 1 and 2 look at the uneven geographical development of capital, and seek to understand the politics of its economic exclusions, and how space and time mediate relations between those that are included in GH1 and those that mediate inside and outside of its disciplinary logics and restrictive spaces.
6 Ashis Nandy, "The beautiful, expanding future of poverty: Popular economics as a psychological defense." *International Studies Review* 4.2 (2002), 107–121.
7 Ibid., 111.
8 Michel Foucault, *The Birth of Biopolitics* (New York: Picador, 2010).
9 David Harvey, *A Brief History of Neoliberalism* (Oxford: Oxford University Press, 2005).
10 Aihwa Ong, *Neoliberalism as Exception* (Durham, NC: Duke University Press, 2006).
11 For background on this crisis and its structural causes from a mainstream (neoclassical) economic perspective, see Robert Shiller, *The Subprime Solution: How Today's Global Financial Crisis Happened, and What to Do about It* (Princeton, NJ: Princeton University Press, 2012), and James Crotty, "Structural causes of the global financial crisis: A critical assessment of the 'new financial architecture.'" *Cambridge Journal of Economics* 33.4 (2009), 563–580. For an empirical analysis of the crisis' impact on Asian economies (including India and China), see Jarko Fidrmuc and Iikka Korhonen, "The impact of the global financial crisis on business cycles in Asian emerging economies." *Journal of Asian Economics* 21.3 (2010), 293–303. For a more critical take on the crisis from the perspective of political economy, see Farshad Araghi, "Political economy of the financial crisis: A world-historical perspective." *Economic and Political Weekly* (2008), 30–32.
12 Examples of this debate are numerous. A few examples from both sides of the debate are the following: Rex Nutting, "Recession will be nasty and deep, economist says." *Marketwatch: The Wall Street Journal Digital Network*, August 23, 2006; Todd

Wallack, "Recession is here, economist declares." *The Boston Globe*, March 15, 2008; "Greenspan says U.S. not headed for recession: Report." *International Business Times*, September 21, 2007; and "Bush denies U.S. economy in recession." *CNNMoney.com*, April 22, 2008.

13 For more on economic virtualism, see James G. Carrier and Daniel Miller (eds), *Virtualism: The New Political Economy* (Oxford: Berg Publishers, 1998) and A. Aneesh, *Virtual Migration: The Programming of Globalization* (Durham, NC: Duke University Press, 2006).

14 Jacques Derrida, *Specters of Marx* (New York: Routledge, 1994), 51.

15 Ibid.

16 David McLellan (ed.), *Karl Marx: Selected Writings* (Oxford: Oxford University Press, 2000), 173, italics mine.

17 Carrier and Miller, *Virtualism*.

18 See for instance, Anthony Faiola, "The end of American capitalism?" *Washington Post*, October 10, 2008, who pointed out just weeks after Lehman Brothers' collapse, "The worst financial crisis since the Great Depression is claiming another casualty: American-style capitalism."

19 Once again, examples are numerous, but a few from both the optimistic and pessimistic sides of the debate: "No impact of subprime crisis in India." *Economic Times*, September 7, 2007; "India safe from global financial crisis: IMF." *Financial Express*, February 5, 2008; "Fundamentals of Indian economy strong: PM." *Economic Times*, November 13, 2008; and "Global crisis impacts India; do everything to push growth: PM." *Association of Indian Individual Investors*, November 4, 2008.

20 Timothy Mitchell, "Fixing the economy." *Cultural Studies* 12.1 (1998), 82–101.

21 Llerena Guiu Searle, "Making space for capital: The production of global landscapes in contemporary India." (PhD diss, University of Pennsylvania, 2010).

22 See my short, experimental video *Delhi in Movement* (2010), particularly the last section entitled "Neo Delhi": https://vimeo.com/16778056.

23 See Seth Schindler, "A 21st-century urban landscape: The emergence of new social-spatial formations in Gurgaon." *Sarai Reader* 7 (2007), 499–508 for an excellent ethnographic description of "new socio-spatial formations in Gurgaon," including slums that house construction works in the shadows of new high-rise buildings.

24 See Fareed Zakaria (ed.), *Newsweek Special Issue*: "Is that all?", December 2009.

25 Ibid.

26 Ibid., 9.

27 Ibid., 33.

28 Ibid.

29 Ibid.

30 For an analysis of discourses on economic reform in India in the 1990s see Himadeep Muppidi, *The Politics of the Global* (Minneapolis, MN: University of Minnesota Press, 2004).

31 Zakaria, "Is that all?", 33.

32 Ibid., italics mine.

33 Anna Lowenhaupt Tsing, "Inside the economy of appearances." *Public Culture* 12.1 (2000): 115–144.

34 Aravind Adiga, "India's mania for malls." *Time*, September 13, 2004.

Bibliography

Aneesh, A. *Virtual Migration: The Programming of Globalization*. Durham, NC: Duke University Press, 2006.

Araghi, Farshad. "Political economy of the financial crisis: A world-historical perspective." *Economic and Political Weekly* (2008): 30–32.

120 *Aura and trace in Gurgaon*

Ashraf, Kazi K. "Raga India: Architecture in the time of euphoria." *Architectural Design* 77.6 (2007): 6–11.

Carrier, James G. and Daniel Miller (eds). *Virtualism: The New Political Economy.* Oxford: Berg Publishers, 1998.

Crotty, James. "Structural causes of the global financial crisis: A critical assessment of the 'new financial architecture.'" *Cambridge Journal of Economics* 33.4 (2009): 563–580.

Das, Gurcharan. *India Unbound.* New York: Anchor Books, 2002.

Derrida, Jacques. *Specters of Marx.* New York: Routledge, 1994.

Fidrmuc, Jarko and Iikka Korhonen. "The impact of the global financial crisis on business cycles in Asian emerging economies." *Journal of Asian Economics* 21.3 (2010): 293–303.

Foucault, Michel. *The Birth of Biopolitics.* New York: Picador, 2010.

Harvey, David. *A Brief History of Neoliberalism.* Oxford: Oxford University Press, 2005.

Khanna, Tarun. *Billions of Entrepreneurs: How China and India Are Reshaping their Futures and Yours.* Boston, MA: Harvard Business School Press, 2007.

Krishna, Sankaran. "Notes on the dramatic career of a concept: The middle class, democracy, and the anthropocene. *Alternatives: Global, Local, Political* 40.1 (2015): 3–14.

McLellan, David (ed.). *Karl Marx: Selected Writings.* Oxford: Oxford University Press, 2000.

Mitchell, Timothy. "Fixing the economy." *Cultural Studies* 12.1 (1998): 82–101.

Muppidi, Himadeep. *The Politics of the Global.* Minneapolis, MN: University of Minnesota Press, 2004.

Nandy, Ashis. "The beautiful, expanding future of poverty: Popular economics as a psychological defense." *International Studies Review* 4.2 (2002): 107–121.

Nilekani, Nandan. *Imagining India: Ideas for the New Century.* London: Penguin, 2013.

Ong, Aihwa. *Neoliberalism as Exception.* Durham, NC: Duke University Press, 2006.

Schindler, Seth. "A 21st-century urban landscape: The emergence of new social-spatial formations in Gurgaon." *Sarai Reader* 7 (2007): 499–508.

Searle, Llerena Guiu. "Making space for capital: The production of global landscapes in contemporary India." PhD diss, University of Pennsylvania, 2010.

Shakuntala, Rao. "The globalization of Bollywood: An ethnography of non-elite audiences in India." *The Communication Review* 10.1 (2007): 57–76.

Sheppard, Eric, Helga Leitner and Anant Maringanti. "Provincializing global urbanism: A manifesto." *Urban Geography* 34.7 (2013): 893–900.

Shiller, Robert. *The Subprime Solution: How Today's Global Financial Crisis Happened, and What to Do about It.* Princeton, NJ: Princeton University Press, 2012.

Tsing, Anna Lowenhaupt. "Inside the economy of appearances." *Public Culture* 12.1 (2000): 115–144.

3 The district

Old Gurgaon

Long before its uneven and volatile transformation into India's so-called Millennium City, Gurgaon had three designations: it was the name of a district in the state of Haryana, the name of a medium-size industrial town and district headquarters, and it was also the name of a small but dense village located approximately two miles north of the town. Historically, over the last millennium the region was a part of successive Rajput kingdoms that ruled swaths of the north Indian gangetic plains and desert regions until overtaken by Muhammad of Ghor of Central Asia in 1196. With the onset of Muslim rule in north India Gurgaon's fate was largely intertwined with that of Delhi to its north. Beginning with the reign of Akbar (1556–1605) the area was contained within the *Subahs* of Agra and Delhi, the latter of which later became the Mughal capital.[1] Gurgaon district was transferred to the Maratha ruler Daulat Rao Sindhia in the eighteenth century, who later relinquished it to the East India Company through the Treaty of Surji Anjungaon in 1803. As the *Gurgaon District Gazetteer* of 1883–1884 states,[2] "With this treaty the history of Gurgaon as a British district commences."

As a result of its proximity to Delhi, Gurgaon was drawn into the violent sequence of events associated with the great sepoy rebellion of 1857 in north India. In May of that year mutinous Indian soldiers belonging to the 3rd Light Cavalry from the United Provinces attacked the administrative town on their march to Shahjahanabad, where the plan was to re-install the Mughal king back as the rightful ruler of Hindustan. Government buildings were ransacked and burned down as the District Magistrate W. Ford of the Bengal Civil Service fled for safer grounds. Gurgaon remained a "liberated" space until October of that year when it was forcefully brought back under British control following the brutal suppression of rebellious groups in the area.[3]

After 1857 Gurgaon remained administrative headquarters of the district under direct British Crown rule. By the late-nineteenth century Gurgaon town consisted of "public offices, the dwellings of European residents, Sadar [wholesale] bazaar," as well as a railway station and the settlements of natives.[4] In 1881 the population of the town was 3390. Yet outside the town, Gurgaon was a poor

122 *Aura and trace in Gurgaon*

agricultural district marked by high levels of malnourishment among peasants and debt bondage to powerful landowning castes and money lenders in the region. According to the *Town Survey Report of Gurgaon (TSRG)*, published by the government of Haryana, in the years and decades following the Mutiny, Gurgaon was "deliberately kept backwards," as "no steps were taken to develop the Gurgaon region educationally or economically."[5] It described the region in 1886 as being comprised largely of "peasant-proprietors," or subsistence farmers, "a large and annually increasing portion of whom are sinking into debt and becoming serfs to money lenders."[6]

In 1928 the Anglo-Indian deputy commissioner of Gurgaon Frank L. Brayne wrote on the need for "rural uplift" in the region and described Gurgaon as "a very poor and backward area" populated with uneducated villagers, unskilled farmers and under-productive alluvial lands.[7] Gurgaon's topography was described as a sandy, dry, famine-stricken area on the fringes of the Rajasthan desert. Its crops were said to be poor. Cultivators grew drought-resistant millets for subsistence and small-scale exchange.

Despite its ostensibly under-productive agrarian lands and low levels of industry, Gurgaon's population doubled soon after India's break from British rule in 1947. From 9935 people in 1941, Gurgaon grew to 18,613 in 1951 (see Table 3.1 for equivalent figures for the whole of Gurgaon District). This jump was largely a result of refugees coming in from western Punjab in the aftermath of Partition.[8] Gurgaon's urban population would continue to rise rapidly in the decades following independence, doubling once again to 37,868 by 1961. In 1966, the state of Haryana was separated from the state of Punjab as a result of linguistic politics in the region (with Haryana being primarily Hindi speaking and Punjab being primarily Punjabi speaking). The district of Gurgaon was subsequently earmarked for industrial development and planned growth of residential sectors on the basis of its proximate location to both Delhi and National

Table 3.1 Population of Gurgaon District (1901–2011)

Year	Population	% variation from previous decade
1901	182,978	–
1911	159,558	–12.80
1921	148,627	–6.85
1931	162,464	+9.31
1941	186,775	+14.96
1951	201,727	+8.01
1961	259,655	+28.72
1971	348,151	+34.08
1981	471,695	+35.49
1991	606,791	+28.64
2001	874,695	+44.15
2011	1,514,432	+73.14

Source: Census of India: www.censusindia.gov.in/2011census/dchb/DCHB_Haryana.
html (accessed June 26, 2016).

The district   123

Highway 8, which connected Delhi to the western states of Rajasthan and Gujarat.[9] The growth in registered industrial factories from 1951 to 1983 testifies to Gurgaon's expanding manufacturing base and its emergence as a hub for industrial production in its own right. Whereas in 1951 there were just twenty-seven registered industrial factories in the district, most of which were located in and around the town of Gurgaon, by the end of the first five year plan this number jumped to seventy-one. By 1983, there were 125 registered large and medium scale industries and 2586 small-scale industries.[10]

Economic and industrial growth in Gurgaon coincided with a dramatic rise in population in the town, from 57,151 in 1971 to 89,115 by 1981. Much of this growth was directly related to the creation of the state of Haryana, whose newly formed government incentivized manufacturers to locate in the district by providing cheap financing from state banks and readily available industrial land. This "brought streams of immigrants into the town in the form of entrepreneurs, traders, industrial and sales workers, construction and transport workers, government servants, etc."[11] Some of these incoming workers moved into planned residential neighborhoods close to Old Gurgaon like New Colony and Model Town. But most housing in the area consisted of post-Partition refugee camps that had concretized incrementally over the decades since independence into sprawling multi-story residential flats and homes. According to the *TSRG*, by the mid-1980s living conditions and urban amenities varied quite dramatically from neighborhood to neighborhood in the town of Gurgaon. While some neighborhoods were unplanned clusters of *kutcha* homes built upon earlier settlements out of mud and stone, other parts of town were "nicely planned areas where roads and streets [were] '*pucca*' (well built) having sewerage and electricity facilities."[12] Beyond the working-class neighborhoods was the original village of Gurgaon, as well as scores of other villages and their associated ancestral lands that existed within the district of Gurgaon. So the town itself was interwoven with the agricultural and village lands surrounding it, such that "cows, buffalo, goats, sheep, dogs and cats are the common domestic animals found in the town."[13] As district headquarters of a largely rural district, the town of Old Gurgaon also featured a mini-secretariat building that housed the municipal government and a district courthouse in the same area, the nearby Civil and Police Lines that housed government employees and a small railway station that linked to Delhi a few kilometers away.

New Gurgaon

By the mid-1980s Gurgaon possessed "all the characteristics of an indigenous town and some characteristics of modern urban planning," but what marked it as unique was its geographical location:

> Gurgaon is surrounded by agricultural lands, a part of which are being developed by [Haryana Urban Development Authority] HUDA for planned urban development. Planned development has also been noticed in [Delhi

124 *Aura and trace in Gurgaon*

Land and Finance] DLF Colony.... Agricultural land in the north and northeast and southeast is available for further development.[14]

In the two decades after *TSRG* was published, public and private developers would indeed target these areas to the northeast and southeast of the existing town, in the village-owned lands east of NH8. HUDA, a state-level development agency in charge of land acquisition and executing the city's official urban master plan, and DLF, the largest real estate developer in the area, would play major roles in the subsequent development of New Gurgaon.

Gurgaon's proximity to India's capital and to National Highway 8, which connected Delhi and Jaipur, was an inescapable part of its growth story. This fortuitous location spurred initial industry in the district, especially around the existing town, leading to steady population growth and urban expansion. Industries like Maruti Udyog (an auto manufacturing company) and Indian Drugs Pharmaceutical made Gurgaon their manufacturing home as early as the late 1970s and early 1980s.[15] The opening of factories brought thousands of skilled and unskilled workers to the area as a variety of ancillary industries sprung up close to the existing town. Gurgaon's strategic location also led to its incorporation into the National Capital Region (NCR) following the NCR Planning Board Act of 1985. Citing high population growth rates in urban Delhi the NCR planning board was constituted with the objective of "relieving the capital city from additional [population] pressures" by attracting migrants to areas outside central Delhi.[16]

With increasing links to the capital, by the 1980s Gurgaon's potential as an urban hub was beginning to crystallize:

> The layout of the town depicts that sufficient land is now available for further planned development of the town.... The town has a very good future for development as a master plan for its development has already been drawn up.[17]

From 1981 to 2001, Gurgaon's urban population nearly doubled, from 89,115 to 173,542. Geographically, Gurgaon expanded even faster, as the area that was "built up," including land under industrial, institutional, commercial, residential, recreational, transportation and services uses, increased from just 11.36 sq. km in 1971 to 84.2 sq. km in 2002, although this built environment was fractured and disaggregated.[18]

By the new millennium Gurgaon had emerged as a major manufacturing hub within the state of Haryana, a trend that continues well into the present. From 1993 to 2003, the number of registered large-scale manufacturing units in Gurgaon district grew from 241 to 944 as industrial output increased at an annual rate of 36.8 percent over that same time span. This far surpassed the national average for industrial output growth, which hovered at 7 percent during the same period.[19] As of 2010 Gurgaon housed and employed 31 percent of the state's total factory workers despite having less than 5 percent of Haryana's population.[20]

In comparison to the growth of secondary-level industrial manufacturing in Gurgaon, the growth of tertiary-level producer services has attracted more sustained media attention. This is particularly the case in business process outsourcing (BPO), information technology (IT), retail, hospitality and real estate industries, all of which exude a strong visual presence in the built landscape of New Gurgaon. As of 2014, more than half of all Fortune 500 companies reportedly had headquarters or offices in Gurgaon. Gurgaon's dynamic economy supplied 71 percent of total exports coming from the state of Haryana, and Gurgaon district contributed close to half of the state's direct taxes to the exchequer.[21] The district's economy grew at an average annualized rate of 10.5 percent from 2005 to 2010. In that same five-year period, per capita income in the district nearly tripled, from Rs81,478 in 2004/05 to Rs229,208 in 2009/2010 (or in terms of U.S. dollars at constant 2004/2005 exchange rates, from $1810 in 2004/2005 to $5093 in 2009/2010). This rapid growth reflected the steady influx of high-skilled professionals and middle-class workers into the area to work in producer services and manufacturing.

But numbers do not quite tell the right story with respect to Gurgaon's historical transformation from "old" to "new." Rather, numbers in the form of "facts" and "figures" about GDP and income growth can be misleading in that they tend to obscure the complex conditions (social, political, ecological) that made such growth and transformation possible. In Gurgaon, the major condition of possibility for its growing urban economy was the rapid and large-scale conversion of land owned collectively or individually by rural villagers and agriculturalists into "urban" land available for industrial and commercial development. How this spatial transformation, at once abstract and geological, took place, is the focus of this chapter.

Land laws in Haryana

Historically, the colonial British and postcolonial Indian governments placed relatively strict regulations on large-scale exchanges of land in Gurgaon, first with the Punjab Land Alienation Act of 1900 and then with subsequent legislation under the Haryana state government.[22] These restrictions were ostensibly meant to curb the power of money lenders in the region, but they were also a way of securing political loyalty from landowning castes, protecting the latter's influence by legally obstructing the emergence of any rival landholding groups in the state. This limited the speculative potential of land in Haryana while preserving the existing caste-based social order.

Without the interventions of the Haryana state government, which opened up land to private exchange and speculation in the 1970s, the hyper-development of New Gurgaon may never have taken place. The first intervention was the Haryana Development and Regulation of Urban Areas (HDRUA) Act of 1975. This law facilitated the participation of the private sector in the urbanization process by awarding licenses to "big private developers to acquire, assemble and develop a minimum hundred acres of continuous land."[23] With an established legal framework to acquire land from sellers, capital-rich developers like DLF

126　*Aura and trace in Gurgaon*

(see Table 3.2), Ansals and Unitech were able to assemble large land banks ahead of actual development taking place on these lands, thereby allowing these developers to drive the price of such lands up on the basis of their anticipated development.

The Haryana government's second notable intervention in this regard was the 1977 Haryana Urban Development Authority (HUDA) Act, which created the apex "public" land development agency charged with the task of land acquisition for "public purposes" of urban development, such as building infrastructure and prioritized services like education and healthcare. Later "public purpose" was redefined to include the development of urban infrastructures built for new corporate developments, mini-cities and private townships, all of which were exclusive by their very design. HUDA also expanded its role to acquiring "public" land for direct transfer to private developers, provoking contestation by displaced villagers and farmers in the streets and the courts.[24] Using the colonial-era Land Acquisition Act, HUDA was able to "acquire agricultural land for developing residential townships and industrial estates and to contract out development to the private sector."[25]

The third important intervention made by the Haryana state government occurred in 1979, when the government split the existing district of Gurgaon in two, separating Gurgaon from what became the district of Faridabad to its east. Of the two resulting districts, Faridabad was considered more industrialized and wealthier in terms of *per capita* income.[26] Meanwhile the re-constituted Gurgaon district was less densely populated and thus given a "rural" designation, which left it free of any local municipal governments that might have interfered with land transfers already going on in the area. Throughout the 1980s and well into the 1990s, large tracts of land that were once classified as "agricultural" or "rural" were acquired by well-capitalized private developers, who in the absence of any local administration in Gurgaon district, were able to negotiate directly with farmers in order to buy the latter's holdings and develop large land banks of potentially profitable real estate. Of these developers, none was more central to the story of New Gurgaon than DLF, which has developed by far the largest share of Gurgaon's once rural lands.

DLF

Delhi Land and Finance, as it was originally known, was founded by Chaudhary Raghvendra Singh in 1946. Singh was a civil servant who turned to real estate just before India's independence. DLF found initial success building speculative mass housing in farmlands just south of New Delhi, constructing homes for the large influx of refugees that came to Delhi from Western Punjab and Sindh in what was now Pakistan. Foreshadowing the aggressive mode of speculation on farmland that would later give rise to DLF City half a century later, from the beginning Singh persuaded farmers in the southern peripheries of the capital "to hand over their land on the promise of future payment, borrowed money to develop residential neighborhoods and then sold at considerable profit to the influx of newcomers [refugees]."[27] As a part of the larger "urban conquest" of postcolonial Delhi's southern periphery,[28] DLF built numerous townships in Delhi throughout the 1940s and 1950s, including what are today some of the elite neighborhoods of south Delhi, including South Extension, Greater Kailash and Hauz Khas. DLF's private conquest of south Delhi came to an abrupt end in 1957, however, when through central government fiat, the Delhi Development Authority (DDA) came into existence under the Ministry of Urban Development and assumed monopoly control over all land development in the capital. Private speculators like DLF were effectively shut out of the land market, and had to look elsewhere for real estate gold.

In the aftermath of the DDA's state monopolization of Delhi's land market, DLF ventured into other pursuits, including manufacturing electric motors and automotive batteries. By the late-1970s, however, these ventures had floundered and other business strategies were explored. In 1979, Chaudhary Raghvendra Singh's son-in-law Kushal Pal (K. P.) Singh took over as Managing Director of DLF's mostly defunct real estate business. Coinciding rather fortuitously with this transition was the aforementioned bifurcation of the Gurgaon District into Faridabad and Gurgaon on 15 August, 1979. As also mentioned above, Gurgaon District was given a "rural" designation in government books because of its low population density. According to the 1981 census, Gurgaon District's population was 849,898 while Faridabad's was just over one million. But Gurgaon's total geographic area was nearly double that of Faridabad, giving it a population density of 675 people/sq. km compared to Faridabad's of 1350/sq. km.[29] This officially classified "rural" designation meant no Urban Local Body (ULB), or a municipal, third-tier government was required to administer the agricultural lands and barren fields of Gurgaon, particularly those to the east of Delhi–Jaipur Road.[30] The lands were instead overseen from Haryana's capital of Chandigarh, located 275 km to the north. Gurgaon Municipal Council did exist within the district but its jurisdiction only covered the town of Gurgaon.

With the absence of a local authority to institute "countervailing checks on arbitrary conversions of village land to urban areas"[31] Gurgaon caught the attention of the businessman K. P. Singh in the early 1980s, who saw the relatively barren and ungoverned frontier lands in Gurgaon as a potential land bank for future real estate development. K. P. Singh's autobiography *Whatever the Odds* devotes much of its narrative to the story of DLF's speculative real estate developments in Gurgaon from the 1980s on. He writes about his initial vision for Gurgaon:

> I could not stop myself from driving down to the outskirts of Delhi and staring for long hours at the wide open spaces all around with nothing but miles and miles of rocky but austerely beautiful landscape. In my mind's eye I could see modern, tall buildings made of glass and steel. I could visualize wide, tree-lined avenues with smooth-moving traffic and people walking on them and children playing in lush green parks.[32]

Table 3.2 shows how DLF fared in acquiring land during different government regimes in Haryana. I describe this process below.

Table 3.2 Land acquisition by DLF in Gurgaon (in acres of land acquired)

Gov't→Acreage	1982–1987 Congress, Bhajan Lal/Bansi Lal	1987–1991 Janata Dal, Chaudhary Devi Lal	1991–1996 Congress, Bhajan Lal	1996–1999 Haryana Vikas Party, Bansi Lal	2000–2005 INLD, Om Prakash Chautala	2005–2014 Congress, Bhupinder Singh Hooda
0–5	105.2	2.7	52.4	18.8	60.2	111.4
5–10	401.0	68.1	85.7	–	–	72.9
10–20	286.0	–	44.4	–	44.4	242.9
20–70	589.0	196.8	78.5	–	72.9	431.7
70–170	401.0	–	384.8	–	–	100.5
TOTAL	**1782.2**	**267.6**	**645.8**	**18.8**	**177.5**	**959.4**

Source: Town and Planning Department, Haryana, information was compiled at www.livemint.com/Companies/rkUwUVtzAflBP7hPVa1roL/How-Gurgaon-was-built-licence-by-licence-government-by-gov.html (accessed June 24, 2016).

The district 129

But state laws in Haryana at the time posed more of a hurdle to K. P. Singh's dream of speculating on Gurgaon's vast rural land than any local administrators or the absence thereof. By spring of 1981, DLF under Singh's head had only managed to acquire forty acres of farmland in Gurgaon, having failed to convince state-level agencies to de-regulate the land market by loosening restrictions on private land acquisition and land-use conversion from agricultural to commercial or industrial use. In 1975 HDRUA had been passed to "regulate the use of land in order to prevent ill-planned and haphazard urbanization in or around towns in the State of Haryana."[33] The act established a legal framework in which private owners of land could apply for licenses to develop said land into a colony, or "an area of land divided or proposed to be divided into plots or flats for residential, commercial, industrial purposes."[34] But because of its strict limitations on how much land could be developed by private builders, HDRUA was for someone like K. P. Singh a bureaucratic hurdle that limited the amount of land he could acquire on speculation, thus inhibiting the realization of his grand vision for Gurgaon.

In the midst of his increasingly frustrated efforts to acquire land, Singh claims in his autobiography that he had a fortuitous encounter in a local village in Gurgaon District that effectively changed both his fate and that of the town itself.

> A meeting in Gurgaon one afternoon with a young man driving an all-terrain vehicle had much to do with this. His vehicle had stalled because of an overheating radiator. I happened to be near by and arranged for water to cool the radiator. He asked me what I was doing out in the wilderness and heard with great interest about my plans [to build in Gurgaon] and how archaic laws and policies were stifling real estate development. Not long after, he became prime minister of the country and was instrumental in ushering the private sector into urban development. Those reforms would revolutionize the real estate sector and also allow DLF to expand at a scorching pace.[35]

This is the by-now legendary tale of K. P. Singh's "fortuitous" encounter with Rajiv Gandhi in Gurgaon in the early 1980s. It is unclear to what degree the story is factual or apocryphal. But throughout the 1980s, Singh writes, he spent countless days in Gurgaon's rural villages convincing farmers to sell to him their ancestral lands. Over the course of hundreds of hours "under the blazing sun ... [Singh tried] to persuade villagers that giving up their relatively small piece of land would guarantee their children and grand children a better life."[36] Singh insists throughout the book that DLF's business ethos "is founded on the basic premise that land acquisition is a transaction which should be a beneficial proposition for all concerned—the seller, the buyers, the community and the end user."[37] He also insists that every piece of land he acquired from farmers and villagers in rural Gurgaon was the result of consensual, non-coercive exchange. Even though "farmers here were emotionally attached to their land" and were often reluctant to part with it, he writes, "DLF was able to acquire thousands of

130 *Aura and trace in Gurgaon*

acres of land in Gurgaon without a single case of litigation against us or even a hint of violence or protest."[38] This peaceful consensus between a powerful real estate developer like DLF and the multitudes of farmers from whom it success-fully acquired land is important to foreground for someone like Singh. At the time of the publication of *Whatever the Odds* in 2011 the politics of land acqui-sition in rural India and outside large Indian cities had become a deeply conten-tious issue. Persistent and often violent protests by farmers over forced acquisition and unfair compensation for confiscated land by the state had spread throughout the country, including in Gurgaon itself.[39]

Given that most of the acquisitions Singh refers to in Gurgaon took place thirty years ago, it is difficult to corroborate the veracity of his claims regarding the consensual nature of land exchange between DLF and the scores of farmers and villagers of Gurgaon with whom he transacted.[40] Yet Singh seems to preempt any possible suspicion with a two-fold rhetorical strategy that is itself quite revelatory. First, he emphasizes the fact that the land he acquired in Gurgaon was useless anyway and therefore justifiably available for conversion to non-agricultural use. Farmers, he writes,

> were emotionally attached to their land even if it was unproductive.... Most of the land we acquired from local farmers was desolate and barren. There were small patches of green where they grew cyclical crops, but they also faced a severe shortage of water. I based my land-acquisition strategy on those prevailing conditions.[41]

Second, Singh frequently adopts a paternalistic tone that assures the reader that he had only the farmer's best interests in mind by acquiring their ancestral lands. Here Singh effortlessly reproduces an elitist bias typical in rural north India in which the upper caste individual knows what is best for the lower:

> When I set out to buy land in this area, I was firm that we would not take the farmers for a ride. They were simple folk and not many knew what the right compensation [for the land] should be. We wanted to pay them adequately so that they would not feel cheated. I myself came from a rural background so I knew their realities. We never forced or arm-twisted a single farmer into selling his land.[42]

Instead, Singh writes that he spent innumerable hours and days and weeks and months with the villagers, meeting them frequently, sharing meals and tea, medi-ating family disputes, helping with school admissions for children and medical issues for elders, attending birth and marriage ceremonies, funerals and intimate functions. He did all this "even after they had sold the land. I saw them as family. It helped create a relationship of mutual trust and respect, even affection."[43]

Returning to the now mythologized story of the encounter between K. P. Singh and Rajiv Gandhi, whether or not the meeting actually occurred in the

The district 131

precise way Singh describes it in his book, it more generally points to the range of dealings and negotiations that took place between Singh and various politicians and bureaucrats, at the federal and state levels. These associations were crucial for DLF to acquire, convert, develop and sell the agricultural lands of Gurgaon from the 1980s on (Table 3.2). As Debroy and Bhandari argue, the absence of a local governmental authority to mediate land acquisition and change in land use meant that decisions were made from far-away Chandigarh, so that "Within the state government the Chief Minster's office ha[d] the key veto power in allowing land conversion."[44] This had dual ramifications for a company like DLF. On the one hand, all land conversion and development-related issues were highly centralized for Gurgaon, "controlled directly by the CM's office.... Given this centralization, it was possible for the state government to take measures highly specific for Gurgaon. This centralization ensured that decisions could be taken and implemented rapidly."[45] On the other hand, this centralization also meant that political connections with the CM's office were paramount to getting any land developed in Gurgaon at all. Singh himself writes that he "realized that unless one developed a good working relationship with the incumbent chief minister, it was virtually impossible to get things done."[46] Yet it was on the strength of his ability to connect with those in power at the national and state levels that Singh was able to push politicians to grant land development permits that would allow him to acquire farmland in Gurgaon and convert it into profitable real estate without fetter.

Public–private partnership

In the early 1980s Haryana became the first state in India to de-regulate the participation of private developers in real estate.[47] Haryana's easing of restrictions on land development was but a harbinger of similar changes in other Indian states, heralding the entry of private Indian enterprises in real estate and other construction related industries, and the subsequent liberalization of foreign investment in sectors related to urbanization and land development.[48]

Haryana government's change in attitude toward private real estate development enabled DLF most prominently, but also other companies like Ansals and Unitech, to assemble land banks through direct negotiations with farmers and to develop these into residential and commercial colonies in Gurgaon. The ability to negotiate directly with farmers for land transfers at prevailing market rates, without needing to go through a governmental intermediary, was a central enabling condition for the rapid speed of land acquisition. In many cases the market as such did not even exist, particularly given the murkiness of land titles in rural Haryana and the low frequency of land transactions.[49] Many farmers in Gurgaon were lured into selling their lands by lucrative cash offers from well-funded developers like DLF, which offered seductive compensations that were generally three or four times higher than the compensation paid by government agencies that acquired through "eminent domain."[50] As one media report observed:

132 *Aura and trace in Gurgaon*

companies licensed to develop residential areas approached the locals directly, offering a few crores (crore = Rs10,000,000) for each acre. It didn't take long for fancy, colorful houses to dot the village's lanes, and for new-acquired vehicles to bring them alive.[51]

But recently large-scale land acquisition has been the site of increasing tension between farmers and state or private actors in Gurgaon and elsewhere in India. People are challenging large state agencies like HUDA that forcibly acquire land from farmers for "public" development or for land banks to be later sold to private developers incorporated as residential, commercial or industrial sectors in future master plans.[52] Farmer protests against land acquisition for Special Economic Zones and other mega-projects for "public purposes" are gaining increasing attention in the media and in academic scholarship. Yet in his autobiography K. P. Singh writes that he faced little resistance from farmers in the 1980s and 1990s. Like his father-in-law in the years surrounding India's partition, K. P. Singh was particularly adept at negotiating with them, even inviting the latter to join as junior partners in DLF's ongoing business ventures. Singh describes his bullish method of financing land acquisition in Gurgaon:

> After handing over the money for [the farmer's] land I would ask them if they needed all that money. Invariably, they said that they had never seen so much cash and did not need it for their kind of lifestyle. I then asked them to invest the money in DLF and become partners who would progress together with us. There were times when we bought land, handed over the money and then got them to give it back to us as an investment in DLF on the very same day! It was a win-win situation for them and for us. We offered them an interest of 12 percent.[53]

DLF obtained its first license to acquire land in 1981. In the subsequent years, under varying administrations in Chandigarh, DLF managed to grow its land holdings in Gurgaon. By the end of the 1990s Singh had acquired the largest private land bank of urbanizable space in India, as

> DLF was able to amass 3500 acres in Gurgaon and began building some of India's first modern commercial structures.... Land that cost Singh as little as $65 an acre at current exchange rates now sells for about $4 million an acre.[54]

HDRUA's intended purpose, to prevent "ill-planned and haphazard urbanization" in Haryana, was largely bypassed through Singh's direct negotiations with farmers. "Sometimes I marvel at the ease through which I was able to amass 3500 acres of land in Gurgaon," Singh writes in self-admiration.[55] But the absence of any local municipality to oversee and administer land exchanges in "rural" Gurgaon meant that transactions could take place with little or no governmental interference. Where contestations over acquisition on the part of

The Haryana government has been particularly adept at creating favorable conditions for the acquisition of rural land and conversion of the same into speculative real estate. In a recent topographical study of 126 sq. km comprising Gurgaon's urban limits, including both old and new cities and newly developed surrounding areas, the pace of change in terms of land use has been dramatic. In 1971, nearly 81 percent of this area was officially under agricultural use. This fell to 51 percent by 1993 and to 27 percent by 2002. The rate of decline has accelerated during the last decade, the study reported. Meanwhile, the proportion of "built-up" land, including industrial, public institutional, residential, recreational, commercial and service uses, increased as a percentage of the total area under study, from 9 percent in 1971 up to 66 percent by 2002.[57]

Public–private competition

HDRUA was established to oversee licensed land acquisition by private real estate developers and provide a legal framework for negotiations between developers and agricultural landowners. These privately acquired lands were to be incorporated within the expanding urbanizable area under the guidelines of the Directorate of Town Planning in Gurgaon. The bureaucratic process went as follows:

> urban planning here is in the hand of a state level organization—the Directorate of Town Planning (DTP)—which is typical across India. Another state organization, the Haryana Urban Development Authority (HUDA) is in charge of implementation of the master plan through preparation of lower order spatial plans like sector layouts, designs of city centre and other public facilities as well as development of serviced land and citywide infrastructure networks. The HUDA prepares also building byelaws and development controls in consultation with the DTP and implements these across private developments.[58]

Outside of the private acquisition of land that DLF and others carried out since the 1980s, HUDA has orchestrated compulsory land acquisition for "public purposes" through the Land Acquisition Act of 1894, a colonial-era ordinance that has been the cause of political turbulence in different parts of India, leading to its re-writing several times over the past decade.[59]

With regard to forced land acquisition by state authorities like HUDA, "public purpose" does not exclude the participation of the private sector in land and infrastructure development.[60] In practice, much of the land acquired by HUDA is quickly turned over to private developers, over whom the state exercises little control regarding how that land is subsequently developed. In 2010 a public interest litigation (PIL) was filed by villagers from Nathupur within New Gurgaon. It alleged that the same land that villagers were forced to sell cheaply to HUDA for infrastructural development was instead given over to DLF for its Cyber City project back in 2006. Cases relating to land acquisition for such "public purposes" increasingly fill the district and state court's dockets.[61]

The original Land Acquisition Act of 1894 "was partly motivated by the intention of developing railways and acquiring land for these."[62] Today it is used by agencies like HUDA to carry out "bulk land acquisition ... and large-scale land development to meet the demands for serviced land and city-wide infrastructure."[63] According to its official guidelines, HUDA works on a "no profit no loss" basis, in which "funds from land sales of residential, industrial and institutional plots are invested into acquisition of new areas, which enable [HUDA] to generate more plots for the public and more funds for the development works and new acquisitions."[64]

For "public" agencies like HUDA that utilize the Land Acquisition Act, in order to accumulate land banks for future urbanization, a number of mediating factors come into play in determining the compulsory price at which the land will be sold to the government:

> In determining the amount of compensation to be awarded for land acquired under this Act, the Court shall take into consideration—first, the market-value of the land at the date of the publication of the notification ...; secondly, the damage sustained by the person interested, by reason of the taking of any standing crops or trees which may be on the land at the time of the Collector's taking possession thereof.... In addition to the market value of the land as above provided, the Court shall in every case award a sum of thirty per centum on such market value, in consideration of the compulsory nature of the acquisition.[65]

However, in the absence of a local governing body to oversee the conversion of agricultural lands into non-agricultural uses, HUDA has emerged as "the apex land acquisition para-governmental structure" in rural Gurgaon.[66] But in terms of bulk acquisitions of land for urban development, private developers have far outpaced public agencies like HUDA, for whom the land acquisition process "is riddled with bureaucratic tangles of involvement of many organizations as well as legal squabbles over land records and compensation rates."[67] In 1981, starting with forty acres licensed for future development, DLF rapidly expanded its holdings to 556 acres by 1983, according to K. P. Singh's autobiography.[68] Over roughly the same time span, HUDA was able to acquire only half of this total, lagging far behind DLF and other large private builders.[69]

Outside of DLF's massive acquisitions, other developers such as Ansals, Emaar, Sheetal, Unitech, Vatika and others benefited from the *laissez faire* regulatory environment for land acquisition in Gurgaon. From 1982 to 2005, Gurgaon's successive state governments in power in Chandigarh approved the transfer of some 7400 acres of land in Gurgaon, at an average of 320 acres per year. In the nine years between 2005 and 2014, however, the Haryana state government approved another 9400 acres of land to private developers, or about

The district   135

1044 acres per year. Since 1982 a total of 16,795 acres were dispersed to 344 different developers. But just three developers accounted for 38 percent of this total area: DLF (20.5 percent), Ansals (9.2 percent) and Unitech (8.7 percent). The maximum acquisition occurred in 2008, the year before the global financial crisis unfolded in India, impacting Gurgaon's speculative real estate bubble dramatically. Yet even after the credit crisis, the state government continued to issue licenses to builders, leading to the transfer of 6380 acres after 2008, or 38 percent of total land allotted in Gurgaon.[70]

Land acquisition in its dual modes, that is, through the public Land Acquisition Act and through direct private negotiation with farmers, has led to two dramatically different speeds of urban development in Gurgaon, and this has had a profound impact on the built environment and infrastructure of the city. There is an inherent mismatch between these two modes, with "private colonization occurring disjointedly both in space and time" and superseding the planned development strategies drawn up in Gurgaon's master plan. Thus, "the difference between the pace of private development and the pace of extension of city infrastructure by the public agencies aggravates the problem of disjointed growth," leading to private developments completed and sold to investor-residents well before public infrastructure services are in place.[71] As we will see in the next chapter, this disjointed growth and lack of public infrastructure in private townships and enclave spaces has pushed Gurgaon's elite and middle classes into political action in new and ambivalent ways.

The same conditions that allowed for Gurgaon's rapid speculative development, namely the absence of a local municipal authority to oversee and mediate land transfers and changes in land use, has also led to a radically uneven landscape in New Gurgaon. High-end private developments form veritable islands of "luxury" development in the midst of severely under-developed urban infrastructure. As Debroy and Bhandari argue,

> In Gurgaon ... the local government did not impact road building, water supply and sanitation, street lighting, parks, etc. Rather private builders who had purchased and controlled large tracks of land were to be responsible for their own areas, and this was supplemented by the efforts of the state government.[72]

To mediate this uneven landscape, to project a time of anticipated completion and arrival over the disjointed space–time of the Millennium City, a speculative ecology is required to circulate money and hype about changing urban life in the Millennium City.

A speculative ecology

By the time of my research there from 2008 on, Gurgaon's identity as Millennium City was contested on several fronts. First, its status as a "global city" had been challenged by the ubiquity of "Third World" conditions prevalent in the

136 *Aura and trace in Gurgaon*

newly developed areas, including annual flooding due to poor drainage, lack of sewage and trash disposal services, crumbling roads and chronic traffic congestion, frequent power cuts and high rates of crime. These lackluster urban conditions have been documented in a variety of popular media both in India and abroad, and will be explored in the next chapter.[73] Second is a less documented but equally significant development taking place in the industrial and manufacturing zones on the western side of town. Here industrial workers have attempted to unionize or to bargain collectively in order to resist "casualization" of labor and to fight for better working conditions. They have come into frequent and often violent conflict with the capital–state–police nexus that is the brutal "invisible hand" in Haryana's *laissez faire* land development policies over the past quarter century or so.[74] And finally, farmers and villagers in rural Gurgaon actively contest the forced acquisition of their ancestral land on the part of the state, arguing that they were being unjustly compensated for their lands or were otherwise unwilling to give up the only livelihood they knew. All three sites of conflict—(1) the ubiquity of "Third World" conditions in what was supposed to be an elite "First World" city, (2) the violent conflict between industrial labor and the state and (3) resistance amongst villagers and farmers against forced land acquisition for private development—introduce politics into a space that was ostensibly projected as "post-political." Gurgaon was supposed to embody the technocratic efficiency of global economics triumphing over the tired redundancies and populist demands of postcolonial democracy. Gurgaon was in this way the ultimate elite "secession" from the chaos and calamity of "India" more generally. A line of flight for the privileged elite to "elsewhere," to "not-India." Yet this line of flight has been continually interrupted in Gurgaon, constituting so many postcolonial specters and ghosts which haunt the Millennium City's projected "globality."

Gurgaon's ecology of speculation involves an assemblage of public and private institutions, built and unbuilt spaces, elite and non-elite actors, technologies and texts. Their interactions mediate Gurgaon's "global" identity and conjure away the postcolonial temporalities of "development" and "underdevelopment" that continues to haunt this identity. Gurgaon's image and identity is thus contingent upon the complex interactions among these distinct parts, which come together to project Gurgaon as Millennium City.

DLF and HUDA

Gurgaon's hyper-development has been in large part molded by the actions of two powerful institutions, DLF and the Haryana state government, though not always through harmonious collaboration. Though various parts of DLF City boast of modern, futuristic architecture, including notable work by India's most commercially successful architects,[75] the "public" infrastructure in Gurgaon is often seen as lagging behind the private productions of urban space. But there were more hidden conflicts between private and public partners in the speculative development of Gurgaon as Millennium City.

Figure 3.1 DLF Limited headquarters, New Delhi.
Source: Photo by author.

In his autobiography, DLF's chairman K. P. Singh notes, almost in passing, a conflict of interest that emerged between himself and then Haryana Chief Minister Bansi Lal in the mid-1980s. Though Singh fails to elaborate on the cause of the conflict, he does describe how it threatened to jeopardize his dream of speculating on the abundant lands of Gurgaon. Singh writes that because of this conflict with Bansi Lal he had difficulty attaining permits to acquire land. In this context, Singh writes that he had to wait patiently for a more favorable chief minister to come to office. As Table 3.2 shows, across six different regimes in Haryana from 1982 to 2014, DLF's land acquisition activity has coincided quite dramatically with periods of time in which Haryana was governed by the Congress Party, the party from which Bansi Lal split in the late 1980s.

When Bansi Lal's Haryana Vikas (Development) Party came to power in Chandigarh in 1996, DLF's land acquisition activities came to an abrupt stop. Following Bansi Lal's ouster in 1999, Singh returned to acquiring farmland in Gurgaon in order to consolidate his holdings and take advantage of the low cost of land.

> I took this decision as land was cheap and I was convinced that it was the right time to buy. It was a calculated risk. At that time, land in Gurgaon was

138 *Aura and trace in Gurgaon*

available for as low as Rs40,000 an acre.... Today, the same land would cost several millions of rupees for an acre.[76]

At this point in the narrative Singh dispenses with the folksy tales of sitting on the floor of village homes cross-legged, sharing meals and quality time with rustic farmers and their simple families. Instead, he stresses the importance of maximizing his land holdings and taking advantage of the low prices in pre-boom Gurgaon. In order to do this Singh honed his bullish methods for leveraging DLF's real estate ambitions, adopting from his father-in-law the speculative strategy of borrowing back money he paid to farmers for land he acquired in order to finance future construction costs and acquire more land. As one commentator noted in 2014:

> Although other builders don't rival DLF's scale, its way of doing business is now being emulated in places like New Gurgaon (a moniker coined by DLF for marketing purposes). Highly leveraged companies, whose corporate prospectuses feature computer-generated images of luxurious housing colonies—in which many of the units are already sold, have aggressively acquired land here for new construction.[77]

The Haryana state government came in as a key participant in this emergent ecology of speculation in Gurgaon. Large developers benefited from political connections with those in charge of HUDA's growing portfolio of urbanizable land in the district, namely the Chief Minister's office. According to guidelines in Gurgaon's master plan for 2021 (published in 2007 but subsequently revised several times), for land designated as lying in an "Agricultural Zone," the Chief Minister's office "can relax the provisions" of the plan "for use and development of the land into a residential or industrial colony provided the colonizer has purchased the land for the said use and developed prior to the material date."[78] In other words, the master plan contained within its own guidelines an incentive for contradicting existing zoning regulations. This opened the door to myriad forms of collaboration and collusion between urban officials and the real estate lobby, so that,

> Continual revisions of the plan and the free flow of licenses have created a robust trade in insider information between developers and politicians. Since farmland is cheaper but far less profitable than developable land, the trick for builders and speculators is to acquire agricultural plots just before they get rezoned.[79]

Master plans are thusly revised, as privately acquired areas are later converted into highly valued residential and commercial sectors to be developed for profit.

This process of revision is conducted surreptitiously by the state agencies and the information is leaked to a select group or an individual, who would then go and buy land in these sectors.... Once the revised Master Plan is released, the price of land in these areas increases manifold.[80]

Property brokers

Property brokers mediate between large private developers like DLF, which use spectacular architecture and cutting edge urban design to project a seductive image of "globality," and state agencies like HUDA, who are in charge of land-use and zoning regulations. Mediating between these two powerful institutions, brokers surreptitiously collect and share information about future developments in Gurgaon, fueling the ecology of speculation from within. But this ecology is about not just land and geography as such. It is also about the possible future revenue that can be conjured for a particular site after building it up. Here, laws pertaining to maximum ground-floor-coverage and floor-to-area-ratio (FAR) are key to unlocking the potentiality of land as a speculative financial asset. These laws and regulations determine just how many floors will get built, how much land will be used for residential versus commercial space, how much of the projected real estate has already been sold off or leased, and how much remains to be leveraged. These become the often-murky details and unverifiable variables that shape the economy of information within an existing speculative real estate bubble. Often in the service of circulating these opaque details and selling them hard to potential investors and future residents is the figure of the property broker, who as we will see, mediates not merely between public and private partners in urban development but between both of these and the end users that eventually inhabit the resulting near order of the Millennium City.

Figure 3.2 Property broker office in Chakkarpur, Gurgaon.
Source: Photo by author.

140 *Aura and trace in Gurgaon*

Speculative ecosystems are not merely generated from the top, from the actions of powerful institutions like DLF and HUDA. The adaptive and productive ecosystem works through the tension and interaction, indeed, the *friction*, as Anna Tsing has conceptualized it, between large institutions operating from above and afar and smaller players "on-the-ground" who convince resident-investors to invest their life savings (often in cash form) into nothing more, and nothing less, than an image.[81] Thus within a speculative ecology, the far order and the near order of the speculative land market jointly shape an economy of appearances. In this dynamic, ever-changing environment, small-time property brokers take on an important role in the projection of Gurgaon's futuristic and seductive aura, trading on specialized knowledge regarding land titles and upcoming sectoral layouts for residential zones in the master plan. Simultaneously, they prey upon the gullibility and desires of the investors and residents to whom they sell this metrosexual aura. Practices of micro-speculation thus serve to keep the flow of money steady and continuous, constantly bringing new buyers into the ecosystem, keeping prices high and the larger urban spectacle alive.[82]

Through macro-speculations on the part of HUDA and DLF, and the micro-speculations of property brokers working directly with end-users, speculative development in Gurgaon becomes highly leveraged. Revenue earned from selling flats in one upcoming property is often used not to ensure that the property is completed on time and up to promised standards for the resident-investors, but rather to buy up additional land for future developments. The primary task of the broker as intermediary is therefore to book as many of these flats before the development is even finished, generating what are called "pre-sales." Pre-sales also have the benefit of creating an artificial sense of high demand by attracting others to take part in the herd-like behavior.[83] Once flats start selling in a new project, builders then hike-up the rates for the remaining flats. Customers, weary of being priced out of the development, opt for the raised price. Charging commissions of up to 1 percent on each transaction they are able to complete, some upwards of ten million rupees ($150,000 according to 2016 exchange rate), brokers make a substantial cut in each deal.[84]

Property brokers are "the storytellers who talk up Gurgaon's high rises, ensuring that prices remain lofty and that demand always seems to be soaring."[85] They have an understated, yet ubiquitous presence in the newly built parts of Gurgaon. One sees the storefronts of these economic actors along most major roads in New Gurgaon. They are often positioned directly in front of unfinished residential projects and upcoming malls, in temporary stalls or semi-finished glass-front offices. Their signage features computerized imagery of future developments. Many of these brokers were once landowners who sold their property and subsequently decided to join the real estate game and the growing speculative ecology. Together with larger institutions like DLF and HUDA, they spectacularly mediate Gurgaon's global aura. As one Gurgaon-based broker said, "We make the builders. We are his arms, feet, eyes and heart."[86]

Conclusion

How can we situate the geohistory of Gurgaon's hyper-development? That is, how does it fit within the transition from agricultural to industrial to post-industrial space? For in Gurgaon the situation is more complex than a one-way neoliberal transition fueled by privatization, de-centralization and de-regulation. Though private developers like DLF played a major role in Gurgaon's transformation and urban growth, without partnering with "public" institutions like

Figure 3.3 Man in front of construction in Gurgaon.
Source: Photo by author.

142 *Aura and trace in Gurgaon*

HUDA and powerful figures within the Haryana state government, this meta-morphosis would never have been possible. De-regulation in Gurgaon's land market was coupled with anti-market monopolization (a form of re-regulation) by powerful "far order" institutions, namely HUDA itself, which has acquired most of Gurgaon's remaining urbanizable land.[87] This is far from de-centralized governance, as far-off Chandigarh continues to play a major role in influencing the shape and trajectory of Gurgaon's ongoing development in collaboration with large developers like DLF.

In light of the continual imaginal disruptions and counter-mediations of Gurgaon public intelligibility, which is examined in closer detail in the next chapter, Gurgaon's speculative ecology is thus needed to mediate the aura of the Millennium City, projecting its distance from the space and time of Gurgaon's uneven, fragmented present. The next two chapters explore this haunted landscape in more detail, looking at partitioned spaces of white collar residents in privatized enclave spaces (Chapter 4) and working-class urbanized villages (Chapter 5). While the elite enclaves themselves express the resplendent visuality of Gurgaon's speculative machine, the working-class villages, very much in the midst of the former, service this machine from a position of interiorized invisibility.

Notes

1 Government of India, Office of Registrar General, Census Commissioner and Director of Census Operations, Haryana, *Census of India 1981, Series 6, Haryana: Town Survey Report Gurgaon* (Delhi: Controller of Publications, Government of India, 1989), 19. Hereafter *TSRG*.
2 Punjab Government, "Gurgaon District 1883–84" (Lahore: Sung-e-Meel Publications, 2001), 23.
3 Ibid., 27.
4 *TSRG*, 20.
5 Ibid., 19.
6 *Gazetteer*, 8.
7 Frank Lugard Brayne, *Village Uplift in India* (Allahabad: Pioneer Press, 1927), i.
8 Urvashi Butalia, *The Other Side of Silence: Voices from the Partition of India* (Durham, NC: Duke University Press, 2000).
9 *TSRG*, 23.
10 Dalia Wahdan, *Governing Livelihoods in Liberalizing States: A Comparative Study of Passenger Transport in Gurgaon, India and Sitta October, Egypt* (Saarbrucken: Lambert Academic Publishing, 2010), 148.
11 *TSRG*, 147.
12 Ibid., 8.
13 Ibid., 3.
14 Ibid., 2.
15 Interview with Bipin Kumar Awasti: March 7, 2015, Gurgaon, Haryana.
16 National Capital Region Planning Board, Ministry of Urban Development, Government of India, "Regional Plan 2021," accessed March 21, 2015, http://ncrpb.nic.in/regionalplan2021.php.
17 *TSRG*, 23.
18 R. K Gupta, and Sudesh Nangia, "Population explosion and land use changes in Gurgaon city region: A satellite of Delhi metropolis," *International Conference Proceedings of International Union for the Scientific Study of Population* (2006).

19 Gov't of Haryana, Statistical Abstract of Haryana, accessed March 21, 2015, http://esaharyana.gov.in/Default2.aspx?PName=State%20Statistical%20Abstract%20of%20Haryana.

20 Kushal Pal Singh and Ramesh Menon, *Whatever the Odds: The Incredible Story behind DLF* (New York: HarperCollins, 2011), 202.

21 Department of Town and Country Planning, Haryana, "Preparation of sub-regional plan for Haryana sub-region of NCR (2010)," accessed March 20, 2015, www.tcpharyana.gov.in/ncrpb/Draft%20Final%20Report-Haryana%20Sub-Regional%20Plan%202021.pdf.

22 K. C. Yadav (ed.), *Socio-Economic Life in Rural Haryana in the Nineteenth Century: The Fortescue Report by Thomas Fortescue* (Delhi: Haryana Academy of History & Culture, 2012).

23 Tathagata Chatterji, "The micro-politics of urban transformation in the context of globalisation: A case study of Gurgaon, India." *South Asia: Journal of South Asian Studies* 36.2 (2013), 279.

24 See Vikas Sharma, "Haryana farmers protest land acquisitions by DLF." *Business Standard*, October 24, 2012, accessed March 25, 2015, www.business-standard.com/article/economy-policy/haryana-farmers-protest-land-acquisitions-by-dlf-112102402002_1.html.

25 Chatterji, "Micro-politics of urban transformation," 278.

26 Bibek Debroy and Laveesh Bhandari, *Gurgaon and Faridabad: An Exercise in Contrasts*, CDDRL Working Paper, 101 (September 2009), 10.

27 "Soldier of fortune: 60 years of independence." *TIME*, August 2, 2007, accessed May 22, 2008, www.time.com/time/specials/2007/article/0,28804,1649060_1649046_1649030,00.html.

28 Veronique Dupont, Emma Tarlo and Denis Vidal, *Delhi: Urban Space and Human Destinies* (Delhi: Manohar, 2000).

29 Hemanshu Kumar and Rohini Somanathan, "Mapping Indian districts across census years, 1971–2001." *Economic and Political Weekly* (2009), 69–73.

30 Debroy and Bhandari, "Gurgaon and Faridabad," 19.

31 Ibid., 16.

32 Singh, *Whatever the Odds*, 95.

33 Haryana Development and Regulation of Urban Areas Act, 1975, accessed May 22, 2008, http://archive.india.gov.in/allimpfrms/allacts/1907.pdf (hereafter HDRUA).

34 HDRUA, 4.

35 Singh, *Whatever the Odds*, 7.

36 Ibid., 2.

37 Ibid., 97.

38 Ibid.

39 For recent academic studies of the politics of land acquisition and resistance by farmers and agricultural workers, see Praful Bidwai, "The great land grab." *Frontline*, September 9, 2006, and Kenneth Bo Nielsen, "Contesting India's development? Industrialisation, land acquisition and protest in West Bengal." *Forum for Development Studies* 37.2 (2010). Michael Levien, "The politics of dispossession: Theorizing India's 'land wars.'" *Politics & Society* 41.3 (2013), 351–394; and Chatterji, "The micro-politics of urban transformation."

40 In Chapter 5 I share the stories of farmers with whom I spoke in the context of an ethnographic study set in one of the pre-urban agricultural villages within what is now DLF City, where Singh ostensibly acquired land in the early 1980s. Although their stories of interacting with DLF do not necessarily contradict the pristine ethics Singh presents in his autobiography, they do suggest complications in the story that the autobiography attempts to glide over.

41 Singh, *Whatever the Odds*, 99.

42 Ibid., 99.

43 Ibid., 101.

144 *Aura and trace in Gurgaon*

44 Debroy and Bhandari, "Gurgaon and Faridabad," 16.
45 Ibid.
46 Singh, *Whatever the Odds*, 141.
47 Debroy and Bhandari, "Gurgaon and Faridabad," 16.
48 Llerena Guiu Searle, "Conflict and commensuration: Contested market making in India's private real estate development sector." *International Journal of Urban and Regional Research* 38.1 (2014), 60–78.
49 Interview with K. C. Yadav, March 13, 2015 in Gurgaon, Haryana.
50 Suoro D. Joardar, "Development mechanism in Spatial Integration." *42nd ISoCaRP Congress* (2006), 11.
51 Anil Varghese, "It takes a village." *Tehelka*, January 31, 2009, accessed September 10, 2010, www.tehelka.com/2009/01/it-takes-a-village/.
52 V. K. Puri, *Master Plan 2021 for Gurgaon-Manesar* (Delhi: JBA Publishers, 2007), 6–8.
53 Singh, *Whatever the Odds*, 107.
54 "Soldier of fortune: 60 years of independence."
55 Singh, *Whatever the Odds*, 108.
56 Debroy and Bhandari, "Gurgaon and Faridabad," 16.
57 Gupta and Nangia, "Population explosion and land use changes in Gurgaon city region."
58 Joardar, "Development mechanism in Spatial Integration," 9.
59 Kenneth Bo Nielsen, and Alf Gunvald Nilsen, "Law struggles and hegemonic processes in neoliberal India: Gramscian reflections on land acquisition legislation." *Globalizations* 12.2 (2015), 203–216.
60 "Land acquisition for public purpose justified: Supreme Court ruling land acquisition for public purpose justified," accessed May 14, 2009, www.india-server.com/news/land-acquisition-for-public-purpose-3572.html.
61 Praveen Donthi, "The road to Gurgaon." *The Caravan* 6.1 (2014), 24–38.
62 Debroy and Bhandari, "Gurgaon and Faridabad," 2.
63 Joardar, "Development mechanism in Spatial Integration," 10.
64 "Haryana Urban Development Authority, INDIA," accessed May 14, 2009, http://huda.nic.in/about.htm.
65 Department of Land Resources, Government of India, Ministry of Rural Development, "The Land Acquisition Act of 1894," accessed May 14, 2009, http://dolr.nic.in/dolr/LandAcquisitionAct1894.asp.
66 Wahdan, *Governing Livelihoods in Liberalizing States*, 163.
67 Joardar, "Development mechanism in Spatial Integration," 11.
68 Singh, *Whatever the Odds*, 122.
69 Joardar, "Development mechanism in Spatial Integration," 11.
70 "How Gurgaon was built, license by license, gov't by gov't." *Live Mint*, accessed May 24, 2010, www.livemint.com/Companies/rkUwUVtzAflBP7hPVa1roL/How-Gurgaon-was-built-licence-by-licence-government-by-gov.html. These maps were created by howindialives.com, compiled from data sourced from the Department of Town & Country Planning, Haryana. howindialives.com is a Delhi-based start-up that is developing a search engine for public data to make the process of land acquisition and conversion from agricultural to non-agricultural use more transparent.
71 Joardar, "Development mechanism in Spatial Integration," 12.
72 Debroy and Bhandari, "Gurgaon and Faridabad," 17.
73 See, for instance, Jim Yardley, "In India, dynamism wrestles with dysfunction." *New York Times*, June 8, 2011, accessed June 14, 2012, www.nytimes.com/2011/06/09/world/asia/09gurgaon.html?_r=0.
74 P. Sainath, "The class war in Gurgaon." *Indiatogether.org*, August 13, 2005, accessed February 17, 2008, http://indiatogether.org/gurgaon-op-ed.
75 Rohan Kalyan, "Fragmentation by design: Architecture, finance, identity." *Grey Room* 44 (2011), 26–53.

76 Singh, *Whatever the Odds*, 130.
77 Donthi, "The road to Gurgaon."
78 Puri, *Master Plan 2021 for Gurgaon-Manesar*, 12.
79 Donthi, "The road to Gurgaon."
80 Swagato Sarkar, "Speculation in land and the predicament of capitalist urbanization." Unpublished paper available at Social Science Research Network, accessed July 13, 2015, http://papers.ssrn.com/sol3/papers.cfm?abstract_id=2462653.
81 Anna Tsing, *Friction: An Ethnography of Global Connection* (Princeton, NJ: Princeton University Press, 2005).
82 This material was gleaned from a joint interview with two property brokers based in Phase II of DLF City in New Gurgaon. To protect their anonymity, I refrain from using their names and have paraphrased their statements as neither allowed me to audio-record the session on March 12, 2015.
83 Donthi, "The road to Gurgaon."
84 Ibid.
85 Ibid.
86 Ibid.
87 Praveen Jose, "600 acres of HUDA land in city taken over by squatters." *Times of India*, March 19, 2015, accessed August 12, 2016, http://timesofindia.indiatimes.com/city/gurgaon/600-acres-of-HUDA-land-in-city-taken-over-by-squatters/articleshow/46615351.cms.

Bibliography

Benjamin, Walter. "Theses on philosophy of history," in *Illuminations*. New York: Schocken Books, 1968: 253–264.

Bidwai, Praful. "The great land grab." *Frontline*, September 9, 2006.

Brayne, Frank Lugard. *Village Uplift in India*. Allahabad: Pioneer Press, 1927.

Butalia, Urvashi. *The Other Side of Silence: Voices from the Partition of India*. Durham, NC: Duke University Press, 2000.

Chatterjee, Partha. "Democracy and economic transformation in India." *Economic and Political Weekly* 43.16 (2008): 53–62.

Chatterji, Tathagata. "The micro-politics of urban transformation in the context of globalisation: A case study of Gurgaon, India." *South Asia: Journal of South Asian Studies* 36.2 (2013): 273–287.

Debroy, Bibek and Laveesh Bhandari. *Gurgaon and Faridabad: An Exercise in Contrasts*. CDDRL Working Paper 101 (September 2009).

Department of Town and Country Planning, Haryana. "Preparation of sub-regional plan for Haryana sub-region of NCR (2010)," accessed March 20, 2015, www.tcpharyana.gov.in/ncrpb/Draft%20Final%20Report-Haryana%20Sub-Regional%20Plan%202021.pdf.

Donthi, Praveen. "The road to Gurgaon." *The Caravan* 6.1 (2014): 24–38.

Dupont, Veronique, Emma Tarlo and Denis Vidal. *Delhi: Urban Space and Human Destinies*. Delhi: Manohar, 2000.

Gov't of Haryana. Statistical Abstract of Haryana, accessed March 21, 2015, http://esaharyana.gov.in/Default2.aspx?PName=State%20Statistical%20Abstract%20of%20Haryana.

Government of India, Office of Registrar General, Census Commissioner and Director of Census Operations, Haryana. *Census of India 1981, Series 6, Haryana: Town Survey Report Gurgaon*. Delhi: Controller of Publications, Government of India, 1989.

146 *Aura and trace in Gurgaon*

Gupta, R. K. and Sudesh Nangia. "Population explosion and land use changes in Gurgaon city region: A satellite of Delhi metropolis." *International Conference Proceedings of International Union for the Scientific Study of Population* (2006).

Haryana Development and Regulation of Urban Areas Act, 1975, accessed May 22, 2008, http://archive.india.gov.in/allimpfrms/allacts/1907.pdf.

Joardar, Suoro D. "Development mechanism in Spatial Integration." *42nd ISoCaRP Congress* (2006).

Jose, Praveen. "600 acres of HUDA land in city taken over by squatters." *Times of India*, March 19, 2015, accessed August 12, 2016, http://timesofindia.indiatimes.com/city/gurgaon/600-acres-of-HUDA-land-in-city-taken-over-by-squatters/articleshow/46615351.cms.

Kalyan, Rohan. "Fragmentation by design: Architecture, finance, identity." *Grey Room* 44 (2011): 26–53.

Kumar, Hemanshu and Rohini Somanathan. "Mapping Indian districts across census years, 1971–2001." *Economic and Political Weekly* (2009): 69–73.

Levien, Michael. "The politics of dispossession: Theorizing India's 'land wars.'" *Politics & Society* 41.3 (2013): 351–394.

National Capital Region Planning Board, Ministry of Urban Development, Government of India. "Regional Plan 2021," accessed March 21, 2015, http://ncrpb.nic.in/regional-plan2021.php.

Nielsen, Kenneth Bo. "Contesting India's development? Industrialisation, land acquisition and protest in West Bengal." *Forum for Development Studies* 37.2 (2010): 145–170.

Nielsen, Kenneth Bo and Alf Gunvald Nilsen. "Law struggles and hegemonic processes in neoliberal India: Gramscian reflections on land acquisition legislation." *Globalizations* 12.2 (2015): 203–216.

Punjab Government. "Gurgaon District 1883–84." Lahore: Sung-e-Meel Publications, 2001.

Puri, V. K. *Master Plan 2021 for Gurgaon-Manesar*. Delhi: JBA Publishers, 2007.

Sainath, P. "The class war in Gurgaon." *Indiatogether.org*, August 13, 2005, accessed February 17, 2008, http://indiatogether.org/gurgaon-op-ed.

Sarkar, Swagato. "Speculation in land and the predicament of capitalist urbanization." Unpublished paper available at Social Science Research Network, accessed July 13, 2015, http://papers.ssrn.com/sol3/papers.cfm?abstract_id=2462653.

Searle, Llerena Guiu. "Conflict and commensuration: Contested market making in India's private real estate development sector." *International Journal of Urban and Regional Research* 38.1 (2014): 60–78.

Sharma, Vikas. "Haryana farmers protest land acquisitions by DLF." *Business Standard*, October 24, 2012, accessed March 25, 2015, www.business-standard.com/article/economy-policy/haryana-farmers-protest-land-acquisitions-by-dlf-112102402002_1.html.

Singh, Kushal Pal and Ramesh Menon. *Whatever the Odds: The Incredible Story Behind DLF*. New York: HarperCollins, 2011.

Tsing, Anna. *Friction: An Ethnography of Global Connection*. Princeton, NJ: Princeton University Press, 2005.

Varghese, Anil. "It takes a village." *Tehelka*, January 31, 2009, accessed September 10, 2010, www.tehelka.com/2009/01/it-takes-a-village/.

Wahdan, Dalia. *Governing Livelihoods in Liberalizing States: A Comparative Study of Passenger Transport in Gurgaon, India and Sitta October, Egypt*. Saarbrucken: Lambert Academic Publishing, 2010.

Yadav, K. C. (ed.). *Socio-Economic Life in Rural Haryana in the Nineteenth Century: the Fortescue Report by Thomas Fortescue*. Delhi: Haryana Academy of History & Culture, 2012.

Yardley, Jim. "In India, dynamism wrestles with dysfunction." *New York Times*, June 9, 2011, accessed June 14, 2012, www.nytimes.com/2011/06/09/world/asia/09gurgaon. html?_r=0.

4 The enclave

"I feel like I have left India!"

One day, still early into my research in Gurgaon, I was riding in a car with Krishan Kumar, a hired driver and a long-time resident of Gurgaon. We were driving south on the Delhi–Gurgaon Expressway (DGE), past DLF Cyber City on the eastern side of the highway. DLF Cyber City was part of DLF City, a privately developed township built by India's largest real estate developer. This private township, which at one time claimed to be Asia's largest, was divided

Figure 4.1 DLF Gateway Tower in Gurgaon.
Source: Photo by author.

into five incremental phases of residential, commercial and office space spread out over some 3500 acres.[1] Its disjointed and unevenly developed enclaves constituted what was increasingly called New Gurgaon.[2] Upon seeing the sparkling towers of Cyber City from our moving car Krishan suddenly exclaimed: "Jaab me yahan gaari chalata hun, mujhe aisa lagtha hai ke main ne Hindustan chodke videsh gaya!"[3]

I had come across this kind of sentiment before. It began even before my arrival in India, when I started reading about Gurgaon in online newspapers in the United States. This image of escaping "India" was a common way of portraying Gurgaon, especially amongst non-resident Indians (NRIs) in the United States.[4] But Krishan's reaction to the new corporate towers of Cyber City was at first striking to me given that he was a driver, that is, a member of a servant underclass that was prohibited from accessing the interiors of new office buildings or the high-end restaurants of Cyber City. This exclusion is tragi-comically critiqued in Aravind Adiga's novel *The White Tiger*, when Balram Halwai, a driver not unlike Krishan, fantasizes about entering into one of Gurgaon's exclusive shopping malls, which middle and elite classes effortlessly inhabited in front of him and his fellow drivers everyday.[5]

Krishan lived in what was called Old Gurgaon, located south from where we were on the western side of the DGE. Old Gurgaon, which I describe in more detail below, was seemingly a world apart from the newly developed shopping malls and condominium towers in New Gurgaon. Nonetheless, despite such outward spatio-temporal separation, it seemed, the visual encounter with the architecture itself produced a visceral feeling of belonging and attachment to something remarkably *new* and *different*, something decidedly far away from "India." But if Gurgaon did not feel like India, what did it feel like?

In Walter Benjamin's unfinished *Arcades Project*, the German philosopher and cultural critic drew an intriguing and enigmatic distinction between two diametrically opposed experiences in nineteenth-century Paris. Namely, city life was filled with varying apparitions of "aura" and "trace." For Benjamin

> The trace is the appearance of nearness, however far removed the thing that left it behind may be. The aura is appearance of distance, however close the thing that calls it forth. In the trace, we gain possession of the thing; in the aura, it takes possession of us.[6]

As visual concept-metaphors that inform an urban depth of field perspective, trace and aura complicate the distinction made in Part I between the near order and the far order of the modern city.[7] That is to say, trace and aura are specifically *urban* concepts. For Benjamin trace becomes intelligible as the tangible sign of a presence that is no longer present. It is the relative invisibility of the near order from the perspective of the far order. Such traces, unless they are possessed by the far order, can potentially return from "invisibility" in order to haunt it, disrupting its fantasies of total knowledge, mastery and control over the city and its urban society.

150 *Aura and trace in Gurgaon*

Aura is different. It is the visibility and presence of the far order from the perspective of the near order. That is, subjects inhabiting the everyday spaces and times of the city bear witness to and encounter the far order's spatio-temporal logics and its disciplinary rhythms. In most cases they reproduce its ideological discourse and abstract logic. Aura, by "taking possession of us," interpellates us into the ideology of the far order. The visual architecture and urban design of DLF Cyber City, notwithstanding the very real and tangible feelings of distance and escape it evoked in Krishan at an emotional and visceral level, expressed not an escape from "India" as such, that is, as an imagined performative community. Rather, it expressed a re-territorialization of the nation-state conjunction. DLF's corporate motto, proudly displayed ubiquitously in New Gurgaon, is the unsubtle "Building India."

Yet there is a peculiarity in the aura of a place like DLF Cyber City and New Gurgaon more generally, for its projections of distance and proximity are often haunted by traces of that which was supposed to disappear. As we will see in both this chapter and the next one, the semi-urban, semi-rural district of Gurgaon is an intriguing example of aura and trace in the postcolonial capitalist city. I focus on the idea of trace in the next chapter, using visual ethnography to explore an "urbanized" village in the heart of New Gurgaon. By virtue of its visual and haptic exclusion from the temporality of the Millennium City, and the village's common figuration as an "anachronistic" or "archaic" remnant of Gurgaon's ruralism, the village itself constitutes a trace that shapes and haunts Gurgaon's urbanism. I use visual ethnography to "gain possession" of these haunting traces and bring them into dialectical relation with Gurgaon's urban aura, which is the focus of this chapter. Globality as aura in Gurgaon is exemplified in the projection of distance through the spectacular architecture and urban design of DLF Cyber City. This economy of spectacular appearances interpellates mobile subjects like Krishan and I driving down the DGE, bringing us into a "new" and "urbanized" India that is "here" and "now." But much like the aura of globality that was conjured through the hosting of the CWG in Delhi in 2010 (see Chapter 1), aura in Gurgaon remains haunted by the traces of postcolonial development and under-development that Gurgaon's elite investors and inhabitants desperately seek to leave behind. The more intensely the aura is conjured in places like Gurgaon and *Neo* Delhi more generally, the more haunting the traces of co-existing "pasts" that refuse to quietly fade from public consciousness.[8]

"Gurgaon collapsing"

Just a few days after my auratic car ride with Krishan in DLF Cyber City, on September 22, 2008, residents from an elite residential community, executives at several prominent multi-national corporations (MNCs), and even a well-known cricketer on the Indian national team took to the streets in the late-summer heat of Gurgaon. This unlikely group of activists was staging a protest against the unauthorized dumping of garbage just outside Qutab Enclave, one of the elite and exclusive residential communities of DLF City. Many of the well-groomed protestors were depicted in newspapers and television the next day holding up professionally made signs reading "Stop Dumping Now" and "Dengue Center Courtesy MCG and HUDA," the latter referring to two governing bodies in Gurgaon, the Municipal Council of Gurgaon (MCG) and Haryana Urban Development Authority (HUDA). Protestors demonstrated wearing protective masks to cover their mouths and noses, effectively visualizing the smell introduced to the environment. The apparition of this "waste" came up right next to some of the most expensive real estate in the greater Delhi region.[9] Protestors complained to reporters covering the protest about the olfactory effects of the garbage, that the dump was now attracting vermin inside the gates of the otherwise exclusive enclave.[10]

BPO Watch India, an online magazine focused on business process outsourcing,[11] ran an article a few days after the protests in DLF City entitled "Gurgaon should shape up or they'll ship out," referring to the scores of Fortune 500 companies and other MNCs invested in Gurgaon.

> The "Millenium City" it may be, but Gurgaon is dealing with the very basic problem of potholed roads and power outages to worsening law and order. This considering that a large number of companies have pumped in billions in investments in the Delhi suburb. In an unprecedented move to protest against these growing problems, CEOs of a large number of corporations and eminent personalities joined hands in the DLF area to protest against illegal dumping of garbage at Gurgaon-Faridabad road last week. These included CEOs, lawyers, CAs and doctors who are coming forward to protest against HUDA officials. DLF resident and mother of cricketer Yuvraj Singh was also part of this protest. "Gurgaon is probably among the most expensive places to live in India but it is a pity that we have to live in this life-threatening situation," she said.[12]

The protest was described in the media as "unprecedented" precisely because of the class background of those who had taken to the streets to hold up signs and demonstrate: the urban elite of Gurgaon that had migrated to the Millennium City ostensibly to escape the messiness of democratic politics in India and to live in the privately developed, sanitized spaces of the new global city.[13] While one was perhaps used to seeing industrial workers and rural peasants protesting in Gurgaon, against work conditions or loss of land, India's new middle and elite classes were typically seen as removed from political life. This broadly "secessionist" class pursued "first-world" lifestyles in self-enclosed, privatized "islands of prosperity" like Qutab Enclave.[14] As the Indian entrepreneur and politician Nandan Nilekani wrote in his 2009 book, "India's urban rich and middle class are seceding from the public sector by investing in gated communities and private guards for security, pumps and borewells for water, private generators for electricity and private schools and hospitals."[15] Such secessionist desires were justified, according to Nilekani, because the public sector was so inept at providing citizens things like security, water, electricity, education and

152 *Aura and trace in Gurgaon*

healthcare. In such a situation, those with means naturally turned to "the market" to access these urban services the government did not adequately provide, and this market was already supposed to be materialized in Gurgaon.

Just two days after the initial protest at DLF Qutab Enclave, *Hindustan Times* (*HT*), India's second largest English-language daily, began a week-long series entitled "Gurgaon collapsing," sharply criticizing the stunning lack of infrastructure and public services available in the Millenium City: "With over 200 Fortune 500 companies, it is the gateway to the new India. But Gurgaon's rapid slide into the third-world is demolishing its first-world dreams."[16] The week-long "Gurgaon collapsing" series, which addressed different facets of infrastructure in turn (waste management, electrical power, sewerage, roads and policing), served to amplify the voice of the Qutab Enclave protestors, often foregrounding the inherent tensions between "First-World" dreams and "Third-World" realities in Gurgaon. For instance, "Global destination or garbage dump?" was the first headline of the series, with the following sub-heading: "This city of 1.6 million residents with a daily solid waste generation of 400–500 metric tonnes does not have a single garbage disposal facility."[17]

In providing a public platform to amplify the grievances of wealthy urban residents and white collar workers, *HT* also aimed its critique at many of the same targets as the protestors, charging state agencies like MCG and HUDA for holding the Millennium City back from its global dreams. As one article reported, for example, "With no landfill site available, HUDA officials are not only dumping the garbage on vacant plots in the vicinity of inhabited localities but they have also converted a stretch of the Aravalli reserved forest for disposing of solid waste."[18] Nor did public bureaucrats interviewed by *HT* help themselves when asked to explain the sub-par infrastructure of Gurgaon. Often times these representatives were shown evading any personal responsibility for mismanagement or inefficiency. Other times they entirely dismissed the criticism of their performance in delivering urban infrastructure and public services like electricity, garbage collection, sewerage and the like. In an interview with HUDA administrator in Gurgaon, G. Anupama, which was a part of the first installment of "Gurgaon collapsing," *HT* inquired in to why it had taken so long for HUDA to set up a solid waste management facility, to which the administrator's reply was disappointingly terse: "I have joined as HUDA administrator recently. I can't comment on the decisions taken in the past."[19]

Official indifference and evasion of responsibility thus became a running theme in the "Gurgaon collapsing" series. The next day the focus was on road conditions in Gurgaon, with *HT* reporting that "40% of roads in new Gurgaon are potholed."[20] But in the corresponding interview with T. C. Gupta, HUDA's Chief Administrator based in Chandigarh (located some 300 km away from Gurgaon), the latter claimed that "There are only four roads that have problems.… There are no major problems with other roads."[21]

In contrast to the aloofness and distance of HUDA and its unwillingness to take responsibility for its alleged infrastructural failures, *HT* presented in each

The enclave 153

episode a section entitled "Boss speak." Here a CEO, Managing Director or Senior VP of a major company based in Gurgaon would diagnose the situation himself (only men were featured), thus supplying the private sector's perspective on the perceived failures of public agencies like HUDA and MCG. On September 25, for instance, former Managing Director of Maruti Suzuki India Ltd. Jagdish Khattar offered his opinion:

Figure 4.2 HT headquarters in Park Centra Building, Gurgaon.
Source: Photo by author.

154 *Aura and trace in Gurgaon*

> Money is not the problem. The Haryana government has reportedly col-
> lected about Rs1,500 crore as what it calls external development charges
> from developers in Gurgaon.... While the architecture of the buildings and
> companies housed in Gurgaon boast of modern technologies, civic authori-
> ties have yet to move over the old and outdated technologies they have been
> using for roads and other infrastructure facilities for decades.

The technocratic, problem-solving approach of the private sector (it's simply a
matter of updating the technology) was set in stark contrast to the contrivances
and evasions of public sector bureaucrats (who were seen as old and outdated).
This way of framing private versus public echoed the prevailing ideology in
post-reform India, namely that the "global" domain of economics had finally
"come into its own," superseding the "local" domain of politics, with its public
inefficiencies and bureaucratic delays.[22] This juxtaposition was articulated again
and again over the course of the series, but also visualized spatially on the page-
wide layouts in each day's paper.

In an interview at *Hindustan Times'* offices in the Park Centra building in
New Gurgaon, Sanjiv Ahuja, editor of the "Gurgaon collapsing" series and a
long-time resident of Gurgaon himself, informed me that problems with infrastructure had hampered the city since the beginning of its booming growth in the
1990s.[23] "Gurgaon grew too fast," Ahuja argued, "and that too in an unplanned
and uncoordinated fashion." But what pushed *HT* to publish the "Gurgaon collapsing" series were

> the photos of residents and corporates protesting Gurgaon's pathetic infra-
> structure on TV. This was the first time anyone saw rich people come out and
> demand some change in the "chalta hai" approach of the local government.[24]

A common perception, particularly among the wealthier classes of urban India,
was that "the rich do not involve themselves with local politics."[25] Rather, they
perceived politics to be the domain of the struggling masses, who voted and parti-
cipated in public life at far greater rates. In the post-reform period, however, both
Indian cities and the "new Indian middle class" gained increasing visibility, becoming identified as "emerging markets" by global capital. Simultaneously, this urban
middle class, which was actually "elite" by most measures, increasingly made
claims on the normative aspirations of the nation, if not the state. In the rest of this
chapter I look at how the new visibility of the urban elite/middle classes exists in
relations of distant proximity and proximate distance with local politics in Gurgaon.
How is such distance and proximity mediated in Gurgaon and what effects do such
mediations have on changing urban life in India's Millennium City?

Mediating modernity

Partha Chatterjee, in his influential work on the nascent nationalist movement in
colonial India, argued that the middle class of British India were "middle" not so

much in terms of its position on the steep class and caste hierarchy of Indian society (in this sense they were more accurately "elite"), but in a radically different sense: "in the sense of the action of a subject who stands 'in the middle,' working upon and transforming one term of a relation into the other."[26] From its colonial inception, the modern Indian middle class was positioned as a class of interpreters and translators who stood in-between the colonizer, on the one hand, and the indigenous masses, on the other. The middle class thus represented, interpreted and translated each side of the colonial encounter for the sake of the other. In being singularly placed in this in-between role, the middle class also reproduced its privileged position vis-à-vis the colonial state, while distinguishing itself from the "pre-modern" Indians that constituted the vast majority of the indigenous population.

Neither "white" like the colonizer, nor fully "native" like the vernacular masses, this colonial middle class in India occupied a space of mediation. This middle class was conjured into its current form by British administrator Thomas Macaulay in his infamous 1835 "Minute on Indian Education," in which he wrote:

> We must at present do our best to form a class who may be *interpreters* between us and the millions we govern; a class of persons, Indian in blood and colour, but English in taste, in opinions, in morals and in intellect.[27]

Figure 4.3 "Experience the perfect life."
Source: Photo by author.

156 *Aura and trace in Gurgaon*

Macaulay's desire was to create a class of English-educated subjects who, in mimicking British tastes, opinions and morals, were to become *virtually* British while remaining *actually* Indian. From the standpoint of the colonial state, this dual coding would enable the middle class to stand in-between the British and "the millions" of natives otherwise out of direct and immediate contact with the colonizer and its "civilizing" culture. But this class was marked by ambivalence from the very outset, for in mimicking colonial rule on the one hand and representing native culture on the other, the colonial middle class was itself estranged from both colonial and native cultures alike.

Rendering this estrangement cinematically, Satyajit Ray's 1977 film *Shatranj Ke Khiladi* (*The Chess Players*) creatively brings the viewer into the ambivalent world of the Indian middle class in the context of the colonial encounter. Briefly, Ray's film re-tells the story of one of the last Mughal cities to come under the direct rule of the British through annexation, just one year before the great sepoy rebellion of 1857. The city-state of Oudh (modern day Lucknow) is ruled by Nawab Wajid Ali Shah, whose rule is described as "effeminate" by the British because he concerns himself with the arts and culture over and above the "affairs of state." He is an ineffective ruler in the eyes of the British General Outram, whose task it is to oversee the transition of authority from Mughal king to British Crown.

In one particular scene, we are witness to the in-between position of the king's Prime Minister Mudar Ud Daulah, who, as a representative of the Nawab to the office of General Outram, literally stands in the middle of this historical transition, and must communicate Outram's decision to displace Wajid Ali Shah to the Nawab himself. Wajid Ali Shah, the inscrutable aesthete-king,[28] is shown reclining on a plush bed of pillows in a palace room, immersed in a song and dance performance in his palace. The prime minister patiently stands at the side, waiting for the performance to end so that he can share the news of the imminent takeover with the king. As viewers, we share in the suspended sense of time that the prime minister experiences as he waits for the performance to end. Mudar Ud Daulah and viewer alike now see the king with new eyes, understanding that Wajid Ali Shah's esthetic regime of political rule would no longer be intelligible from the perspective of a becoming-dominant discourse of British colonial expansion in South Asia. This historical becoming is communicated critically through a set of time-images.

The scene unfolds patiently, in duration with the temporality of the musical performance, which is shown in its entirety. It is as if Ray is inviting the viewer into the time of the aesthete-king, before his rule is vanquished for good. While the song and dance is performed, the camera cuts between shots of the performers and shots of the king, who watches the masterful performance with great attention, fully immersed in its melody and rhythm. Interspersed between these shots of the performance and the king's undivided attention to it, we get close-up shots of the temporarily frozen and "un-timely" prime minister as the latter waits for the performance to conclude. The prime minister's time is "out of joint" with respect to the temporality of the dance

The enclave 157

performance. This is because of Mudar Ud Daulah's own awareness of this alternative temporality, that of the historical transition from Mughal to British rule in north India. A faithful servant, the prime minister hesitates to bring this despairing news to his king. Meanwhile, the king is figured precisely in the opposite way, fully immersed and thus in synch with the temporality of the song and dance, yet "out of joint" with respect to history. The prime minister's mournful expression indicates his knowledge of the imminent abdication of the king's throne, even as the king himself remains unaware of the historically changing circumstances. The prime minister thus functions as a Deleuzean "attendant" figure, which

> does not signify an observer or a spectator-voyeur (although it might also be one from the point of view of a figuration that remains, despite everything). More profoundly, the attendant only indicates a constant, a measure or cadence, in relation to which we can appraise a variation.[29]

Figuring the prime minister as an attendant, Ray's camera dramatizes the ambivalence of in-betweenness.[30] Through a juxtaposition of countervailing temporalities he manages to render an esthetics of geohistorical difference. When the king and the prime minster are finally brought within a single frame, we bear witness to yet another creative and critical depth of field image. We see the prime minister in the foreground, devastated at the news of the impending overthrow, and the king, in the last moments of his blissful historical ignorance. This is a cinematic interpretation of colonial transition in northern India that is simultaneously performative: as the king's esthetic regime of rule becomes historically anachronistic, colonial modernity becomes dominant, and the prime minister comes to occupy a middle point from which the transition became visible in its horrifying inevitability. The prime minister is the prototypical middle-class Indian subject, standing in between countervailing temporalities of being and becoming. This image of thought as depth of field is particularly relevant in an era of postcolonial urbanism and neoliberal economic reform when this mediating "middle" class gains increasing visibility and recognition as a target market for global investors and corporations. The contemporary middle class, I argue, continues to mediate countervailing temporalities of being and becoming in changing urban life.

In the remainder of this chapter, I will read a contemporary documentary film about the contemporary Indian "middle" class in Gurgaon. I will treat the film's central characters as esthetic subjects in a manner similar to the way in which Ray's *Shatranj Ke Khiladi* treats the prime minister, through the mode of the attendant figure, that is, a figure whose movements and cadences mediate changing life. What the esthetic subjects of Gurgaon attend to is not the ambivalence of the colonial encounter with historical difference, which the alienated Mudar Ud Daulah mournfully mediates in Ray's film, but rather the visual aura of India's Millennium City and the geohistorical difference that surrounds this aura on all sides.

158   *Aura and trace in Gurgaon*

I am Gurgaon

I Am Gurgaon: The New Urban India (2009, hereafter *IAG*) is a haunting documentary film. I will argue that it supplies an uncommon sense of neoliberal globalization in India through its cinematic thinking, that is, its "camera consciousness."[31] This film utilizes the documentary idiom but also departs from the "realism" of the genre in order to intimately present "middle-class" residents of Gurgaon as esthetic subjects (see Chapter 2 for more on esthetic subjects in film). These are subjects whose spatial movements and practices are less interesting in terms of the inner motivations compelling them, and more in terms of how they map and trace geohistorical differences that come into productive friction in a place like Gurgaon. In this way, creative documentary films like *IAG* introduce images of changing urban life that usually resist inclusion in most academic analyses of hyper-development in places like Gurgaon.

Directed by the Dutch documentary filmmaker Marije Meerman in 2009, *IAG* was produced by an Amsterdam-based NGO called VPRO, which provides a summary of the film on its website:

> The shining facades of Gurgaon, a satellite city of New Delhi, are symbols of India's unparalleled economic growth. Gurgaon was built at the turn of this century by the largest project developers in the world. A village 15 years ago, has now grown into a city of 1.4 million inhabitants, but with little or no infrastructure. How viable is this new type of city? Residents of the gated communities of this privatized society offer insights in their hope, desires, and in the new self-confidence of the Indian middle class. Gradually it becomes clear what the consequences of the credit crisis and the growing gap between rich and poor are for the city and the psyche of its inhabitants.[32]

IAG was part of VPRO's "Backlight Series: Future Affairs Program," which espouses two modes of communication through its documentary films. The first mode provides "in-depth analysis of new developments by leading intellectuals and architects of change."[33] The second mode applies "daring cinematic techniques, capturing the effects those changes have on the daily lives of the real world's citizens." But *IAG* creatively departs from this basic formula; the in-depth analysis is provided not by "leading intellectuals" and "experts" on urban development in India per se, but through intimate cinematic portraits of "real world" residents of several new gated communities in Gurgaon, whose everyday spatial practices, discourses and performative interpretations the film treats and analyzes. The film's deft utilization of the second mode of communication—"daring cinematic techniques"—enable it to perform this critical analysis by presenting Gurgaon's residents as *esthetic subjects* of "the new urban India," subjects produced through the esthetic politics of partitioned city spaces and experiential discourses that are encountered and mediated in everyday life.[34]

The most "daring" cinematic technique of the film is its narrative structure, namely, its eschewing of an omniscient, third-person narrator who supplies factual content and socio-historical context (Geohistory 1) for the audio-visual assemblages that are presented. Instead of utilizing a "voice-of-God" narration that is common to the narrative structure of many traditional and contemporary documentary films, the story of *IAG* is stitched together through multiple narrative fragments that come from the film's various esthetic subjects, with an accompanying sound design that mixes familiar north Indian classical melodies with more ambient sounds of meditative suspense.

The film opens with a series of shots from inside the confines of a gated residential community. We see everyday activities of residents and workers: a man walking his dog on a well-paved road; several people dressed in color-coordinated exercise outfits doing yoga on a lush grass lawn; a man washing a car window with a rag. *Hindustani* classical music accompanies the opening montage: we hear a sonorous melodic instrument play a slow, searching melody. The soundscape that accompanies the opening shots of the neoliberal urban landscape evokes the *alap* stage of the Indian classical music form of *raga*, in which the introductory phase slowly hails the listener through its deliberately drawn out melodic explorations of the *raga*'s musical scale, its tonal patterns and themes. The overall ambience of the image–sound assemblage in the opening montage is one of serenity and meditation as we witness the early morning rhythms of everyday life in a gated community, it is peaceful and enchanting. Accompanying the music and images are the placid sounds of birds chirping.

In the middle of the opening progression, we hear a woman's voice that sounds just as tranquil, calm and intimate as the meditative sound–image assemblage it adjoins, though we cannot see her face:

> My first and foremost requirement was space. Three children require a lot of space to move in and around the house. I wanted accessibility to a park, I got that here. I wanted safety and security above everything else. When my children go to the park, I want to be sure that nobody's going to pick one of them or no vehicle is going to run them down.

The woman's voice is played over more shots of the gated community's various protected and secured spaces: its green lawns, trimmed hedges and homogeneous row housing. And then we cut to the interior of a spacious and well-decorated middle-class home, with a woman sitting in front of the camera. She finishes her opening statement, gesturing with her hands: "I wanted a kind of gated community."

This is Shilpa Sonal, a marketing consultant and resident of a gated community in Gurgaon called "Nirvana." Her voice is introduced before her face is, and it is played over images of "Nirvana." It is almost as if the discourse belongs more to the gated community's inter-subjective space than to the particular subject that enunciates it. The displaced sound–image assemblage in the opening montage provides an analytic framework through which we can explore the micro-politics of interpretive practices on the part of the middle class, a class of

160   *Aura and trace in Gurgaon*

interpreters whose interpretations transform the very realities and spaces they move within and encounter.

By rendering the inter-subjectivity of Sonal's narrative discourse, that is, the ways in which it renders the intelligibility of "Nirvana" as a space of security and desire in the "here" and "now" of Gurgaon, her discourse becomes performative rather than merely descriptive or even explanatory. This productive aspect of discourse is presented through the cinematic technique of juxtaposing anonymous voices with the multiple and dispersed spaces (indoor and outdoor, inside and outside the gates) of "Nirvana," suggesting that Sonal's discourse belongs not so much to her innate desire, but rather to the inter-subjective space of the gated community that gives this desire a particular form and intelligibility.

Once again, playing Sonal's voice over images of Gurgaon's high rise office buildings and condominiums, we hear a discourse that is at once descriptive, analytical and poetically performative:

> There was some kind of crunch within Delhi City. It lacked space. Delhi had to expand into nearby areas. Gurgaon happened to be the place where a lot of technically qualified people came and started setting up their base. So when they came, a lot of multinationals from abroad also decided to open up offices. A lot of talent moved in. Talent which was all over the world. The brain drain from India found it comfortable to come back to Gurgaon with the economic growth that India saw. Everything came together at the right time. That's one of the most important factors for Gurgaon to have seen this growth.

As we see shots of glass office towers with "global" signs—Microsoft, Canon, Ericsson—Sonal continues her narrative:

> Gurgaon has been basically created by builders. In my view, Gurgaon is the place where there's globalization. It's the most modern area that people all over the country look forward to. They feel that if something's happening in the country, if something is growing then Gurgaon is one of those places. A Singapore for India.

In the pacing of the sound–image assemblage, the ambient space that pervades the scene, we get the sense that Sonal is attempting to convince herself as much as she is attempting to convince us about why she ended up in Gurgaon.

Bineeta Singh, a loquacious textile designer, supplies another narrative description. While sitting in her living room, which is tastefully decorated with earth-toned art work and furniture, she tells us

> Gurgaon caters to the young urban mobile couple who have just married so they go and live in these high rise buildings. Two-bedroom apartments, a studio kind of look. And also to young families with one or two children. Which is where we feature. So they are progressive, moving and modern. They have been exposed to the world.

The enclave 161

As we hear her words, which are spoken with a real estate agent's familiarity with advertising rhetoric, we are shown a roadside billboard depicting a future mall in Gurgaon. The camera pans over the length of the billboard, and the virtual image of the mall, with its amplified design and pristine landscaped environs, eventually takes up the entire screen. The billboard stops being a representation of a future development and becomes *presented* in its virtuality, its simulacral present. In the virtual image that occupies the screen, all signs of locality/Gurgaon are erased: there are no cows, no stray dogs, no slums, no piles of garbage, no surrounding farmland within the image. The grass is lush and green as opposed to dry and parched. The utopic vision of this as yet unbuilt commercial retail space is accompanied by Singh's discourse, which describes the emergence of a globally minded middle class in Gurgaon:

> They expect the good things of life. And that is what Gurgaon offers: clubs, infrastructure, commercial space, shopping areas, malls. These are the things we see when we travel. It's what we expect back in return when we come back to our country.

The effect of these descriptive/performative analyses by the likes of Singh and Sonal is visualized powerfully in *IAG* through the peculiar discursive and imaginative power of cinema. As Ranciere writes, cinematic images do not merely represent objects, subjects, spaces and relations that exist in "real life." The cinema changes "the very status of the "real."

> It does not reproduce things as they offer themselves to the gaze. It records them as the human eye cannot see them, as they come into being, in a state of waves and vibrations, before they can be qualified as intelligible objects, people or events to their descriptive and narrative properties.[35]

By detaching objects, people or events from their descriptive and narrative properties, cinema offers the possibility of re-articulating and re-distributing the experience and intelligibility of these. It is in this way that the "common sense" discourse of the likes of Sonal and Singh, when presented in *IAG* through a cinematic technique that foregrounds the ambivalent spaces in which this discourse circulates, restores perception to an uncommon sense that invisibly structures any dominant discourse.

Cinema articulates "relations between a whole and parts; between a visibility and a power of signification and affect associated with it; between expectations and what happens to meet them."[36] Such expectations, mediated through Meerman's image–sound assemblages, come to constitute the transformative realities of Gurgaon as an inter-subjective space that is at once real and imagined, virtual and actual. Cinema as a medium is particularly attuned to rendering such a complex virtuality, showing spaces of expectation and anticipation and how they become *real* through the temporal discourses of middle–class interpreters like Singh and Sonal.

162 *Aura and trace in Gurgaon*

By juxtaposing their discourses with images of real and imagined spaces, *IAG* works within a simultaneous logic of resemblance and dissemblance that Jacques Ranciere argues is unique to cinema and is indicative of its singular and critical power.[37] The cinematic image, for Ranciere, refers to two different things:

> There is the simple relationship that produces the likeness of an original: not necessarily its faithful copy, but simply what suffices to stand in for it. And there is the interplay of operations that produces what we call art: or precisely an alteration of resemblance.[38]

The dissemblance practiced by Meerman's camera, juxtaposing disconnected spaces with detached voices, allows her to provide more than "in-depth analysis" of urbanization in Gurgaon, it involves us as viewers in the disjunctive near and far orders of Gurgaon as Millennium City, the various perceptual exclusions and spatio-temporal mediations required for such an image to even make sense.

"I am Gurgaon"

Later in the film we are introduced to Henry Ledlie, a boisterous and aristocratic man who is a member of an organization called World Spa Action Group, a Residential Welfare Association (RWA). As I will explain more fully in the next section, RWAs are an increasingly active site of middle-class politics in Indian cities. These associations are comprised of representatives from neighborhoods with like-minded residents (usually upper-class neighborhoods) that collectively pressure local and state governments for particular urban reforms. These initiatives are mostly directed at their own neighborhoods but sometimes reach out to touch upon larger spatial issues, such as urban infrastructure, public space in the city and urban esthetics.[39] World Spa Action Group (WSAG) is unlike other RWAs in the sense that the neighborhood it ostensibly represents does not yet exist; its construction is on hiatus in the aftermath of the global financial crisis. WSAG represents the disgruntled investors of the World Spa, a gated high rise luxury complex that was promised to the future residents by an already past date.

Meerman introduces us to the political world of this group by foregrounding the temporal imaginary of someone like Ledlie, juxtaposing his narrative with time-images of Gurgaon's incomplete and halted hyper-development. Once again, slow and meditative classical music completes the ambivalent *mise-en-scène*. We see a bored security guard in the foreground scratching his crotch, with an unfinished high rise complex in soft focus behind him: he's shown as bored because all he has to guard is an empty, unfinished and abandoned building. Then we get a wider shot that shows us the juxtaposition of a billboard advertisement for DLF Park Place, with lush green and landscaped environs within its simulated image, and the dusty and parched landscape over which this simulation is projected. Ledlie's narrative is played over this montage:

The enclave 163

Swedish massage rooms, aromatic therapy centres, meditation rooms, gymnasiums, indoor and outdoor pools, poolside wireless connectivity, putting greens, golf. Who doesn't want to live there, especially if you've got the money. Who does not want to live here? Of course, we understand that you can't get heaven on earth. But when you're playing with sentiments of people with money we want to believe that there is going to be heaven on earth.

Then the camera joins Ledlie in the car as he drives to World Spa. Through the passenger side window we see a city frozen in incomplete development, half-finished buildings with scaffolded skylines:

We are going to this residential complex where I and 300 others have invested our money, not in terms of an investment but in terms of the promise of better living. The dream. We are all dream merchants. We want to live and have good dreams. But this is turning into a bloody nightmare.

The camera follows Ledlie as he enters the unfinished spaces of World Spa, eventually taking us up to his own apartment on the seventeenth floor of the high rise: "We bought these apartments six years ago," Ledlie tells us, "They were supposed to be delivered four years back." The camera follows Ledlie into his apartment, which was delivered to him even though most of the other apartments remain unfinished.

This is my apartment here on the seventeenth floor. I took possession, but as you see, I've broken everything down. You're asking me why I'm breaking it all down. Well, this is the reason I'm breaking it all down. So that my children, my mother, and my home, my investment is solid and safe as promised.

We see Ledlie peeling away crumbling plaster from the walls, showing the shoddy construction. He walks to the balcony in the master bedroom, accessed through a glass door that is missing the glass. "This is what they gave me!" exclaims Ledlie as he steps back and forth through the nonexistent glass door. "Shocking! Thank you very much for taking my money and giving me this!"

Through what we called pre-sales in Chapter 3, Ledlie and many others like him paid the full price of the apartment before construction even began, because there was a 10 percent discount for early investors. "By the way, we are not talking a small 100 or 200,000, we're talking half a million [dollars] plus." WSAG was formed by resident-investors like Ledlie, who were screwed over by Gurgaon's speculative ecology.

Latika Tukral, also part of the WSAG, later informs us, "We're after [the developers] to give us our apartments. But they can't deliver, because the money is not there." According to Ledlie, the construction company took the pre-sale money he and others put down for their apartments and used it to finish other developments. "That is where greed has entered. They have taken loans, our

164   *Aura and trace in Gurgaon*

money, everything, and suddenly there's a crash. These guys are in trouble. They're business model is a Ponzi scheme."

After showing us the half-finished development of World Spa, and the disappointment on the part of resident investors whose expectations were unmet, the film turns to "I am Gurgaon," a citizen's initiative comprised of largely middle-class and wealthy residents who challenge private builders and para-statal agencies alike to deliver on their promises of creating "world-class" urban spaces in Gurgaon. The camera cycles through a series of shots depicting urban calamity in Gurgaon: flooded streets due to inadequate sewage treatment, traffic jams, slums next to elevated highways and skyscrapers. Then it cuts to an interior shot: a meeting room in a corporate office, with a polished wood desk, tinted glass walls, and a group of women and men in business attire sitting and holding a discussion.

Deep Kalra of "I am Gurgaon" explained the genesis of the group:

> Why has something like "I am Gurgaon" come up? Because there is a gap. If it were as well planned as Singapore, which is one extreme, or the hundreds of new suburbs that come up outside cities anywhere in the world there wouldn't be a need for someone like I am Gurgaon. We are addressing issues which lie with the responsibility of the government and the big developers, who I think have run amok.

A self-funded group comprising elite activists, citizen's initiatives like "I am Gurgaon" enact a politics of expectation and exclusion similar to that exemplified in the "Gurgaon collapsing" episode at the beginning of this chapter. In both cases their cause was immediately publicized in the English-language print media. *The Times of India* on May 30, 2010, for instance, featured an article about "I am Gurgaon" in which journalist Sumit Sukanya described the group as "solutions driven," oriented more toward problem-solving than any ideological or "political agenda."[40] "Our mantra is cooperate, don't confront," one member is quoted as saying. Another member, an accountant at a large multi-national firm, described the initiative as a pressure group that uses "corporate methods" and "business strategies" to organize as efficiently as possible: "We have a talent pool of experts as we assign tasks to members according to their area of expertise."

In its business-oriented and cooperative approach to urban reform, the group is depicted as non-partisan and even apolitical, though the issues it pursues are decidedly "middle-class issues": "shortage of parking [in the city], littering of garbage, and ill maintained parks." Moreover, one can trace a distinct politics of class-partitioned urban experience in the following anecdote found in Sukanya's article, in which one of the founders of "I am Gurgaon," Latika Thukral, faced hurdles from local businesses and vendors when she tried to get permission for building a parking structure in Gurgaon.

> Thukral identified a vacant plot and approached the municipality for turning it into a parking lot. Once ready, it will house 100 cars. But crusaders

The enclave   165

always face their share of troubles. Thukral has been advised not to use that road because vendors uprooted from the vacant spot are angry with her.

Of course, we might reasonably ask, how could this plot of land be "vacant" if vendors had to be uprooted from it? Such a contradiction exemplifies the ways in which media-driven middle-class discourses de-limit fields of vision and intelligibility, so that vendors, squatters, slum dwellers, hawkers, beggars and others are obscured from view. Once rendered unintelligible, Thukral becomes intelligible as a "crusader" for the "common" cause of building a parking garage for urban elites that can actually afford cars.

If we follow the narrative trajectory of the film *IAG*, we might come to commiserate with the "elite activists" whose expectations for World Spa in particular and Gurgaon in general were disappointed. At a narrative level, the film does not offer an explicit critique of the construction of elite life-worlds as such. And yet, through its cinematic technique, the film does more than present a merely *moralistic* critique of elite activism; it renders these life-worlds as strange, as structurally haunted by what they exclude, more specifically, the untimely presences in Gurgaon's landscape that must be conjured away.

Haunted auras

At the beginning of this chapter I briefly mentioned the Indian entrepreneur and central government bureaucrat Nandan Nilekani. In his book *Imagining India: The Idea of a Renewed Nation*, Nilekani writes that "India's urban rich and middle class are seceding from the public sector by investing in gated communities and private guards for security, pumps and borewells for water, private generators for electricity and private schools and hospitals."[41] These secessionist projects are praiseworthy for Nilekani, for they "are showcasing themselves as small-scale models of how cities ought to be run."[42]

But the results of these elite urban enclaves have been far from "showcase" worthy. Among Gurgaon's elite residents, it is by now cliché to complain about the potholed roads, the toxic waste sites, the cows and pigs running around, the violent clashes between industrial workers and the Haryana state police, farmers protesting forced land acquisition. Perhaps someone like Nilekani is so readily seduced by gated communities because they allow elite residents to distance themselves from these postcolonial urban realities. To invoke Pavan Varma's grim assessment of the "great Indian middle class," the contrast between today's socio-political apathy on the part of elites and the middle class and the pre-neoliberal years is jarring, which says a lot since this was already a class that was largely blind to its own class-based privileges.

> In the beginning, in the years just after 1947, there was at least the awareness that India is a poor country and the poor exist and something needs to be done for them. No longer. In all these years the numbers of the poor has gone up, but paradoxically and tragically, the middle class' ability to notice

them has gone down. The poor have been around for so long that they have become a part of the accepted landscape. Since they refused to go away, and could not be got rid of, the only other alternative was to take as little notice of them as possible.... For the burgeoning and upwardly mobile middle class of India, such poverty has ceased to exist. It has ceased to exist because it does not create in most of its members the slightest motivation to do something about it. Its existence is taken for granted. Its symptoms, which would revolt even the most sympathetic foreign observer, do not register any more. The general approach is to get on with one's life, to carve out a tiny island of well-being in a sea of deprivation ... not unlike a system of apartheid, rendered more insidious because the perpetrators no longer even notice the conditions of those they have banished.[43]

All this leads Varma to a rather damning indictment of the Indian middle class, which he argues "must be one of the few classes in the world where the extreme sensitivity to intra-material hierarchies coexists so effortlessly with the most blatant insensitivity to the conditions of the world 'external' to such interests."[44]

But even if we take Varma's critique of Indian middle class, what are we to make of the sudden turn to democratic politics by the ostensibly secessionist subjects of Gurgaon, like those in Qutab Enclave described at the beginning of

Figure 4.4 Real estate billboard, Gurgaon.
Source: Photo by author.

this chapter? And what of NGOs like "I am Gurgaon," who organize resident-investors in the Millenium City in order to articulate a voice for change? What of the print and digital media itself, which gives synchronic voice to disparate experiences of frustration at the apparent lack of "globality" in Gurgaon? An increasingly visible middle class comes to actively mediate in an increasingly visual urban political economy of appearances.

Back in 2008, I met with *Hindustan Times* reporter Sanjeev Ahuja in the aftermath of the "Gurgaon collapsing" story, and the journalist directed me to people directly involved in organizing the Qutab Enclave protests.[45] This led me to the world of Residential Welfare Associations (RWAs) and elite local politics in Gurgaon more generally.

Kishore Arora lived in a palatial house in Phase I of DLF City. On a pleasant, sunny January afternoon we sat at a patio table on his front lawn, secluded from the neighborhood by raised walls that surrounded the compound. Arora was one of the earlier investors in Gurgaon, having bought the land for his large home in the 1990s.

> That was when many changes began to come to Gurgaon. See before that it was a sleepy town. People wanted to leave Delhi to come here. They saw that there was more space here, less crowds. This was a peaceful place.[46]

After learning that I was a researcher coming to India from the states, Arora informed me that his son and daughter also lived there. Both had graduated from Ivy League schools, he said proudly. And they were now successful professionals with families of their own. He spent much of his time traveling back and forth between Gurgaon and the U.S., visiting his children and grandchildren with his wife.

Arora was retired, having worked for thirty years in corporate consultancy and business management in Delhi. Following his retirement, which coincided with his full-time shift to Gurgaon, Arora got involved with the local residential welfare association that included other property owners in the neighborhood. Several years later he helped inaugurate a federation of residential welfare associations that sought to pressure the local government of Gurgaon to improve its infrastructure delivery. "Gurgaon was unplanned," Arora argued, "the Haryana government sold the land and told the private developers to build every-thing. But the developers didn't think about infrastructure. This is why we have problems today."[47]

The RWA federation that Arora helped found was having its monthly meeting at Arora's house that afternoon. In attendance were presidents and leaders of several disparate residential welfare associations in the area. Their discussion that day was on the idea of initiating "an out-of-the-box Corporate Model for the Governance of Gurgaon." Aurora led the meeting with a colorful slide-show presentation orchestrated from his laptop computer. The slides, which were projected on a large white wall in the dining room of him spacious home, began with jarring pictures of urban chaos and dysfunction in Gurgaon: flooded streets,

168 *Aura and trace in Gurgaon*

traffic jams and stray cows and dogs on the road side. According to Arora, the "present mess" in Gurgaon had easily identifiable causes: lack of vision and political willpower, absence of basic urban planning, multiplicity of governing authorities, inadequate application of resources, and perhaps most of all, decisions made in far-off Chandigarh that bore little relationship to the realities of Gurgaon. All this could be changed, Arora argued. In place of the existing dysfunction, he proposed a "corporate model" of governance that would take "best practices" from the private sector and implement them in running the public affairs of Gurgaon. This included importing "good management principles" and a corporate leadership structure, complete with a Chief Executive Officer and Board of Directors. In the "Gurgaon City Authority Organizational Structure" that Arora outlined in his presentation, this leadership would work in an integrated manner with the existing Municipal Council of Gurgaon, thus comprising a kind of hybrid public–private model of local government.

The aim of the Gurgaon City Authority would be to make Gurgaon a "well-planned, vibrant community, rich in its social diversity."[48] But this was not yet another "development authority," like HUDA or DDA in Delhi, which were marked by corruption and bureaucratic inefficiencies. As Arora told the other federation members, "I have deliberately not used the word 'Development' in [Gurgaon City Authority's] name, for this is a loaded word and it is inadequate for the role I envisage for this long-term Authority."[49] If Gurgaon followed this post-developmental model of corporate governance, Arora argued, "By 2020 Gurgaon should be counted amongst the top 10 cities in the world, as far as the quality of life and environmental parameters are concerned. Liveability would be the paramount consideration in the development of the City."[50]

Rather than "citizens" Arora spoke of "shareholders" in Gurgaon, but all aspects of governance were to be covered by the City Authority: from education and health services, roads and parking, public transport and infrastructure, to planning and emergency preparedness. Arora's audience was captivated by the slide-show presentation; it was an alternative "far order" to that of HUDA and DLF, one that was designed to be more responsive to the needs of Gurgaon's elite citizens eager for a global lifestyle in a post-developmental context. But this "far order" was still quite distant from existing political realities in Gurgaon.

Another branch of RWA politics in Gurgaon sought to intervene directly in the political process through electoral politics. Sanjay Kaul was younger than Arora, and exuded a more charged, impatient and aggressive demeanor. He spoke in rapid English about local government in pejorative terms, expressing frustration and anger toward what he called "dirty politics." But Kaul was similarly transnational, having traveled to the U.S. and England through his work in advertising and corporate communications. By the time we met in 2009, Kaul was also an active organizer of RWAs in both Delhi and Gurgaon and started a public advocacy group called People's Action that sought to address corruption and bureaucratic inefficiency in government. He informed me quite bluntly that many middle-class residents in Gurgaon turned to RWAs to solve local issues rather than petition municipal governments or agencies like HUDA, which were

The enclave 169

usually unresponsive. In fact, many residents of New Gurgaon did not even vote in local elections because "all the parties are lousy," according to Kaul.[51]

In 2004 People's Action began to organize RWAs to join together and put up a "clean" candidate for the legislative assembly seat of Gurgaon in the February 2005 Haryana state elections. According to Kaul,

> the act was a response to the common refrain of the middle class that they did not vote due to poor choice of candidates. This event became a watershed as a majority of the RWAs in the constituency forged an agreement to support such a move.[52]

In January 2005, People's Action facilitated the creation of the Gurgaon Resident's Party and fielded a candidate in state elections. The group attempted to consolidate residents around a "clean" candidate that represented "middle-class" issues and was not beholden to "vote bank"—read populist—politics. As Kaul explained

> political parties are more interested in addressing slum issues than the problems which effect middle-class citizens. They know they will get many votes from the slums and so they don't waste time in contacting us. They are useless to us and we are useless for them.[53]

In response, People's Action sought to register voters for the February elections, particularly among those that had recently moved to Gurgaon over the previous five-to-ten years.

By speaking specifically to the concerns of residents in the rapidly growing elite sections of Gurgaon, Kaul attempted to politically mobilize citizens who, though already economically privileged, often felt disconnected from local politics. According to Kaul, his political organizing led to "an unprecedented participation of urban vote in Gurgaon, with close to 35 percent polling in some areas. This was up from just 10 percent in earlier elections."[54] Thus, Kaul's desire was to challenge the logic that the middle-class voter was alienated from political life in India. As Pavan Varma has argued, this was a self-defeating logic for the middle class, one that was "strikingly circular: politics is dirty because good people do not enter it, and because good people do not enter it, politics is dirty."[55] Kaul proposed to nominate "clean candidates" free of "political baggage." Although his party lost the February 2005 elections for state assembly, primarily because elite voters in Gurgaon at that time still comprised a minority of the overall electorate in the district, Kaul continued his political organizing, eventually joining the Hindu-nationalist Bharatiya Janata Party, which won state assembly elections in Gurgaon in 2014, riding a larger wave of anti-incumbency around the country.[56]

As ostensibly "middle-class" subjects mediating between countervailing temporalities of development and globality, Kishore Arora and Sanjay Kaul practiced different strategies of political mediation in Gurgaon. In his slide-show presentation at

170 *Aura and trace in Gurgaon*

his home Arora projected an alternative "far order," the Gurgaon City Authority, to replace the existing municipal structure. Meanwhile, Kaul attempted to work within this existing structure in order to change how it operated, actively registering new voters and putting up "clean" candidates that would be more attractive to the middle-class electorate. Yet both shared an elite disposition toward postcolonial politics that was marked by deep ambivalence. This ambivalence was mediated by modes of distancing that were obvious in the case of Arora (distance enacted through corporate governance) and less so in the case of Kaul. For Kaul often used terms like "aam aadmi" or "common man" to articulate the problems citizens faced in Gurgaon and Delhi. This image of the common man struggling against the bureaucratic inefficiencies and outright corruption of the postcolonial state has gained increasing prominence in mainstream Indian politics, leading to the election of the anti-corruption Aam Aadmi Party in Delhi and the BJP in Haryana.[57] Simultaneously, imagery of India's expanding "middle class" continues to circulate both within the country and abroad, promising to finally reconcile the dynamics of electoral politics and the anticipated demographic dominance of the normative liberal middle class. Yet the vast distance that exists between this entrenched "middle class" and the majority of the country means that such forms of political mediation as practiced by the likes of Arora and Kaul reproduce the very forms of distance they seek to overcome, so that the self-defeating logic Varma outlines above remains pertinent when it comes to theorizing the possibilities and limits of middle-class politics in neoliberal India.

In one particularly telling scene in *I am Gurgaon*, Bineeta Singh is driving in a car with her two young children. They are on their way to an exclusive country club to go swimming. Singh speaks to her children in English, who respond in kind, performing their economic and cultural privilege on camera. "Let us find a poor person to give some money to," she tells the boys, as the car navigates the roads of Gurgaon. The kids seem uninterested in the forced charity, instead wrestling with each other in the back seat of the car. Eventually they look out the window, searching for beggars on the streets. "How much money will we give them?" one of the boys asks. "Ten rupees," Singh replies. "Ten rupees is a lot for these people."

But we never actually see them give any money to anyone. Whether this is edited out of the film or they simply fail to find a beggar, in the very next scene we see that, in any case, Bineeta Singh and her privileged kin have already moved on. After passing through guarded gates, they enter the grounds of the country club. "Lets look for peacocks!" Singh now commands the children, who in their excitement seem to have forgotten all about the beggars that were previously their locus of attention.

Notes

1 Reinhold Martin and Kadambari Baxi, *Multi-National City: Architectural Itineraries* (Barcelona: Actar, 2007), 114.
2 Ibid.
3 My translation: "When I drive here I feel like I have left India and traveled abroad!"

The enclave 171

4 Somini Sengupta, "Inside gate, India's good life; outside, the servants' slums." *New York Times*, June 9, 2008, accessed August 19, 2010, www.nytimes.com/2008/06/09/world/asia/09gated.html.
5 Aravind Adiga, *The White Tiger* (New York: Free Press, 2008).
6 Walter Benjamin, *The Arcades Project*, trans. Howard Eiland and Kevin McLaughlin (Cambridge, MA: Harvard University Press, 1999), 447.
7 These concepts are introduced in the Introduction and in the preface to Part I and come from Henri Lefebvre's essay "The specificity of the city," in *Writings on Cities* (Oxford: Blackwell, 1996), 100–103.
8 Walter Benjamin, "Theses on philosophy of history," in *Illuminations* (New York: Schocken Books, 1968), 253–264.
9 For more on "waste," see Awadhendra Sharan, "In the city, out of place: Environment and modernity, Delhi 1860s to 1960s." *Economic and Political Weekly* 41.47 (2006), 4905–4911, and Vinay Gidwani and Rajyashree N. Reddy, "The afterlives of 'waste': Notes from India for a minor history of capitalist surplus." *Antipode* 43.5 (2011), 1625–1658. For more on the commercial real estate industry in Delhi and Gurgaon, from critical ethnographic and spatial perspectives, see Véronique Dupont, "The dream of Delhi as a global city." *International Journal of Urban and Regional Research* 35.3 (2011), 533–554, and Llerena Guiu Searle, "Conflict and commensuration: Contested market making in India's private real estate development sector." *International Journal of Urban and Regional Research* 38.1 (2014), 60–78.
10 "Protest on Sept. 22 in Gurgaon against garbage dump." *Right to Information*, accessed September 29, 2008, www.rtiindia.org/forum/7329-protest-sept-22-gurgaon-against-garbage-dump.html.
11 For more on business process outsourcing in India, see A. Aneesh, *Virtual Migration* (Durham, NC: Duke University Press, 2006) and Rohan Kalyan, "Ghostly images, phantom discourses, and the virtuality of the global." *Globalizations* 7.4 (2010), 545–561.
12 "Gurgaon should shape up or they'll ship out." *BPO Watch India*, accessed September 29, 2008, www.bpowatchindia.com/bpo_news/gurgaon_clean/September-26–2008/gurgaon_ceos_cleanliness.html.
13 Saskia Sassen, "Why cities matter." *Catalogue of the 10th International Architecture Exhibition, Venice Biennale* (2006), 26–51.
14 Pavan Varma, *The Great Indian Middle Class* (Delhi: Penguin Books, 1998).
15 Nandan Nilekani, *Imagining India: The Idea of a Renewed Nation* (New York: Penguin, 2009), 207.
16 "Gurgaon collapsing." *Hindustan Times*, September 24, 2008.
17 Ibid.
18 Ibid.
19 Ibid.
20 "Gurgaon collapsing." *Hindustan Times*, September 25, 2008.
21 Ibid.
22 Himadeep Muppidi, *The Politics of the Global* (Minneapolis, MN: University of Minnesota Press, 2004), 31.
23 Interview with Sanjeev Ahuja, October 23, 2008 in Gurgaon, Haryana.
24 For more about this 'chalta hai' attitude and the way it is deployed rhetorically in India, see my blog: http://virualpolitics-india.blogspot.com/2008/10/chalte-chalte-vs-india-inc_21.html.
25 Interview with Sanjay Kaul, November 13, 2008, New Delhi, India. For more on rates of political participation in voting for middle class Indians, see Eswaran Sridharan, "The growth and sectoral composition of India's middle class: Its impact on the politics of economic liberalization." *India Review* 3.4 (2004), 405–428.
26 Partha Chatterjee, *The Nation and its Fragments: Colonial and Postcolonial Histories* (Princeton, NJ: Princeton University Press, 1993), 35.

172   *Aura and trace in Gurgaon*

27 Quoted in Pavan Varma, *The Great Indian Middle Class* (Delhi: Penguin Books India, 1998), 2 (italics mine).

28 Ashis Nandy argues that Satyajit Ray inherits an orientalist position in his rendering of the Mughal king Wajid Ali Shah. I argue against this interpretation in an upcoming essay. See Ashis Nandy, *The Savage Freud and Other Essays on Possible and Retrievable Selves* (Delhi: Oxford University Press, 1995).

29 Gilles Deleuze, *Francis Bacon: The Logic of Sensation* (Minneapolis, MN: University of Minnesota Press, 2003), 59.

30 Homi Bhabha, *The Location of Culture* (London: Routledge, 1994).

31 Michael J. Shapiro, "Towards a politics of now-time," in *Cinematic Political Thought* (New York: NYU Press, 1999), 23.

32 Website for VPRO, accessed January 15, 2010, http://tegenlicht.vpro.nl/backlight.html.

33 Ibid.

34 In Chapter 2 I discuss esthetic subjects in the context of Kathputli Colony and a recent documentary produced on the slum.

35 Jacques Ranciere, *Film Fables* (Oxford: Berg, 2006), 2.

36 Ibid., 3.

37 My usage of the political is indebted to philosopher Jacques Ranciere's sense of politics as involving the "re-partitioning of the sensible." See Jacques Ranciere, *The Politics of the Aesthetics: The Distribution of the Sensible* (New York: Bloomsbury Books, 2004).

38 Ibid., 6.

39 Jonathan Shapiro Anjaria, "Street hawkers and public space in Mumbai." *Economic and Political Weekly* 41.21 (2006), 2140–2146.

40 Sumit Sukanya, "They've a Gurgaon action plan." *Times of India*, May 30, 2010, accessed July 13, 2012, www1.lite.epaper.timesofindia.com/getpage.aspx?article=yes&pageid=6&edlabel=CAP&mydateHid=30-5-2010&pubname=Times+of+India+-+Delhi+-+Front+Page&edname=&articleid=Ar00600&format=&publabel=TOI&max=true.

41 Nilekani, *Imagining India: The Idea of a Renewed Nation*, 207.

42 Ibid., 213.

43 Varma, *The Great Indian Middle Class*, 132.

44 Ibid., 137.

45 Interview with Sanjeev Ahuja, October 23, 2008 in Gurgaon, Haryana.

46 Interview and field notes with Kishore Arora (name changed upon request), January 17, 2009, in Gurgaon, Haryana.

47 Ibid.

48 Ibid.

49 Ibid.

50 Ibid.

51 Interview with Sanjay Kaul, February24, 2009 in Delhi.

52 Ibid.

53 Ibid.

54 Ibid.

55 Pavan Varma, *The Great Indian Middle Class* (Delhi: Penguin Books, 1998), 147.

56 Sandali Tiwari, "15 years on, BJP rises in Gurgaon." *The Indian Express*, October 20, 2014, accessed March 28, 2015, http://indianexpress.com/article/cities/delhi/15-years-on-bjp-rises-in-gurgaon/.

57 Rohan Kalyan, "Did India just elect its Ronald Reagan?" *Economic and Political Weekly*, May 31, 2014, web exclusive.

Bibliography

Aneesh, A. *Virtual Migration*. Durham, NC: Duke University Press, 2006.

Anjaria, Jonathan Shapiro. "Street hawkers and public space in Mumbai." *Economic and Political Weekly* 41.21 (2006): 2140–2146.

Benjamin, Walter. "Theses on philosophy of history," in *Illuminations*. New York: Schocken Books, 1968: 253–264.

Benjamin, Walter. *The Arcades Project*. Trans. Howard Eiland and Kevin McLaughlin. Cambridge, MA: Harvard University Press, 1999.

Bhabha, Homi. *The Location of Culture*. London: Routledge, 1994.

Deleuze, Gilles. *Francis Bacon: The Logic of Sensation*. Minneapolis, MN: University of Minnesota Press, 2003.

Dupont, Véronique. "The dream of Delhi as a global city." *International Journal of Urban and Regional Research* 35.3 (2011): 533–554.

Gidwani, Vinay and Rajyashree N. Reddy. "The afterlives of 'waste': Notes from India for a minor history of capitalist surplus." *Antipode* 43.5 (2011): 1625–1658.

"Gurgaon should shape up or they'll ship out." *BPO Watch India*, accessed September 29, 2008, www.bpowatchindia.com/bpo_news/gurgaon_clean/September-26-2008/gurgaon_ceos_cleanliness.html.

Kalyan, Rohan. "Ghostly images, phantom discourses, and the virtuality of the global." *Globalizations* 7.4 (2010): 545–561.

Kalyan, Rohan. "Did India just elect its Ronald Reagan?" *Economic and Political Weekly*, May 31, 2014, web exclusive.

Lefebvre, Henri. "The specificity of the city," in *Writings on Cities*. Oxford: Blackwell, 1996: 100–103.

Martin, Reinhold and Kadambari Baxi. *Multi-National City: Architectural Itineraries*. Barcelona: Actar, 2007.

Muppidi, Himadeep. *The Politics of the Global*. Minneapolis, MN: University of Minnesota Press, 2004.

Nandy, Ashis. *The Savage Freud and Other Essays on Possible and Retrievable Selves*. Delhi: Oxford University Press, 1995.

Nilekani, Nandan. *Imagining India: The Idea of a Renewed Nation*. New York: Penguin, 2009.

Patke, Rajeev S. "Benjamin's Arcades Project and the postcolonial city." *diacritics* 30.4 (2000): 2–14.

"Protest on Sept. 22 in Gurgaon against garbage dump," *Right to Information*, accessed September 29, 2008, www.rtiindia.org/forum/7329-protest-sept-22-gurgaon-against-garbage-dump.html.

Ranciere, Jacques. *The Politics of the Aesthetics: The Distribution of the Sensible*. New York: Bloomsbury Books, 2004.

Ranciere, Jacques. *Film Fables*. Oxford: Berg, 2006.

Sassen, Saskia. "Why cities matter." *Catalogue of the 10th International Architecture Exhibition, Venice Biennale* (2006): 26–51.

Searle, Llerena Guiu. "Conflict and commensuration: Contested market making in India's private real estate development sector." *International Journal of Urban and Regional Research* 38.1 (2014): 60–78.

Sengupta, Somini. "Inside gate, India's good life; outside, the servants' slums." *New York Times*, June 9, 2008, accessed August 19, 2010, www.nytimes.com/2008/06/09/world/asia/09gated.html.

174 *Aura and trace in Gurgaon*

Sharan, Awadhendra. "In the city, out of place: Environment and modernity, Delhi 1860s to 1960s." *Economic and Political Weekly* 41.47 (2006): 4905–4911.

Shapiro, Michael J. "Towards a politics of now-time," in *Cinematic Political Thought*. New York: NYU Press, 1999: 10–38.

Sridharan, Eswaran. "The growth and sectoral composition of India's middle class: Its impact on the politics of economic liberalization." *India Review* 3.4 (2004): 405–428.

Sukanya, Sumit. "They've a Gurgaon action plan." *Times of India*, May 30, 2010, accessed July 13, 2012, www1.lite.epaper.timesofindia.com/getpage.aspx?article=yes&pageid=6&edlabel=CAP&mydateHid=30-5-2010&pubname=Times+of+India+-+Delhi+-+Front+Page&edname=&articleid=Ar00600&format=&publabel=TOI&max=true.

Tiwari, Sandali. "15 years on, BJP rises in Gurgaon." *The Indian Express*, October 20, 2014, accessed March 28, 2015, http://indianexpress.com/article/cities/delhi/15-years-on-bjp-rises-in-gurgaon/.

Varma, Pavan. *The Great Indian Middle Class*. Delhi: Penguin Books, 1998.

5 The village

> Before beginning Chapter 5: The village, the reader is encouraged to watch the musical video *Street Ethnography and Rhythmmanalysis: Chakkarpur, Gurgaon* (9 min). The video was produced by Rohan Kalyan in collaboration with Praveen Verma. Shot over a series of micro-ethnographic explorations within Chakkarpur Village in 2015, the video thinks through photo-montage, musical rhythms and spatial movements in order to piece together a virtual experience of this "urbanized" village. To view the video, visit: www.neodelhi.net/videos/.

> Perhaps the cultural logic of the Indian city demands the presence of the village.
>
> Ashis Nandy, An Ambiguous Journey to the City

Ambiguous journeys

In the above work, Nandy theorizes the interaction between two imaginary spaces—the village and the city—in modern Indian political life.[1] Nandy argued that this foundational split between village and city, also often articulated as the conflict between tradition and modernity, was undermined by the way in which each side bled into the imagination of the other, structuring it invisibly from within. The resulting mediations between the two sides meant that the village was never far from the city and vice versa, even if both could be separated physically, cultural, politically and economically.

In this chapter I share the results of my own ambiguous journey that was Nandy's in reverse, a journey not to the (ruralized) city but to the (urbanized) village. During March 2015, my research partner and I traveled regularly from the city of Delhi to the village of Chakkarpur, the latter located in the district of Gurgaon. Rather than finding traces of the village in the city, as Nandy does in his masterful essay, our goal was to find traces of the city in this "urbanized" village.

In the composite, virtual journey below I share the results of recorded conversations, documented encounters and ethnographic observations in the streets of

Chakkarpur. This accompanies a cinematic version of this visual ethnography.[2] The reader should also consult Map 3 at the front of this book to follow the composite journey through Chakkarpur I describe below.

Street ethnography in an "urbanized" village

Chakkarpur Village stands in the southwestern quadrant of an intersection between two major roads in New Gurgaon: Mehrauli–Gurgaon Road (MG Road—which runs west to east across DLF City) and Golf Course Road (which runs north to south from DLF City to other private townships and residential sectors in the southeast corner of the district). MG Road, which forms the northern border of the traditional village land of Chakkarpur, traverses some of the iconic architectural landmarks of DLF City, including places like Sahara Mall, DT City Center, Beverly Park Apartments, MGF Mega City Mall. As such, the thoroughfare showcases the Millennium City in all its commodified globality.

The architectural spectacle of New Gurgaon as seen on MG Road all but erases Chakkarpur's not-so-distant agrarian past. Just three decades ago, the now developed spaces of DLF City were farmlands and pastoral fields belonging to small farmers and villagers. The original village of Chakkarpur still stands where it has long stood, but today the village has become urbanized in its own right, its population growing dramatically from 1808 in 1981 to 14,216 by 2011.[3] While its population density increased manifold the village's once extensive farmlands

Figure 5.1 View from MG Road Metro Station 1, Gurgaon.
Source: Photo by author.

The village 177

and grazing pastures rapidly shrank, the latter having been acquired by private real estate developers like DLF and state agencies like HUDA (see Figure 5.3), leaving a dense cluster of tightly-packed "village" settlements enveloped in a sea of high-end real estate.

While much has been made of the macro-level spatial and structural changes taking place in Gurgaon (this was the focus of the previous two chapters), much less has been written about the various village settlements that pre-date Gurgaon's transformation and persist today, developing alongside, yet differentially, from elite spaces.[4] This unbalanced attention is most likely due to the fact that macro-structural changes like policy reform at the national level are now regularly associated with the signs and discourses of neoliberal urbanism, which Gurgaon exudes in surplus, with its malls, condominiums, office buildings and golf courses.

Less visible, at least for Gurgaon's "normative" middle-class subjects, are the equally dramatic changes taking place just behind the architectural facade of the Millennium City. Gurgaon's urbanized landscape contains scores of villages that pre-date recent hyper-development chronicled in the previous chapter. But many of these villages are "urbanized" to the extent that they have become intimately entangled with newly built up spaces around them, even if the lives of the former are largely invisible from the perspective of the latter.

This chapter presents a particular kind of visual ethnography that is not merely cinematic, but also decidedly "street." "Street ethnography" combines improvised urban exploration, open-ended conversations with local workers and residents, sensory-geographic mapping, thick description of built environments and audio-visual documentation. It seeks to explore how changing life is mediated at the intersection of near and far orders.

From the point of view of Gurgaon's official master plan, Chakkarpur is classified as a village *abadi*, or village land/zone, located in Sector 28 of Gurgaon. In English Chakkarpur is better described as an "urbanized" or "urbanizing" village on the new side of town, that is, on the east side of the Delhi Gurgaon Expressway (aka National Highway 8). Its erstwhile agricultural land is for all purposes gone. Since the early 1980s DLF had aggressively targeted it for acquisition and speculative development. In fact, Chakkarpur Village is where K. P. Singh officially acquired the first piece of land in Gurgaon for DLF, "from Surajmal, a farmer, on 29 October, 1980. It was a small plot of land—just 0.375 acres."[5] DLF quickly expanded its holdings in the area around Chakkarpur. This history of private land acquisition in Gurgaon was detailed in Chapter 3.

At first glance Chakkarpur seems an anachronistic relic in the midst of a hyper-modern Gurgaon that appears to be swallowing it whole. Yet this is a classically far order perspective, one that inhabits and reproduces the universal constitution of what Sheppard et al. call Geohistory 1 (see Introduction). This perspective betrays a denial of coevalness and entanglement between village and city, and between working-poor and working-elite classes. This is an "urban" entanglement that is deep, even if often invisible from the perspective of the elite city. These entanglements are manifest as soon as one enters the dense, hybrid, polyrhythmic spaces of Chakkarpur, which is neither urban nor rural, but something much more complex.

178 *Aura and trace in Gurgaon*

Figure 5.2 View from MG Road Metro Station 2, Gurgaon.
Source: Photo by author.

On the Metro

The field research for this chapter was conducted in March 2015 in collaboration with Praveen Verma, a researcher based at Delhi University (DU). We began our trips to the field each day on the Metro train. Praveen was coming from the north campus of DU, and I from the AIIS guesthouse in Defense Colony. We would meet up at the Saket Metro Station in the morning and then take the Yellow Line south to DLF City in Gurgaon. The journey began underground but would later transition to elevated concrete tracks just as the train passed Qutab Minar, built in the thirteenth century during the reign of the Delhi Sultanate. The tracks then passed through picturesque forests with rolling hills and ravines that belonged to the ancient Aravalli range. This protected "green belt" in the southern fringes of Delhi was punctuated by human settlements that either predated the zoning laws, or developed in relative indifference to them.[6]

Continuing south, soon enough one began to see the tall buildings of Gurgaon in the distance, office skyscrapers and mass-residential towers, scores of them spread out along the hazy horizon. Passing from peri-urban Gurgaon into the thick of DLF City, with its visually loud architecture and rampant consumerism, was like traveling through Gurgaon's pre-urban history: on the outskirts of Gurgaon one saw newly excavated sites for upcoming shopping malls and condominium towers, transitioning gradually to existing malls and apartment buildings that were constructed in the late 1990s and early 2000s. Many of these structures already looked dusty and dated, notwithstanding their once futuristic facades.

The village 179

Each day we would get off at the MG Road Metro Station, which was the third stop in Gurgaon, after Guru Dronacharya and Sikhanderpur stops. From here our journey into Chakkarpur Village would commence by foot. During each visit we mapped out different itineraries, exploring various routes into and out of the village, moving between and across the condensed neighborhoods, tightly packed into a space a little more than one square kilometer in size. The village was composed of tightly-packed multi-story buildings, street markets and dense mixed-use neighborhoods. Our goal was to navigate the village's neighborhoods and strike up conversations with different passersby in a more or less improvisational manner. I took digital photos and videos with my smart phone (after replacing the one I lost during field work in 2012) while Praveen would directly interview our subjects. After obtaining their permission to talk with them and take photos we would sit down and record for as long as an hour with each subject. The journey is presented in edited form below.

MG Road

As soon as we descended the stairs from the elevated Metro Station platform we were on the southern side of MG Road. From here we would walk east a few blocks and take a right turn on a long straight road that would lead us directly into Chakkarpur. On MG Road we encountered a twelve-year-old boy slouched nonchalantly behind an *aloo tikki* stand. We were hungry so we decided to grab an *aloo tikki* burger—a little "local" street flavor on this "global" boulevard.

Deepak

His name was Deepak. His stall was positioned in front of DT City Center, a popular mall on MG Road. Deepak lived in another urban village called Chattarpur in south Delhi (not to be confused with Chakkarpur—where we were heading). The *tikki* stand belonged to his father. Deepak worked there after school, taking the Delhi Metro each day from Chattarpur to MG Road. It was about a fifteen-minute ride, he said.

Parhayi bhi karta hun, aur ye kaam bhi karta hun.[7]

Deepak told us that on a typical day he got up at five in the morning to go to school. The school day finished at one in the afternoon and he began work at 1:30. He got off from work at around six in the evening and then went home to Chattarpur.

Deepak's father owned a total of six *tikki* stands, all in Gurgaon. There were two others in Phase III of DLF City (we were currently in Phase II), and another one in sector 56, which was outside of DLF City proper and in another privately developed part of the city. Deepak didn't seem to know or remember where the others were located. His particular stall was stored each night in a *godown* behind Sahara Mall, less than 100 meters down the road.

180 *Aura and trace in Gurgaon*

He told us he earned around Rs3000 per day selling *aloo tikki*. This seemed a bit high to us. But then again, it was a busy pedestrian-friendly road (one of the few streets with an accessible sidewalk in Gurgaon). In any case, he said that he didn't get to keep the money, that his father collected it at the end of each day. His uncles, brothers and cousins all took turns operating the other stalls in Gurgaon, with his father moving from location to location throughout the day, mostly to collect money. Deepak was the youngest of the siblings. We asked him if this was what he wanted to do when he got older. Deepak replied at once: "Nahin!"

Then what did he want to do?

He said he had one older brother who used to work at one of his father's stalls but now worked in a computer store in Delhi. Deepak wanted to follow in his brother's footsteps.

Manu

We met Manu just a few meters down the sidewalk from Deepak's *tikki* stall, still a full block before the road to Chakkarpur. Manu was standing on the side-walk holding a flier that read "English for Professionals." He was a marketing agent, and soliciting people on the street to sign up for "accent neutralization" English-courses. Gurgaon was a big hub for Business Process Outsourcing (BPO) operations, where many American businesses outsourced part of their producer services to "Third World" countries like India, and Gurgaon has been a major site of business process re-location for multi-national corporations. In other words, it was hardly surprising to find someone selling the chance to learn or improve one's English on MG Road.

Bina English ke koi growth nahi hain, kise bhi line main.[8]

Manu moved to Gurgaon from Uttar Pradesh five years ago. He himself had started out working in a call center, he told us. It wasn't too difficult to get a job at one, he said. You just needed good communication skills in English.

Manu wanted to work in sales, so he left the call center after just one year and began working in his current occupation, which he described as market research. On days like the one on which we met him on MG Road, he would stand on the pavement for the entire afternoon, soliciting potential clients for the company. On other days he was in the office, making phone calls.

Mujhe sales ki kaam acha lagta hain, kyunki sales main naya log milta aur bhaat karna mujhe acha lagta hai.[9]

He also switched to sales because Manu anticipated that he could earn more money there. Though in both jobs the starting salary was roughly the same, about Rs10,000 per month, according to Manu, in sales one's pay could rise rapidly through commission. After just three to four months working six days a week he was already making Rs15,000 per month, which is what he earned now.

The village 181

Manu moved to Gurgaon after completing high school in Uttar Pradesh (UP). He was now twenty-six years old. His sister also lived in Gurgaon, with a family of her own. But Manu and his sister's family did not live together. He seemed to value this freedom he had in Gurgaon. He could meet friends at the mall or go to Payal Cinema in Sector 14 of Old Gurgaon. This was also a big commercial market, with lots of "foreign" restaurants and shops where he and his friends would hang out.

We soon started talking about the rental market in Gurgaon, of which Manu seemed quite privy (like most of the people we later talked to in Chakkarpur itself, a point to which I return in the next section). He told us that, compared to the older parts of Gurgaon, it was much more expensive to rent in New Gurgaon, even in villages like Chakkarpur. In Old Gurgaon, where both he and his sister lived, one could find a one-bedroom apartment for Rs5000 per month, 7000–8000 for a two bedroom flat. In New Gurgaon, on the other hand, Rs6000 would only get you a small non-AC room in someone else's home, called PG (paying guest) accommodation. AC-equipped PGs started at Rs8000 in New Gurgaon. Gurgaon was more expensive than even Delhi, at least if one wanted decent housing. In both Old and New Gurgaon, it was common to see as many as three to four people or a small family sharing a cramped one-bedroom apartment, usually in former single-family homes that were only recently expanded into multiple rental units.

We asked Manu if he wanted to stay in Gurgaon in the long term, raise a family here, try to buy an apartment or a plot of land.

> Baas ye hai, mere vichaar me Gurgaon me to makaan nahi banega. Ye fix hai. Sab se ganda Gurgaon hai. Ek to costly jagga hai. Doosri baat yahan to kuch khas cheez hai nahi. Environment ko acha nahin lagta. Aaght ya nau bajhe ke baad gumne jao. Phir pata lagega. Yahan ke logo todasa … baar ke log ko parishani karna ke adat hogai. Kabi bhi dek na jo banda Bihar ya UP se aya hue, to tanasahi to chaleygi.[10]

Chakkarpur Village Road

Between Vipul Agora, a greenish-blue glass-covered office building, and Sahara Mall, a bombastic, if somewhat past its prime, structure built by DLF back in the mid-1990s, there was a long, straight road heading south that formed a T-junction with MG Road, forming a boundary line between the two structures. This was the road we walked down to enter Chakkarpur, and it was as if these two post-modern buildings were standing guard at the entry-way into the post-rural village.

Ashish

About 100 meters down this road we encountered a middle-aged man sitting on the curb, his back leaning against a street light. His name was Ashish, and he

182 *Aura and trace in Gurgaon*

Figure 5.3 The road into Chakkarpur Village, Gurgaon.
Source: Photo by author.

was a barber by profession and caste. He was also a janitor by necessity. At the moment Ashish did not have any customers, and so after making acquaintances we were able to sit down with him.

Ashish had moved to Gurgaon from Calcutta eight years before, and now lived in Chakkarpur with his wife and two children. In addition to cutting hair at a small rickety stall on the side of the road here, Ashish also worked as a cleaner in several office buildings and malls on MG Road. Every day from early morning until 1pm, he cleaned floors using *jardoo* (broom) and *pocha* (wet rags). After cleaning he would come to work at his stall until the evening, when he'd retire for the night at home.

Araam raat ko kartha hun.[11]

He told us he earned around Rs7000 per month cleaning and an additional Rs6000 from cutting hair. His wife also worked and made about half of what he earned. She was a housekeeper and also cleaned offices. They had two girls, aged six and four. Like many locals we spoke with in Chakkarpur, Ashish reported a steep increase in the cost of living since moving to the area. When he first came to Chakkarpur eight years ago, a small one-room apartment went for

The village 183

Rs2000 per month. But that price had by now doubled, and they were currently paying Rs4000 per month for such an apartment. Another example of inflation that Ashish provided was the price of rice, which used to cost just Rs20 per kilogram a few years ago, but now was close to double that at Rs35.

Many workers in Chakkarpur were Bengalis like Ashish and his family, meaning they had come from the eastern state of West Bengal. According to Ashish, Bengalis mostly performed jobs like cleaning office buildings and domestic homes, but they also could operate cycle rickshaws and perform delivery services, transporting fruits, vegetables and grains from the central market (*mandi*) to various neighborhoods. Meanwhile, migrants from the state of Bihar, who were also numerous in Chakkarpur, tended to be drivers or deliverymen, either operating their own taxis or working for a private company.

Kal party hua, office main.[12]

At one point we saw that Ashish had a small bottle of whiskey behind the stool where his customers would sit to get their hair cut. Ashish told us that he drank almost every night after work. Not a lot, he said, just enough to fall asleep, or just to pass the time when business was slow. The previous night he was cleaning up after an office party for white collar workers. After the party finished Ashish and some of the other janitors stayed late and drank a bottle someone had taken from the bar, which they drank late into the night. He might have still been a little bit tipsy when we spoke to him that afternoon. Perhaps this was why he was so talkative with us.

We were not so eagerly received in our next site of encounter, just down the road from Ashish and at the entrance of Chakkarpur Village proper.

Nambardar **market**

Down the road about 100 meters from Ashish's barber stall the relatively open spaces around the street condensed into walls of shop entrances and buildings on both sides. There were stores selling household goods, clothes and fabrics, snacks and tea shops, fruit and vegetable stands. There was also a Universal Gym and several property broker offices, with large glass windows for their storefronts that were covered with mirrors, so that those on the inside could see outside but not vice versa.

On the left side of the road we saw one such office with a sign that read "Sangwan & Yadav: Real Estate Agent." Next to the large text was a computer-generated image of a modern multi-story apartment building.

This was the *nambardar* market, a major landmark in Chakkarpur both in terms of local geography (since it was located right at the entrance to the village) and in terms of local politics. For the Yadav in question was Jeelay Singh Yadav, and he was not merely a property broker (along with his partner Mr. Sangwan), but he also held the influential title of *nambardar* in the village.[13] *Nambardar* referred to a title prevalent in northern India that was used by powerful land

184 *Aura and trace in Gurgaon*

owning families (*zamindars*) in rural villages and towns. The *nambardar* often mediated social and familial disputes, especially pertaining to land. In his office Jeelay Singh had pictures hanging up on the wall showing him at public functions and events, cutting ribbons, shaking hands, accepting awards. There was also a portrait of his father who had previously held the hereditary title. A bright orange garland hung across the frame.

When we encountered Jeelay Singh in his office one day in the *nambardar* market we were excited as researchers. For the *nambardar* himself seemed to be involved with real estate as a property broker (not uncommon in Gurgaon, since the *nambardar* was someone who came from a dominant landowning caste). If Chakkarpur was where K. P. Singh of DLF had first acquired land in Gurgaon back in 1980, then this seemed like an important part of that story, not revealed in K. P. Singh's account. Instead, as you'll recall from the previous chapter, Singh portrays himself as a scrupulous business man, with never even the slightest hint of friction between he and the hundreds of farmers from whom he was able to acquire land. Here we could engage those that actually sold their land to K. P. Singh and other developers, either through consent or through compulsion. Number one amongst these erstwhile farmers that had sold land to DLF would be the *nambardar* himself, or so we thought.

But Jeelay Singh was not interested in talking to us. In our brief and hasty encounter with him in his office, Singh repeatedly would walk out and talk on his phone, only to come back in and sit with us for a few minutes, before up and leaving once again. He informed us that DLF and HUDA had acquired the land in this area in the 1980s (which we already knew), and that this included the site where the Sahara Mall is now located (which we also already knew). Thus our

Figure 5.4 Interior, *nambardar* office, Chakkarpur Village.
Source: Photo by author.

The village 185

brief interaction with the *nambardar* yielded little useful ethnographic material. Instead, he directed us to two of his associates, who turned out to be interesting informants in their own right. But even during our brief encounter with Jeelay Singh, two things stood out that *were* of ethnographic significance. First, according to him the lands that were sold off were not barren and uncultivated, as K. P. Singh claims in his autobiography (Chapter 3), but were rather fertile and productive. He didn't elaborate on this and we didn't get the chance to follow up on it, but this idea was echoed in the words of others with whom we spoke, as we will see later. And second, the *nambardar* had a curious habit of speaking in the present tense when referring to the land he and others from the village had sold, some of it as long as thirty years ago. When referring to this land he spoke not only in the present tense but also in the possessive sense, as if the land was still his (or the village's) and he could reclaim it at any time.

Sahara Mall se yahan tak lekhe sara zamin hamare hain.[14]

Bipin Kumar

Arre hum bhi outsider hai![15]

The *nambardar*'s first associate, Bipin Kumar, was more inclined to speak with us. When we returned on another day to the office we interviewed Kumar, who was born in Ludhiana, Punjab and studied engineering in Chandigarh, the shared capital of both Punjab and Haryana. He came to Gurgaon in 1984 to work at the newly established Maruti car assembly plant. Following a bad leg injury, Bipin Kumar (BK from here on) was forced into early retirement after working for eighteen years at Maruti. He subsequently became a full-time landlord and property broker, like many others whose arrival in Gurgaon pre-dated its speculative boom. BK had bought a house in Maruti Vihar back in the 1980s. The neighborhood, which was adjacent to Chakkarpur, was originally designed to accommodate managers and workers at Maruti but it soon turned into a speculative rental market for workers of varying classes and professions in Gurgaon. After adding another floor to his home BK started renting out space too.

Ab summe me parivartan aa chukhe hain.... Hamare dekthe dekthe, ye sara badalahua ye.[16]

Having lived in nearby Maruti Vihar for three decades, Bipin Kumar witnessed first hand the radical changes that were to take place in conjunction with the larger speculative development of Gurgaon described in the previous chapter. After Maruti came to Gurgaon, he told us, other ancillary units re-located to the area, making car parts and providing services for the managers and workers of Maruti. In the early days there was a small market that surrounded the Maruti plant and smaller ones around other automobile plants in the area. Workers and their families would get their vegetables and dairy from Chakkarpur, where

186 *Aura and trace in Gurgaon*

villagers sold milk from their cows and buffalos. Back then, Bipin Kumar recalled, Chakkarpur was much different. There were none of the hotels, restaurants and malls that now characterized this space. People went to Delhi for all of that.

> Hum bhi Dilli jaya karthe the![17]

Change in Gurgaon was especially pronounced on the eastern side of the expressway. With the arrival of manufacturing also came dozens of export units, ancillary automobile units, education institutions, small joint ventures and collaborations (mostly with Japanese investment). Bipin Kumar would often identify the "flow of money" (*paisa ki flow*) as the main fuel for change in the area. Namely, with the establishment of manufacturing and outside investment from Japan (for Maruti and Hero Honda), 90 percent of which was in automotive-related industries, wages increased and more people came in. Along with disposable income, the requirements of Gurgaonites increased, BK said. People wanted to send their children to good schools to make them engineers and doctors. Those that sold their land often invested in creating new businesses, including restaurants and hotels or building rental housing. Even *sabzi wallahs* who built on their small parcels of land were soon making money off of rent, BK informed us.

> Yahan kuch bhi kaam karlo, paisa ki flow bahut hai.[18]

As money flowed in through industrial employment and new entrepreneurial activities in Chakkarpur and Gurgaon more generally, the cost of housing increased dramatically. Today, Bipin Kumar said, a single-bed PG went for Rs8000–10,000 per month with AC and Rs5000 per month without AC. The area was expensive because it was so well connected with the capital and other towns in southern Haryana, like Faridabad and Riwari. BK rented out a whole floor in his house for Rs20,000 a month (around $300 as of August 2016 exchange rates). This was an inflated price, he admitted, but not uncommon for the area. As recently as 2001, Bipin Kumar said, he rented the apartment out for Rs3800 per month. But manipulation in real estate was very high, and everyone was making money off the bubbling rental market.

> Yahan koi aisa aadmi nahi hai jo kamai nahi rahe.[19]

Gurgaon was expensive and getting increasingly more so with the continuous flow of money that was coming in, and this inflationary bubble impacted Chakkarpur directly. One needed to make at least Rs50,000 per month to enjoy a good life in Gurgaon, BK told us. As we would discover, however, this salary was significantly higher than the average monthly income of most we encountered in the course of this study. It seemed that BK spent most of his time with rich and powerful men like Jeelay Singh, wealthy farmers that sold their land and now traded in economic and political power. This was a class that benefited

The village   187

greatly from the sale of strategically located land, so that the far order speculative boom in Gurgaon (orchestrated by DLF and HUDA) produced a near order boom in Chakkarpur.

Inniko charro taraf se lottery nikalghi.[20]

Before all the land was sold and developed into what you see today, Bipin Kumar told us, this area consisted of fields and un-irrigated lands, which were largely under-productive because they were dependent upon the annual rains. DLF came in and bought this land from villagers in places like Chakkarpur, Sukrali, Sikanderpur, Nathupur, Jharsa and others. All located around what is today MG Road and Golf Course Road. DLF then went to the government, which approved its plans to develop the land, and subsequently cut out plots for residential housing. At first there were just a few plots here and there, but then it became more densely populated throughout the 1990s and into the 2000s, picking up even more by around 2005.

Many farmers that originally sold their land, including Jeelay Singh, still lived in Chakkarpur. But not everyone sold willingly. There were disputes with people who did not want to sell. They did not wish to leave behind farming, which was the only life they knew, and so many that reluctantly sold their land would turn around and buy land elsewhere, where it was comparatively cheaper. Jeelay Singh was one of the first to sell part of his land and persuaded many others to do so as well, so as to increase the value of the remaining lands he still held. Many took their money and transitioned profitably into new professions, becoming contractors and property brokers, or going into local and state politics. But many more wasted away the money they made, Bipin Kumar told us, dying as a common man. BK spoke of the latter as if it were a wasted opportunity, one that he was not fortunate enough to have himself.

Walk around Chakkarpur, BK said, and note how certain homes (*kotis*) look much nicer that the others surrounding it. They have nicely finished roofs and ornate verandas and balconies, conspicuous satellite dishes and often multiple cars parked out front. These houses belonged to farmers that sold their land and made a lot of money. The landowning caste in Chakkarpur comprised almost exclusively the *Ahir* community, which had been the dominant caste in this region since colonial times. According to BK *Ahirs* were a gentle lot, much softer than the *Jaats*, the other major landowning caste in the area that dominated regional politics in Gurgaon and Haryana for decades. *Ahirs* don't fight, he told us, although they do tend to discriminate against non-*Ahirs*, particularly when it came to adjudicating local disputes and competing claims over land. This last statement might have been a reference to his own experiences as an "outsider" in Chakkarpur. But for his part, by closely associating with *nambardar* Jeelay Singh, BK had hitched his wagon to a highly influential and powerful figure in Chakkarpur. We saw BK in several of the *nambardar*'s pictures hanging up in the latter's office. We also saw Jeelay Singh's other associate, Chandra Prakash, in some of these photos.

188 *Aura and trace in Gurgaon*

Chandra Prakash

When we met Chandra Prakash (hereafter CP) in the *nambardar*'s office on another day when we visited, he was reading a Hindi-language newspaper. The office had the aforementioned pictures and portraits hanging on the wall, as well as a clay *hookah* in the middle of the room, around which were arranged plastic chairs. CP was sitting and reading in one of these chairs.

Like Bipin Kumar, Chandra Prakash moved to Gurgaon to work for Maruti. But he came a bit later, in 1991. CP was a lawyer by training and worked for a number of years in the Gurgaon district court as an advocate. He had worked for the *nambardar* for a number of years too, advising him on legal matters. He told us that Jeelay Singh performed a lot of service (*sewa*) for the people in the village. For instance, he was president of the Residential Welfare Association of Saraswati Vihar, a middle-class residential colony that was directly adjacent to Chakkarpur. In fact Jeelay Singh lived just across the street from his office. The *nambardar*'s elder son, who was talking to some people at a nearby juice stand, owned and operated the Universal Gym that was across the street.

When we asked him what Chakkarpur was like when he first moved here, CP told us that besides Maruti Vihar and the *nambardar* market, there was not very much development. Maruti Vihar was built for middle-class workers, including accountants, engineers, teachers and the like. They paid in installments for apartments in multi-story buildings, totaling between 800–1200 units. Outside of this, however, the area was desolate when he first moved here.

> Yahan sare single-story makkan the. Yahan koi rahene wale nahi …. Iffco chowk se yahan tak siraf ekhi bus aya karte the.[21]

The area had a reputation for being dangerous after dark. The village of Chakkarpur was not developed back then, CP told us. There were small flats, concrete (*pucca*) and mud (*kutcha*) homes and the market you see in front of this place, which had a few chicken shops and vegetable stands but little else.

But people started moving here in the 1990s because it was close to Maruti and other industrial plants, and was increasingly surrounded by new middle- and upper-class residential neighborhoods, built by DLF and other private developers. By this time the village's land had already been sold and plotted for development. In the village, locals started to build upon the small single-story homes they owned in order to create rental units for migrating workers and families.

> Ye zamin to gaon ke hai.[22]

Like the *nambardar*, CP spoke in the present tense when referring to the village land that was now commodified and transformed into private real estate. Perhaps by speaking in this mode about this land, folks like Jeelay Singh and CP could produce a discursive place for themselves within this radically transformed landscape.

Kadam Singh's *jhuggi*

Down the road from the *nambardar* market, there was a crowded intersection with several restaurants, small shops and apartment buildings. There were also businesses of various kinds selling household items, electronic repair shops, grocery stores and the like. If one took the road straight through this intersection one came to an open area with flimsy looking slums and shacks on the left and right sides and slightly more built up tenement apartments on two floors in the rear. This area was unmapped, too new and too impermanent to merit a formal or even informal name. Residents we spoke to here called it simply a *jhuggi* (slum) that belonged to someone named Kadam Singh, who they referred to as *malik* (landlord). The *malik* owned various other plots of land in Chakkarpur but lived in a *koti* in DLF Phase I, which bordered the village on its eastern side.

Mathihur

Mathihur was a bit distant at first. This was perhaps to be expected. We were two young men with backpacks and sunglasses who clearly were not from the *jugghi*. I was taking pictures and capturing video with an iPhone that had a detachable wide-angle lens affixed to it while Praveen was walking around slightly less conspicuously with a small digital recorder in his hand.

We walked into the *jugghi* area, which constituted a courtyard of sorts, surrounded as it was on three sides by the makeshift structures in which the residents lived. In the rear was a two-story row of tenements, made of reinforced concrete and painted blue. Each unit had one bedroom with a front door and a

Figure 5.5 Jhuggi, Chakkarpur Village.
Source: Photo by author.

190   *Aura and trace in Gurgaon*

window. Clothes hung out to dry in front of each apartment. On the left and right sides the dwellings were little more than shacks and tents, made of loose brick and sheets of iron or plastic tarp. The grounds were of dirt and mud, with puddles and deep tire-tracks marking the recent occurrence of rain. There was a great deal of debris and the scattered possessions of the thirty or so families that lived there. Several young children were playing in the clearing, running around without shoes or sandals and climbing on the various tables, chairs, carts and rickshaws that were strewn about. There were also three cars lined up on the left side of the space. Two were small white Maruti sedans and one was a Tata Innova, a larger four-wheel drive truck. Mathihur was standing next to one of the cars, talking to another man, when we entered the scene.

Malda ke aadmi aur aloo sab jage milega.[23]

Mathihur came to Chakkarpur with his wife Kohinoor a few years ago from Malda, a district in West Bengal on the border of India and Bangladesh. Mathihur identified as Bengali. The reason why they landed up in Chakkarpur was that they knew some people from their village that came here. When Mathihur and Kohinoor first arrived, they stayed with these people for about two months before moving into their own place here in the *jugghi*.

They paid Rs3500 per month to rent a small one-room. One couldn't find cheaper rent than this in Chakkarpur, Mathihur told us. Other places around the area went for Rs5000–6000 for one room, with extra for electricity and water. For working-class people, he said, there were not too many places to live. One could not find a place in Sushant Lok, DLF City or other high-end neighborhoods in Gurgaon. There *kotis* and plotted residences went for Rs20,000 per month. In Chakkarpur it was cheaper, Rs10,000–12,000 for one floor of a flat. But that was well out of range for Mathihur.

For work, Mathihur was a transporter and ran a delivery service, moving fridges, coolers, ACs and the like from shops that hired him in Chakkarpur to homes all over the town. "Hum to pochayenge,"[24] he assured us, even a heavy fridge that needed to be moved up a few flights of stairs. He and Kohinoor had four children, two older boys and two younger girls. Kohinoor worked as a cleaner and domestic maid, earning Rs5000–7000 per month working in Sarasvati Vihar. They managed to save money each month. That's why they left the village in the first place, Mathihur said. If they spent all the money they earned, then why would they leave the village? He told us he sent money back to his sister in Malda every month.

Kamai teek hai, agar kam karne wale hai.[25]

The two boys worked with their father as well as in an office, doing cleaning work and providing services for professionals (such as supplying *chai* [tea] or *pani* [water]). The girls were younger, in 5th and 8th class, but the older one was soon to drop out of school for work.

Gaon jab chodke paise ke liye aye, to bachchon bhi kam karna padega.[26]

The village 191

We asked Mathihur if he liked living in Chakkarpur?

> Ye to apne desh todi hai? Apna gaon todi hai? Jab yahan makan leliya, to tabhi gaon samaj sakenga.[27]

Still, if he ended up staying here, we asked if he would get his children married in Chakkarpur or in Malda, to which he responded that they had no community here so marriage would be impossible.

> Gaon me sari rishtidar hai. Yahan har banda hai, ek to milega Bangi, ek milega Adivasi, ek milega Hindu, doosra milega Bihari, tisra milega UP wala, chotha milega Bengali, ab kis log ke saath karenge?[28]

In any case, the prospect of staying where they currently lived, in Kaddam Singh's *jugghi*, seemed a temporary one. It was already rumored that the land was sold off for the construction of a hospital. This would lead to their inevitable removal. Mathihur told us that the open area in the middle of the slum previously housed thirty to forty additional *jugghis*, but that these had been demolished by the *malik* before Mathihur arrived. There were only about thirty families remaining today.

Kadam Singh was already in the process of building PG housing in the four-to-five-story buildings right next to the *jugghi*. Who will stay in the upcoming PG housing, we asked? Mathihur's response suggested that he thought we were personally interested in the housing.

> Aap agar office me kaam karte, ab kahan rahene chatta? Is jugghi pe rahenge? Nahi rehe payge. To aap ke liye wo room teek hai.[29]

In our extended conversation (we spoke with Mathihur for close to an hour), one got the sense that it was inevitable that they would eventually have to leave their *jugghi*, and that this future horizon might be fast approaching. Mathihur seemed resigned to this fate and the underlying logic of the land market that informed it.

> Kya karega wo gaon wale? Agar paisa aya kya karega paise ke saath? Building karda kardo, bus ye kam hai, paise tho iss se araha hai.[30]

Much like Bipin Kumar, who spoke frequently about "the flow of money" in Gurgaon, from Mathihur's perspective, locals who owned land were fortunate to be able to make money without really working. They could easily make Rs30,000–40,000 per month just from renting to others. So what would be the point of working?

> Ab gaon wale jo hai, wo to paise wale hai.[31]

Mathihur then excused himself because he had to take his younger daughter to the doctor. She was sick.

Uttaranchal Hotel

Mahesh

>Chakkarpur to bahut bada hai. Aadmi chakkar ko jayega, wase wahan nikalgaye, ye charro taraf gumke, jaga ekhi ayegi.[32]

Mahesh operated a small restaurant called Uttaranchal Hotel. The signage displayed this name as well as the following information: "Veg and Non-Veg Thali/Tiffin Service Also Available." Inside were several tables and an open kitchen. The menu was written in Hindi on a white board hanging on a wall. It was divided between vegetarian and non-vegetarian entrees, and further distinguished by half versus full plates. He also served *paratha* and *rotis* to go along with the entrées. We met Mahesh in the middle of the afternoon, when the restaurant was empty. But we were hungry so we ordered food, and engaged in conversation while Mahesh cooked it.

True to his restaurant's name, Mahesh came from the mountainous state of Uttaranchal, from the northern district of Pithoragarh, which bordered both Nepal to the east and China to the north. He came to Gurgaon back in 2001 with his wife. Together they had a son in 10th class and a daughter in 4th. His wife stayed at home, which was located just down the street from the restaurant. She did house work, he told us.

Figure 5.6 Uttaranchal Hotel, Chakkarpur Village.
Source: Photo by author.

The village 193

Before opening up his own restaurant in 2008 in Chakkarpur, Mahesh was a supervising manager at the chain restaurant Haldi Ram from 2001 to 2007, working at locations in Sahara Mall and DT Mega Mall. He left because of the low pay, he said, earning just Rs9500 per month.

Mahesh bought his restaurant from a Rajasthani man. He made much more money operating his own business than working as a manager at Haldi Ram. When he first started with Uttaranchal Hotel, he used to make Rs2000 per day. But at its height in 2010 and 2011 he was earning Rs7000 in revenue daily. Of late, however, times had been much harder in Chakkarpur, if not Gurgaon as a whole. Construction had slowed down dramatically, and many call centers that were flourishing four or five years ago either reduced their operations or closed shop and re-located elsewhere. Malls too witnessed a steep decline, even on the heralded MG Road.

Yahan to katam hai market.[33]

The biggest problem here, Mahesh told us, was the inflated price of property and rent. Many offices moved elsewhere where rent was cheaper, places like Manesar and Sohna Road just a few kilometers from Chakkarpur and DLF City, which was now one of the most expensive parts of Gurgaon. High rental and property prices meant that margins were cut for businesses based here. Call centers didn't need fancy offices, Mahesh argued, and they didn't need to meet face-to-face. So they could locate elsewhere. They just needed a phone and computer, so they went where rent was cheaper.

So who stayed in this area? Mahesh told us that many who lived in Chakkarpur worked in the nearby malls and restaurants or the remaining call centers in the area. The poorer workers were Bihari or Bengali and lived in crowded *jugghis* that were constructed fast and cheap by contractors. The *maliks* put little effort into making these places nice or providing any amenities because they could rent them out without any problems.

A family with a couple of children needed at least Rs15,000 per month to survive in Chakkarpur, Mahesh told us. Five thousand for rent, another five for food and another five for other expenses. Yet despite the sluggish local economy, rent had not come down. Mahesh claimed that in the time he had lived in Chakkarpur, rent increased around 10 percent every year. Back in 2001 when he first moved to the area, he paid just Rs1500 per month for a small one-room apartment. Now such a room rented for at least Rs5000.

Something else that dramatically affected Chakkarpur, at least according to Mahesh, was the election of Narendra Modi in the central government. After the government changed, Mahesh said, black money disappeared from the local economy. This was in contrast to when Congress was in power, when there was a lot of black money coming in and thus a lot of investment happening in construction and business. That has now changed with the election of Modi. The black money, which drove informal economies like that of Chakkarpur's, has largely disappeared.

194 *Aura and trace in Gurgaon*

Yet Mahesh was optimistic about the future. Modi is planning for the long term, he told us, as we finished up our lunch of *daal, matar paneer* and *roti*. Other leaders planned for the short-term but Modi was thinking about the long term. I noticed a small *mandir* in the back of the restaurant with a statue of the Hindu god Ganesha. This was the elephant god, the remover of obstacles. There was burning incense next it.

Numbers 90 and 91

Street ethnography consists of improvised wanderings where one is pulled and directed by the varying ambiance of the built environment.[34] Something attracted us down a dirt road with wide and deep puddles that were difficult to navigate, especially on foot. After walking a few yards we came to a tall, well-appointed *koti* that was behind a fancy metal gate with high adjoining walls. There was a marble plate next to the gate that had the words "Yadav" engraved and below that "No. 90." Since Yadavs in Chakkarpur belonged to the *Ahir* caste, which at one time owned most of Chakkarpur's lands, we were quite certain that this home belonged to a (now) wealthy family of former farmers that sold its land and used the money to improve its large family home, which was a modern day *haveli* (mansion). The gate was left a bit ajar

Figure 5.7 Numbers 90 and 91, Chakkarpur Village.
Source: Photo by author.

so we decided to peak in and see if there was someone with whom we might be able to talk. Inside there was a nicely manicured front lawn, a swinging bench hanging from the ceiling in the veranda and concrete pillars. But no one was around so we decided to move on.

Hajera

Right next to No. 90 there was a structure with a very different spatial layout. There was no entry gate but instead a short concrete wall with an opening to a narrow alley. On either side of the alley were two floors of single-room units made cheaply of brick and concrete. The ground was made of laid bricks that were jaggedly and loosely arranged, so that one could see the mud ground

Figure 5.8 Number 91, Chakkarpur Village.
Source: Photo by author.

196 *Aura and trace in Gurgaon*

beneath. There were two cycle rickshaws parked inside the courtyard space in between the two rows of tenements. A water tank sat at the end opposite the entrance. Clotheslines were tied from one concrete structure to the next. There were a handful of small children running around. One held a pet white rabbit with red eyes. The children and the rabbit were playing on one of the parked rickshaws.

As we entered the space, hesitatingly at first, we were motioned to come further in by a middle-aged woman who appeared to be keeping one eye on the children and another eye on a meal she was in the process of cooking. She seemed eager to talk, and we sat with her for an hour while she finished cooking her meal and told us about her life in Chakkarpur.

Hajera moved to Chakkarpur with her husband back in 2001. They were from Dinajpur District in West Bengal, just a few kilometers from the border with Bangladesh. Hajera worked as a domestic maid, cleaning *kotis* in Chakkarpur, Sarasvati Vihar and Maruti Vihar. Every morning she cleaned three homes and one in the evening. Typically she cleaned dishes and clothes, and swept and mopped floors at the homes of middle- and upper-class residents. She earned Rs3000 per month in total. She said she could make more money but because of her son's disability she could not spend too much time away from home.

Door nahin jati hu main.[35]

Her son Raju was seventeen years old but had a mental disability, she told us. He required treatment but they could not afford it. Raju seemed a curious teen, following the conversation we were having with his mother in their apartment but often drifting away to play with the kids outside. Raju used to attend school and was doing fine until 2nd class, when some kids hit him badly and he didn't want to go back. After that he stayed at home.

At one point during out conversation with Hajera he started singing the alphabet song in English. He heard his mom talking about his schooling and the song must have popped into his head. He was mostly correct with the alphabet but confused the order of a few of the letters.

Hajera also had five daughters, four of whom had already been married off, as she put it. The youngest one was unmarried and going to school. She was thirteen.

Four people stayed in their small one-bedroom apartment, which was packed with clothes, kitchen supplies and utensils, suitcases, a small TV and radio. Her daughter, son and husband all slept on the bed that took up the vast majority of the space in their room.

Hajera's husband was not home when we visited. He operated an auto-rickshaw that he rented from someone. He had to park it outside because if he parked it inside the *malik* would demand more money each month, Rs250 extra.

Their family had lived in the small room at No. 91 for three years. There was an empty room next to theirs but it seemed that all the others (perhaps twenty in total) were occupied.

The *malik* was fine if you paid rent on time, Hajera told us. But he could be quite brutal if you were late with the money. He frequently harassed and threatened to expel delinquent tenants, most of whom were Biharis and Bengalis. Many of the men in the area drank in the evenings, Hajera said, but not her husband. He didn't drink or smoke, nor did he eat out. He was a good man.

Hajera showed us her Aadhaar (unique identification) card, which she could use to vote.[36] She also had an LPG ration card for the gas cylinder she was using to cook.

At No. 91 there were three toilets that twenty families shared. Two were on the first floor upstairs and one was on the ground floor. Water was delivered in the large black tank in the middle of the loose brick courtyard that divided the two rows of tenements. This tank was filled up every week, Hajera said. Usually there was no problem with water, but in the summer months there were shortages and they would have to wait up to a month for someone to come and fill up the tank. In such instances they had to get water from other tanks in the neighborhood, if people were generous enough to share with them.

Living in Chakkarpur was getting more expensive every year, Hajera said.

Kamana pahle bahut tha, paisa tora bahut bache thi, abhi kuch nahi bachtha, karai bahut manga karliya.[37]

Rent was Rs1800 per month when they moved into No. 91 three years ago. Now it had climbed up to Rs2600. They had to pay extra, Rs200–400, for water and electricity. Meanwhile,

Rate nahin badtha. Bahut kaam wale aagaya humare jaise. Agar hum nahi karte kaam doosre log karenge. Wo bhi saste lag jaate hum se.[38]

Life seemed hard but Hajera was kind and most hospitable. She invited us to eat some of the food she had made. When we later asked her if she wanted to stay at No. 91, she replied with the kind of stark realism that I learned was typical of many working-class poor in Chakkarpur.

Hum log to kirai mai hai, aagar aaj yahan khali karte hai to hum doosre jage par jawenge.[39]

Chaupal

Walking past Hajera's tenement through a series of two-story brick buildings housing garages and shops on the ground floor and apartments above, we came to the historical core (*chaupal*) of the village. This was a relatively dense collection of old and crumbling *havelis*, or large, gated homes, made of red stones and brick, patched up in parts with mud. This area had cleaner roads and pathways than the others in Chakkarpur. The small open square in the center was made of bricks arranged in an artful pattern. There was space for gathering, sitting or just walking through.

198 *Aura and trace in Gurgaon*

Soiza

We met Soiza walking across the *chaupal*. He was with his cousin, who looked at least a few years younger than Soiza, who we learned was twenty-eight. The cousin had just moved to Chakkarpur the previous day to look for work. Soiza was taking him around the village looking for restaurants that were hiring workers. Soiza himself worked in a restaurant, but not in Chakkarpur. He worked at a chain restaurant on MG Road and figured he might know of a few places in the village or on MG Road that were looking for someone to hire.

Soiza invited us up to take a look at his apartment, which was on the third floor of a building with open hallways leading to the front door of each unit. Soiza's apartment was relatively sparse and neat. The room was about twice the size as Hajera's in No. 91. But Soiza's apartment was also in a building made of concrete and brick, whereas Hajera's was a small and narrow structure that was only slightly more built up than the *jugghi*'s of Kaddam Singh. Soiza was much younger than Hajera, more educated, and thereby more upwardly mobile. He could speak English, which qualified him to work in higher-end restaurants in Gurgaon, including fast food chains. Like Hajera, Soiza had migrated from eastern India, but not West Bengal. He came from the northeastern state of Manipur, along with his wife and his wife's sister. Migrants from northeastern states were often considered foreigners by locals. Sometimes Soiza heard people call him and his wife "Chinks" to their face. Many assumed they were from Nepal.

Sometimes Soiza experienced trouble with locals here in Chakkarpur. In fact, he only moved to Chakkarpur after being forced to leave Nathupur, another village just a few kilometers away. Nathupur was too rough of a place, he said, full of aggressive locals and Bihari migrants. He told the story of how one day, his sister-in-law was walking home from work and saw some men in *dhotis* washing themselves on the street out in the open. Feeling offended at the sight she informed Soiza, who went down to confront the men and ask that they stop washing themselves in public. Taking offense to this request, the locals beat him badly, with one of the men hitting Soiza on the back of the head with a metal pipe, causing an injury that required emergency treatment in the hospital. "I was in the newspaper," Soiza said, with ironic pride. But after that incident it was clear that they would have to move. Chakkarpur was comparatively more peaceful, he said.

I asked him if the police punished those who beat him. He said he didn't know.

But I am a Christian, and so I forgive them.

On the wall near the front door of their single-room apartment there was a framed painting of baby Jesus and the mother Mary. Above it was a sign made out of cloth with the following text embroidered into the fabric: "Don't be perfect, be true."

Amma

On one of the last days of our street ethnography in Chakkarpur, we re-visited the *chaupal* area in the hopes of talking to someone who might tell us how old the village was, or at least how old the *havelis* here were, and to whom they belonged. We were fortunate to meet three older women sitting outside their house on wooden chairs. They were smoking *hookah* between the crumbling architecture on one side, and refurbished homes and apartment buildings on the other. They had a large cow tied to one of the pillars of the *haveli*. The rustic scene could have been from half a century earlier if not for the untimely presence of a white car next to the sitting women. Quite fittingly, it was a Maruti.

The women seemed amused by the idea of our research project. But they invited us to sit with them and talk, even offering us *chai*. Just as we were about to begin recording, however, another woman, much older than the rest, walked out and started yelling at us.

> Tum log kya kar rahe hai?! Jao yahan se![40]

This was Amma, by far the oldest resident we spoke with in Chakkarpur during the course of our month-long street ethnography. She was angry that we were

Figure 5.9 Old *haveli* and cow, Chakkarpur Village.
Source: Photo by author.

200 *Aura and trace in Gurgaon*

taking photos of women smoking *hookah*. She claimed that we would bring shame to these women and the village by photographing them, especially if the pictures ended up in the newspaper or TV. Amma's friends tried to calm her, explaining that we were students from Delhi that had come to Chakkarpur for historical research, to see how the village has changed over time. Soon she joined the circle and told us about her life in the village. The four women spoke jointly, often completing each other's sentences or adding details to what others said. But Amma did most of the talking.

These *havelis* were very old, she told us. Many were empty now. They belonged to *Ahirs*, the dominant caste in Chakkarpur. She pointed to another *haveli* just down the road and several others inside the village—all belonging to *Ahirs*. These structures were here long before Amma came to Chakkarpur more than sixty years ago, following her marriage to her husband. In those times this area was surrounded by jungle. Jackals used to howl at night. It was frightening at first. She recounted a popular rumor of *lakkad bagha* (cougar) roaming the area after dark. Amma and her family were afraid that the cougar would take away their younger children so they would stay awake the whole night.

Chakkarpur really started to change after Maruti moved here, Amma recalled, about thirty years back. Most of the land belonged to *Ahirs*, but people of all different castes lived on the other side of the village—*Chamaars*, *Chuddei* (both lower castes), barbers, weavers, *dhobi* (washermen), *Brahmans* (upper castes). Actually, she said, there were more *Chamaars* than *Ahirs* in Chakkarpur, but the latter were historically dominant.

Today there is no land left—not much, Amma lamented. A few families might have still held on to one acre here or a half-acre there. But by and large their elders (referring to the established families in the village) had sold all the land. And the land was sold very cheap—Rs39,000 per acre. "We have been robbed—we have been victims of the government's heavy handedness," Amma alleged and the other women agreed. Now the land was worth more than Rs1 *crore*, but there was no land left to sell.[41]

All that was left were these old dilapidated buildings. Amma claimed that the *havelis* were once well made with heavy stones and thick foundation walls. But now they lived in *pucca* houses, where it was difficult to adjust. She pointed to the newer *kotis* across from the crumbling *haveli* to which the cow was tied. She preferred the older *kutcha* homes because the family knew how to take care of repairs themselves. Now with *pucca* homes made out of reinforced concrete and clay bricks, they could not handle these materials and so they went unrepaired.

We asked *Amma* if the land around Chakkarpur was at one time fertile. She told us emphatically that it was. They had very robust crops—*jawaar* (sorghum), *baajra*, wheat, *mauth*, *moong daal*, *urad daal*, *masoor daal*, *gajjar*, *mooli*, peanuts, sugarcane. Before, Amma said, they used to roam the area collecting wood or fodder for animals. They used to have a lot of cattle, mostly buffalo. But these livestock had gradually disappeared with the land. The authorities recently had closed the dairies in the village. They now had only one cow, which was tied by a rope to the *haveli*. They kept this cow for their own dairy needs.

They did not like the processed milk in a pouch that was sold in the market. They still liked to have their own milk.

We asked *Amma* how old she was. She laughed: "maybe 100 years old—definitely more than seventy." We pressed her for a more exact age. We asked her if she could recall significant historical events that she lived through. After some time she remembered that she was around seven years old at the time of India's independence. So that put her at about seventy-five years of age. She was married at a young age. Her husband, a native of *Chakkarpur*, died three years back. He was about twenty years older than Amma.

So how has Chakkarpur changed over the years, we asked? Everything has changed, Amma claimed. For one thing, there were more renters now than owners. A lot of Bengalis had moved in. They were a problem—they had big families (ten members or more) and they fought and argued a lot. She told us that Bengalis were very secretive and did not give information about their neighbors to the authorities. When challenged, Amma claimed, they all tended to become united. Just recently there was the murder of a woman in one of their neighborhoods but the police were unable to find the criminal. Before there used to be mostly Biharis and Rajasthanis in Chakkarpur, Amma recalled. Now the character of the village had completely changed—there were more Bengalis than the original residents, most of whom had moved out to the city. Only a few like them remained here today.

The post-rural village

In this chapter I have tried to demonstrate how access to the "ordinary" and the "everyday" potentially restores perception to geohistorical processes that are obscured from the perspective of what we earlier called Geohistory 1.[42] Geohistory 1 is that of the state and capital, they are processes that are Euro-centric in two related senses: as universalizing discourses that position Europe as the theoretical subject of history, and as globalizing processes that positioned Euro-America as centers of imperialism, benefiting materially from exploitative trade/investment relations with colonial outposts. Unlike Geohistory 1s, which are universalizing and globalizing discourses, explorations of everyday life in places like Chakkarpur are not meant to be exhaustive. Nor do they collectively represent reality "as it is." Rather, these studies are transductive, to use Lefebvre's neologism. Transductions move between the actual and the virtual, underlining the limitations of dominant conceptions of the urban while seeking to open up space for investigations of new kinds of urban phenomena, without fully subsuming them into existing frameworks of the state and capital.

As an experimental methodology for studying changing urban life at multiple scales, street ethnography seeks to restore perception not to an "actual" urban reality that pre-exists the audio-visual assemblage, but rather to a critical image of thought rendered by the virtual assemblage itself. This image is not that of an "authentic" Geohistory 2 as an alternative urban assemblage. Rather, Geohistory 2s are performative, they emerge as both a reproduction (of Geohistory 1) and a

202   *Aura and trace in Gurgaon*

rupture, forcing us to re-think Geohistory 1 and its affective capacities in our everyday political lives, altering us to how alternative experiences of changing urban life silently co-exist with dominant far order projections in the near order of the city.

Three sets of far order–near order relations captured my attention in the composite journey through Chakkarpur. The first far order was the one diagramed in the previous chapter, the partnership between DLF and HUDA, its public–private vision for Gurgaon as Millennium City. Chakkarpur Village resides in the middle of Phase II of DLF City in New Gurgaon, that is, right next to some of the most expensive real estate in this already elite suburban satellite town. This proximity means that residents in Chakkarpur often worked in the nearby office buildings (as janitors or security guards), gated residential communities (as domestic servants, caretakers, gardeners, cooks, public cleaners or security guards) and shopping malls (as retail service workers, marketing agents, restaurant workers or, again, security guards). The proximity of DLF City and Chakkarpur was actually the cause of its socio-economic distance from the elite city. For this proximity not only attracted many workers to the area, raising the supply of labor and bringing down average wages, but it also created a shortage of housing in a city where almost all of the new formal housing is for the rich. Thus rental prices have increased dramatically, as the narratives of Manu, Ashish, Bipin Kumar, Mahesh, Mathihur and Hajera all corroborate in various ways. Meanwhile, the downward pressure on wages meant that less money was left over for other necessities after paying rent, leading to increasing hardship on already low-income, low-consuming families. Insofar as this local wage and rental economy was shaped by the larger speculative ecology of Gurgaon, the latter articulated a far order that projected socio-economic realities, relations and rhythms onto the near order of the village.

A second far order that was projected from a distance in Chakkarpur was more geographically and temporally remote than DLF and HUDA. It was "home villages" from where many of the working-class families that now lived in Chakkarpur originally came. For Bengalis like Ashish, Hajera and Mathihur, and for other residents from states like Bihar and Uttar Pradesh, the home village continued to exert an important presence in everyday life. This was not just an abstract space of memory, but a site of regular return (for many seasonal migrants that traveled east for farm work and then came back to Chakkarpur after the cultivation season was over). The home village was also where many workers sent home portions of their income, sacrificing their present urban existence for a temporally and spatially removed purpose. For someone like Mathihur, for instance, the fact that Chakkarpur was so socially heterogeneous only confirmed that his ultimate locus in life was Malda, his home district in West Bengal. That was where he imagined he'd get his children married, and perhaps where he too would one day return after he was finished working in Gurgaon.

The imagined distance and proximity of the "home" village was also manifest in the near order of the village through the construction of community and identity. Notwithstanding the social heterogeneity of Chakkarpur, with its diverse array of ethnic groups, caste communities and social classes, blocks of apartment buildings were in general separated by relatively homogeneous micro-communities, usually based on caste or ethnicity. So that Bengalis lived here and Biharis there, Punjabis on this side of the street and local *Ahirs* on the other. These closely assembled bodies, brought together by virtue of their imagined and practiced belonging to a community of identity, could also, quite predictably, lead to violence. Just as this book was being sent for publication my research partner Praveen sent me a story from Chakkarpur.[43]

On August 15, 2016 a "friendly" sporting competition amongst local youth was hosted in the village. The competing teams represented different caste communities, one comprised of *Chamaar* and *Valmiki* communities (both part of Dalit or untouchable castes) and the other the powerful Yadav or *Ahir* community. The latter, as we saw in this chapter and the previous one, traditionally owned most of the land in and around Chakkarpur, selling it to DLF in the 1980s and preserving their economic and political power in "post-rural" Gurgaon. That day the Dalits were winning the competition when local men from the *Ahir* community began taunting and shouting insults at the Dalit youth. A fight ensued and several of the young Yadav men were seriously injured and taken to a nearby hospital. For the Dalits interviewed in the article they alleged that these kinds of caste conflicts, especially intimidation and violence from upper castes, were common and had a long history in Chakkarpur. Local politicians, representing the village in Gurgaon's municipal council, downplayed the importance of caste. Sunil Yadav, a local councilor from the dominant *Ahir* caste himself, claimed that the incident had nothing to do with caste:

> The argument happened like it does in any game played by youngsters, and it just went a little overboard. Some people may try to give it a caste angle but there is nothing like that. This is a peaceful village and will continue to be one.

Notes

1 Ashis Nandy, *An Ambiguous Journey to the City* (Oxford: Oxford University Press, 2001).
2 "Street Ethnography and Rhythmanalysis: Chakkarpur Gurgaon," Directed and edited by Rohan Kalyan (2015) can be viewed here: https://vimeo.com/128682979.
3 Government of India, Ministry of Home Affairs, Office of the Registrar General and Consensus Commissioner. "2011 Census of India," accessed April 12, 2015. www.censusindia.gov.in/2011census/population_enumeration.html.
4 One notable exception is V. Narain, "Growing city, shrinking hinterland: Land acquisition, transition and conflict in peri-urban Gurgaon, India." *Environment and Urbanization* 21.2 (2009), 501–512.
5 K. P. Singh, *Whatever the Odds* (London: HarperCollins, 2011), 100.
6 See Anita Soni, "Urban conquest of outer Delhi," in Veronique Dupont, Emma Tarlo and Denis Vidal (eds) *Delhi: Urban Space and Human Destinies* (Delhi: Manohar, 2000), 75–94.
7 My translation: "I study and I also work here." All subsequent translations are mine from recorded interviews conducted in March 2015 in Chakkarpur, Gurgaon.

204 *Aura and trace in Gurgaon*

8 "Without English there are no opportunities for growth in any career line."

9 "I like sales jobs because you get to meet and talk to people, which I enjoy."

10 I don't want to buy a place in Gurgaon. This is certain. Gurgaon is a dirty place. First of all, it is too expensive. Second, there isn't anything special about this city. It's not a good environment, especially if you come out around nine or ten in the evening. Then you will see. The locals have made it a habit to harass people who are not originally from here. Just look at the plight of people who come from Bihar or UP.

11 "I relax at night."

12 "Yesterday there was a party in the office."

13 S. R Ahlawat and Neerja Ahlawat, "On the floor and behind the veil: The excluded in the Panchayati Raj in Haryana," in B. S. Baviskar and George Matthew (eds) *Inclusion and Exclusion in Local Governance: Field Studies from Rural India* (New Delhi: Sage Publications India, 2009), 137.

14 "The land from here until Sahara Mall is ours."

15 "Of course I too am an outsider!"

16 "In this time changes have come.... I have seen how everything here has changed."

17 "I also used to go to Delhi for fun!"

18 "Here whatever line of work you are in, there is a lot of money flowing in."

19 "There is nobody here who isn't making some money."

20 "These guys (farmers that sold their land) have won the big lottery."

21 "Here there were only single-story apartments. No one really wanted to stay here. From IFFCO circle to here only one bus would come daily."

22 "This land belongs to the village."

23 "People from Malda are as common as potatoes."

24 "We can deliver anything."

25 "The money is good here if you are willing to work for it."

26 "If we left our village to earn some money here, then it only makes sense that our children too will need to earn."

27 "This is not our country, nor it is our village. If we someday buy an apartment here (instead of renting), then we will understand this place as home."

28 In our village we have all of our relations [i.e., people in the same caste/religious group for marriage]. Here there are too many different kinds of people. You will meet one Bengali, one tribal, one Hindu, another Bihari, a third UP person, a fourth Bengali. But with whom will you arrange a marriage?"

29 "If you want to work in an office, where will you stay? Will you stay in a slum like this? No, you won't be able to stay here. So for you a PG room will suffice."

30 "What will the villagers do with all the money they are getting [from selling land or renting space]? They will make buildings. This is the only work here. That is how the money is made."

31 "The villagers are the people with money."

32 "Chakkarpur is a big circle. They say that if you walk around, no matter how far you go, you will always end up in the same place."

33 "Here the market is finished."

34 In this sense street ethnography shares a family resemblance with what Guy Debord called *derive*, which he also defined as a mode of urban wandering in which one was pushed and pulled by the psycho-geographic variations of the built environment. Guy Debord, "Theory of the derive," in Ken Knabb (ed.) *Situationist International Anthology* (Berkeley, CA: Bureau of Public Secrets, 1981), 50–54.

35 "I don't go very far for work."

36 For more on Aadhaar from the state's perspective, see Nandan Nilekani, "Building a foundation for better health: The role of the Aadhaar number." *National Medical*

Journal of India 24.3 (2011), 133–135. For a more critical take, see Jean Drèze, "Unique facility, or recipe for trouble." *The Hindu*, November 25, 2010.
37 "Before we used to earn enough money. We could save a little bit each month. Now the money all goes towards rent."
38 "Wages do not go up. There are many people who come here looking for the same kind of work. And they can do it cheaper than I can."
39 "We are just renters. If they want to empty this plot out someday, we will be forced to look for another place."
40 "What are you people doing here? Leave at once!"
41 One *crore* = ten million.
42 See Introduction, "Image 6."
43 Sakshidayal, "As Dalits start winning, 'friendly' Kabadi match turns violent." *Indian Express*, August 16, 2016, accessed August 18, 2016, http://epaper.indianexpress. com/c/12532560.

Bibliography

Ahlawat, S. R and Neerja Ahlawat. "On the floor and behind the veil: The excluded in the Panchayati Raj in Haryana," in B. S. Baviskar and George Matthew (eds) *Inclusion and Exclusion in Local Governance: Field Studies from Rural India*. New Delhi: Sage Publications India, 2009: 137–168.

Debord, Guy. "Theory of the derive," in Ken Knabb (ed.) *Situationist International Anthology*. Berkeley, CA: Bureau of Public Secrets, 1981: 50–54.

Drèze, Jean. "Unique facility, or recipe for trouble." *The Hindu*, November 25, 2010.

Government of India, Ministry of Home Affairs, Office of the Registrar General and Consensus Commissioner. "2011 Census of India," accessed April 12, 2015, www. censusindia.gov.in/2011census/population_enumeration.html.

Lefebvre, Henri. *The Urban Revolution*. Minneapolis, MN: University of Minnesota Press, 2003.

Martin, Reinhold and Kadambari Baxi. *Multi-national City: Architectural Itineraries*. Barcelona, Actar, 2007.

Nandy, Ashis. *An Ambiguous Journey to the City: The Village and other Odd Ruins of the Self in the Indian Imagination*. Oxford: Oxford University Press, 2001.

Narain, V. "Growing city, shrinking hinterland: Land acquisition, transition and conflict in peri-urban Gurgaon, India." *Environment and Urbanization* 21.2 (2009): 501–512.

Nilekani, Nandan. "Building a foundation for better health: The role of the Aadhaar number." *National Medical Journal of India* 24.3 (2011): 133–135.

Sakshidayal. "As Dalits start winning, 'friendly' Kabadi match turns violent." *Indian Express*, August 16, 2016, accessed August 18, 2016, http://epaper.indianexpress. com/c/12532560.

Sassen, Saskia. "Why cities matter." *Catalogue of the 10th International Architecture Exhibition, Venice Biennale* (2006): 26–51.

Singh, K. P. *Whatever the Odds*. London: HarperCollins, 2011.

Soni, Anita. "Urban conquest of outer Delhi," in Veronique Dupont, Emma Tarlo and Denis Vidal (eds) *Delhi: Urban Space and Human Destinies* (Delhi: Manohar, 2000): 75–94.

Conclusion
Partitioned communities of sense

"The aim is to engage political thought without closing the question of 'the political.'"

Michael J. Shapiro, *Cinematic Political Thought*

As a virtual city, *Neo* Delhi can be contrasted with the actual cities normally imagined in contemporary urban studies. Rather than posing the question, what *is Neo* Delhi? I ask the following: what is possible at the level of urban experience and changing urban life? The question is not what is the city as such, but rather what kind of city is possible, what kind of urban experience is imaginable? And in what ways does the virtual city structure our interpretations of the actual one? How do our ideas of what is possible shape, often invisibly and imperceptibly (as a haunting), our representations of what is actual? How is the material city always already structured by the imagined one? And what is the politics of this haunted structure?

The preceding chapters were presented as trans-disciplinary methodological interventions designed to study changing urban life in *Neo* Delhi. I employed visual ethnography, media archival research and theoretical argumentation in order to construct my interventions. In "concluding" a set of experimental studies such as those assembled here and on neodelhi.net, I wanted to underline the speculative nature of such a set of investigations. Perhaps they are less valuable in terms of what they disclose about the essential nature of "the political" than in how they engage in open-ended explorations of urban politics that might help us re-imagine the possibilities of changing urban life. In this conclusion, I set out one further speculation, connecting (1) the relations of distance and proximity that I explored through visual ethnography and media archival research in *Neo* Delhi and (2) the theoretical concept of sensible milieu, or the esthetically partitioned communities of sense that invisibly structure political life in cities and other urbanizing spaces across the Global South.[1]

The concept of communities of sense, or sensible milieu, comes from the Prussian philosopher Immanuel Kant. In his *Critique of Judgment* Kant argued for a philosophy of esthetic experience that could inform judgments that were both subjective (i.e., based purely on sensory perception and not cognition) and

Conclusion 207

universal (i.e., whereby everyone could nevertheless agree upon some work of art's "objective" beauty, notwithstanding our lack of unmediated access to the "thing-in-itself"). This presumed subjective necessity of esthetic judgment, its guarantee of universal public communicability, its quasi-objectivity, was tied to Kant's late eighteenth-century imperial political imaginary. This becomes clear not so much in the *Critique of Judgment* (although it is strongly suggested in Kant's analytic of the sublime), but in another work: *Perpetual Peace*.[2] As Michael Shapiro has brilliantly shown, Kant saw his own "European" moral culture as a universalizing force pointing in the direction of cosmopolitan society and a world government by consent.[3] Liberal world government was underpinned, in Kant, by the universality of common sense that was ultimately sutured together through an appeal to universal moral reason. For this was how Kant finally guaranteed esthetic judgment's universal communicability. The fact that subjects could universally agree on experiences of the beautiful as surely as they could agree on public ideas of moral goodness and virtue is what connected Kant's global imperial politics with his esthetics of sensory perception. Reading the "signs of the times" from his own locality in post-Enlightenment Europe, Kant presupposes that his moral cultural training begets a universal community of sense, emboldening the prognostication of global cosmopolitan governance, or perpetual peace, in the future to come.

Post-Kantian thinkers have taken Kant's proposition of a community of sense, while taking heed of the historical horrors of European domination in most of the world, and have effectively pluralized it.[4] They have done so by replacing subjective necessity, which is bound up in a universalizing logic of common sense apprehension, with subjective contingency, which looks not only at multiple communities of sense within a city or urbanizing space, but also considers the uncommon sense that passes through them all, the latter attaining the ontological status of virtual. Thus, contingent, fluid, relational communities of sense co-exist and shape one another in the virtual city. This complex co-existence and inter-relation is nowhere else more intense than in the contemporary postcolonial city, where multiple, overlapping, yet often times mutually unintelligible communities of sense come into contact and everyday inter-mediation. My aim in this book has been to document, analyze and theorize from these specifically urban encounters and ask: what do *Neo* Delhi's possibilities portend for our understandings and theorizations of urban politics?

In Chapter 1 on the urban, I described an urban elite/middle class in Delhi that was increasingly invested in an ongoing process of globalization in and through cities. Through this investment in the aura of a new and increasingly urbanized and globally recognizable "India," this middle class was also haunted by the old, provincial, socialist, bureaucratic past of the Nehruvian postcolonial nation. This hauntology was publically communicated in the media debacle and aftermath of the Commonwealth Games from 2008 to 2010, which I followed both in India and from the U.S. But the communities of sense in contention here were not just the mobilized elites and middle classes versus inefficient bureaucrats like Lalit Bhanot who "brought shame" to the economically renewed nation. More so it

208 *Conclusion*

was between varied elites that could effortlessly inhabit new spaces of access and mobility, and working-class residents that lived in slums and working-class tenements, the latter of whom were required to disappear in order for new spaces of elite consumption and global recognizability to materialize, to become actual.

Virtual cities are characterized by inter-temporal, and often contending communities of sense: the state and big capital, on the one hand, and urban subalterns who are as under-represented within the state as they are distanced from dominant elite and middle-class imaginaries of "normative" political community. In Chapter 2 I described the neighborhood of Shadipur and the slum community of Kathputli Colony, a community of performance artists and street-smart cultural survivors. My focus was on the distance between the urban elite and subaltern classes, particularly as it was explored in the film *Tomorrow We Disappear*. This innovative documentary dramatized the encounter between the far order of the state and the near order of the slum. Through an exploration of differently positioned esthetic subjects whose movements brought different sensible milieu into a common (urban *qua* cinematic) space of encounter, we saw how gender, class, ethnic and other forms of socio-cultural division mediated alternative experiences of changing urban life, presenting a variety of strategies and tactics of spatial negotiation.

In an era of globalization, virtual postcolonial cities are sites of mediated relations of proximity and distance between different social groups and inter-temporal spaces. In the district of Gurgaon, just to the south of New Delhi, we saw distancing at proximity through state laws regarding land acquisition and collusions with private real estate developers. In this rapidly urbanizing, yet intensely variegated economic space, we also witnessed the increasing distance between New Gurgaon and Old Gurgaon. This history of transition through distanciation (in many ways a reiteration of New Delhi and Old Delhi) was presented in Chapter 3. Yet the urban projection of a far order—Gurgaon as Millennium City—was haunted by the lingering presence of the older, rural district, as well as the emergence of new unintended "villages" of the "informal working class." The analysis revealed multiple communities of sense that contended over the "global" intelligibility of Gurgaon's fragmented and unevenly urbanized landscape.

In elite enclave communities within the newly developed parts of Gurgaon, the hetero-normative middle-class resident assumed an historical role as cultural and political mediator between tradition and modernity, between the pre-modern native society and the modern West. But as we saw in Chapter 4, this class remained haunted by problems that were structural to their own social geography. In the working-class village of Chakkarpur, in the very shadows of new elite skyscrapers and condominium towers, but hidden from "public" visibility, urban subalterns hustled to survive in economically volatile times, fighting inflationary rents and precarious employment. Having moved recently and settled in Gurgaon, they formed micro-communities of sense with those who spoke their language, shared their ancestors and cultural sensibility. Meanwhile, native elites in the urbanized village, besieged by heterogeneous communities of sense on all sides, conjured a utopian pre-developmental past in the relatively privileged spaces they inhabited in the present.

Conclusion 209

To study these multiple, often contending communities of sense, I found an urban depth of field perspective to be useful as a trans-disciplinary concept-methodology. Such a perspective placed into analytic focus shifting relations of distance and proximity at multiple scales of changing urban life. The urban depth of field critically framed an understanding of spatio-temporal multiplicity and plural normative horizons, showing multiple histories, multiple senses of the present and multiple pathways into the future. This was because the unbridled depth of field that opened up between near and far orders in the various milieu explored in this book was not merely spatial, but temporal. Such a framing is an investment in a kind of politics that remains open to different experiences of changing life and that demands just accounting from the dominant institutions that disproportionately engineer socio-spatial transformation to fit their specific interests and little more. To invest in such a politicized framing of the post-colonial city is to recognize the limits of modern conceptions of the political as the nexus of liberal democracy and market economics, both mediated by the fetishized image of the subject as naturalized (and de-politicized) *individual* and little more. It is to invest in an understanding of subjects as historically and geographically produced and of politics as structured and haunted by multiple communities of sense.

The legacy of colonialism and the historical violence of underdevelopment continue to define the terrain of "global" political sense-making in postcolonial cities like Delhi. This sensibility is anything but "common," "shared," or "universal," no more in Delhi, India than in Newark, New Jersey. It is plainly futile and politically imperialistic to expect the emergence of a planetary common sense (like Kant did) before first recognizing the multiplicities of sensible milieus that may (or may not) share inter-subjective commonalities. The city is both laboratory and stage.

Notes

1 In contrast to the critiques of mainstream urbanists like Storper and Scott (see Introduction, "Image 3"), I understand the term Global South less in strictly geographical terms and more in terms of an inter-temporal globality. The Global South names the dark side of the planet, a globality that is studied and experienced and imagined through the experience of historical oppression, exclusion, marginalization or extermination.

2 Immanuel Kant, *Critique of judgment*, trans. Werner S. Pluhar (New York: Hackett, 1987). See also Immanuel Kant, *Perpetual Peace and Other Essays: On Politics, History, and Morals*, New York: Hackett, 1983.

3 Michael J. Shapiro, *Cinematic Political Thought: Narrating Race, Gender, and Nation* (New York: New York University Press, 1999). See also Michael J. Shapiro, "The sublime today: Re-partitioning the global sensible." *Millennium: Journal of International Studies* 34.3 (2006), 657–681.

4 Shapiro, "The sublime today."

Index

Page numbers in *italics* denote tables, those in **bold** denote figures.

Aam Aadmi (Common Man) Party 66, 170
abstract labor concept 21–2
activism, elite 150–2, 158–65, 166–70
Adiga, Aravind 72n91, 149
Ahir community 187, 194, 200, 203
Ahuja, Sanjeev 154, 167
Ambience Mall, Gurgaon **7**
Amin, Ash 11–12
Amma (Chakkarpur resident) 199–201
Ansals 126, 131, 135
Arabtec Construction LLC 85
Aristotle 17
Arora, Kishore 167–70
Ashish (Chakkarpur resident) xii, 181–3
Asian Games (1982) 44–5, 62
assemblage urbanism 15–18, 22–3
aura 149–50
automotive industry 124, 153–4, 185, 186, 188, 200

Baviskar, Amita 62–3, 66
Beijing Olympic Games (2008) 61
Benjamin, Walter 149–50
Bersani, Leo 93
Bhandari, Laveesh 131, 135
Bhanot, Lalit 47, 48, 63–4
Bharatiya Janata Party 169, 170
Bhat, Puran 76, 81, 89, 91, 94–5, 96–7
Bhatt, Kailash 79–80, 86, 87
Bollywood films 107
Bombay, Victorian 52–3
BPO Watch India 151
Brayne, Frank L. 122
Brenner, Neil 8–9, 10, 12, 17–18
British colonial rule: Delhi 27, 51–5, 82; Gurgaon 121–2, 125; and middle classes 154–7

Cairo 27
capitalism 15, 19, 21–2; *see also* global financial crisis; neoliberal reforms; neoliberalism
Cartesian ideas of space 14
caste conflicts 203
Castells, Manuel 6
Chakkarpur Village 175–203; Chakkarpur Village Road 181–3, **182**; Chaupal xii, **9**, 197–201, **199**; *jhuggi* xii, 189–91, **189**; maps xi, xii; MG Road 176, 179–81; MG Road Metro Station xii, **176**, **178**, 179; *nambardar* market xii, 183–8, **184**; Numbers 90 and 91 xii, 194–7, **194**, **195**; panorama of **26**; Uttaranchal Hotel xii, 192–4, **192**
Chakrabarty, Dipesh 21–2, 23
Chamaar community 203
Chatterjee, Partha 52, 58–9, 82, 154–5
Chaupal, Chakkarpur Village xii, **9**, 197–201, **199**
Chess Players, The (1977) 156–7
China 61
cinema, depth of field shots 24–5, 94–5
Citizen Kane (1941) 24–5
cleanliness standards 47, 63–4
colonial city 51–4
colonial rule *see* British colonial rule
Commonwealth Games (2010) xi, 43, 44–8, **46**, 61–4, 65, 66–7
communities of sense 206–9
compulsory land acquisition, Gurgaon 126, 132, 133–4, 135
conceived spaces 13, 14
Congress Party 66, 71n82, 83
Contempt (1963) 93
Cyber City, Gurgaon xi, 134, 148–50

Index 211

Dalits 203
Datta, Abhijit 56, 57
DDA *see* Delhi Development Authority (DDA)
de Certeau, Michel 3–4
de-territorialized theories of urbanization 8–11
Debroy, Bibek 131, 135
Deepak (Chakkarpur resident) xii, 179–80
Delanda, Manuel 16–17
Deleuze, Gilles 16, 23–5, 41n5, 92
Delhi 43–67; colonial city 51–4; Commonwealth Games (2010) xi, 43, 44–8, **46**, 61–4, 65, 66–7; developmental city 54–60; immigration 55, 56–7, 58; Master Plan for Delhi (1962) 54, 55–8, 59–60, 105; Master Plan for Delhi (2021) 79, 83, 84–6; panorama 1, **2**, 3, 4–5; population *28*, 56–7, 58, 98n17; Shahjahanabad/Old Delhi xi, 1, **10**, **16**, **19**, 27, 54–5, 56, 71n82, 82, 121; unintended city 56–60, 78; *see also* slum demolitions and re-development
Delhi Development Authority (DDA) 55–6, 79, 84–6, 88–9, 127
Delhi Improvement Trust (DIT) 54–5
Delhi in Movement (2010) 41n13, 105
depth of field shots 24–5, 94–5
depth of field, urban 6, 23–5, 40, 88, 149, 157, 209
Derrida, Jacques 111
developmental city 54–60
Directorate of Town Planning, Gurgaon 133
DIT *see* Delhi Improvement Trust (DIT)
Dixit, Sheila 45, 66
DLF (Delhi Land and Finance) 125–32, *128*, 134, 135, 136–8, **137**, 140, 143n40, 176–7, 184
DLF City xi, 136, 143n40, 148–9, 150–2, 166, 167–70, 176, 202
DLF Cyber City, Gurgaon xi, 134, 148–50
DLF Gateway Tower, Gurgaon **148**
DLF Qutab Enclave, Gurgaon xi, 150–2, 166
documentary filmmaking: *I Am Gurgaon: The New Urban India* (2009) 158–65, 170; *Letter to the City Yet to Come* (2015) 35, 36, 37, 41n4; *Tomorrow We Disappear* (2015) 91–7
Dubai 85
Dutoit, Ulysse 93

ecology of speculation 135–40, 163–4

economic reforms 43–4, *45*, 64–5, 76–8; and financial crisis 111–12, 115–16; in popular media 106, 107–8
Economist, The 76–8
Elden, Stuart 14
elite activism 150–2, 158–65, 166–70
elite local politics 166–70
elite, urban *see* middle classes
Emergency period 71n82, 81, 82–3, 87–90
Engels, Friedrich 21
English-language media 47, 69n23
esthetic subjects 92–6, 157, 158–9, 208

Fanon, Frantz 51–2
far and near orders 13–14, 25, 29, 40, 49–50, 59, 67, 105, 149–50, 202–3
Farias, Ignacio 17, 18
Faridabad 126, 127
financial crisis, global 110–18, 135
Ford Foundation 57, 58
foreign direct investment 44, *45*
Foucault, Michel 109
Fukuyama, Francis 115

Gandhi, Indira 71n82, 81, 83
Gandhi, Rajiv 129, 130–1
Geohistory 1 22–3, 25, 91, 95, 97, 118n5, 177, 201–2
Geohistory 2 22–3, 25, 95, 118n5, 201–2
global city 6–8
global financial crisis 110–18, 135
globalization 6–8, 21
Godard, Jean-Luc 93
Gurgaon 105–7, 108, 109–10, 121–42, 148–54; economic and industrial growth 123, 124–5; and financial crisis 113–14, 117–18, 135; geographical location 123–4; "Gurgaon collapsing" series 152–4, 167; history of 121–3; *I Am Gurgaon: The New Urban India* (2009) 158–65, 170; land acquisition 125–35, *128*; Mall of India project **106**, **107**, **110**, **112**, **114**, 117–18, **117**; map xi; Master Plan for Gurgaon (2021) 138–9; middle class activism 150–2, 158–65, 166–70; Millennium City identity 106, 135–6, 142; population 122, *122*, 123, 124, 127; private developers 125–32, *128*, 134–5, 136–8, 140, 176–7, 184; property brokers 139–40, **139**; Residential Welfare Associations (RWAs) 162–4, 167–70, 188; "rural" designation 126, 127; speculative ecology 135–40, 163–4; *see also* Chakkarpur Village

212 *Index*

Gurgaon City Authority 168, 170
"Gurgaon collapsing" series 152–4, 167
Gurgaon Resident's Party 169

Hajera (Chakkarpur resident) 195–7
Harvey, David 15, 18, 109
Haryana Development and Regulation of
Urban Areas (HDRUA) Act (1975) 125,
129, 132–3
Haryana state: land laws 125–6, 129, 131,
132–3, 134, 135; *see also* Gurgaon
Haryana Urban Development Authority
(HUDA) 126, 132, 133–4, 136–9, 140,
151, 152, 176–7
havelis, Chakkarpur Village 199–200, **199**
Hindustan Times 152–4, **153**, 167
historicism 22
Hong Kong 27
Housing and Land Rights Network
(HLRN) 62
HUDA *see* Haryana Urban Development
Authority (HUDA)
hygiene standards 47, 63–4

"I am Gurgaon" initiative 164, 167
I Am Gurgaon: The New Urban India
(2009) 158–65, 170
image of thought concept 5–6, 23–4
in-situ rehabilitations 84–6
informal settlements 56–60; *see also* slum
demolitions and re-development; slums
infrastructure development 44, 45–6, 61,
62, 64–5, 66–7

Jama Masjid mosque 1, **2**, 3, 4–5
Jamuna Bazaar 88–9
Jha, Gangadhar 56, 57
jhuggi, Chakkarpur Village xii, 189–91, **189**
Jhuggi Jhonpri Removal Scheme (1958) 82

Kalmadi, Suresh 43
Kalra, Deep 164
Kant, Immanuel 206–7
Kathputli Colony xi, 78, 79–81, 83, 84–6,
87, 89–90, 91–7
Kaul, Sanjay 168–70
Khattar, Jagdish 153–4
Kumar, Bipin 185–7
Kumar, Krishan 148, 149, 150

Lal, Bansi 137
Land Acquisition Act (1894) 126, 133,
134, 135
land acquisition, Gurgaon 125–35, *128*

land-use guidelines 57–8, 59–60
Ledlie, Henry 162–4
Lefebvre, Henri 12–15, 38, 41n13, 48,
49–50, 56, 67, 69n29
Lehman Brothers 110
Letter to the City Yet to Come (2015) 35,
36, 37, 41n4
lived spaces 13, 14

Macaulay, Thomas 155–6
Mahesh (Chakkarpur resident) 192–4
Mall of India project, Gurgaon **106**, **107**,
110, **112**, **114**, 117–18, **117**
Manhattan 3–4
Manu (Chakkarpur resident) 180–1
Maruti Suzuki India Ltd. 124, 153–4, 185,
186, 188, 200
Maruti Vihar, Gurgaon 185, 188, 196
Marx, Karl 21, 111
Marxian theory 12–15, 18–19
Massey, Doreen 14–15
Master Plan for Delhi (1962) 54, 55–8,
59–60, 105
Master Plan for Delhi (2021) 79, 83, 84–6
Master Plan for Gurgaon (2021) 138–9
Mathihur (Chakkarpur resident) 189–91
Meerman, Marije 158–65
Mehrauli–Gurgaon Road (MG Road),
Chakkarpur Village 176, 179–81
metis 38, 39, 40, 90–1, 96, 97
Mexico City 27
MG Road, Chakkarpur Village 176,
179–81
MG Road Metro Station, Gurgaon xii, **176**,
178, 179
middle classes 51, 59, 60, 64–6, 69n23;
activism 150–2, 158–65, 166–70; and
British colonial rule 154–7; and
Commonwealth Games (2010) 47, 61,
64; critique of 165–6; and local politics
166–70; unauthorized colonies 58
Midnight's Children (Rushdie) 79, 81,
89–90
migration, urban 7, 55, 56–7, 58, 122, 123
Ministry of Urban Development 127
Moody's ratings agency 47
movement-images 24
moving slum concept 79–81, 88, 89–90
Municipal Council of Gurgaon 151, 152,
168

nambardar market, Chakkarpur Village
xii, 183–8, **184**
Nandy, Ashis 58, 65, 81, 97, 108, 175

Nathupur village 133–4, 187, 198
National Capital Region (NCR) 28, 124
National Capital Territory of Delhi (NCTD) xi, 1, 27–8, *28*
National Emergency period 71n82, 81, 82–3, 87–90
NCR Planning Board Act (1985) 124
near order *see* far and near orders
Nehru, Jawaharlal 54
neo-colonialism 21
neoliberal reforms 43–4, *45*, 64–5, 76–8; and financial crisis 111–12, 115–16; in popular media 106, 107–8
neoliberalism 109–10, 115
New Delhi xi, **13**, 27, **53**, 54, 55
Newsweek International 115–16
Newtonian conceptions of space 13, 14
Nilekani, Nandan 151–2, 165

Old Delhi/Shahjahanabad xi, 1, **10**, **16**, **19**, 27, 54–5, 56, 71n82, 82, 121
Ong, Aihwa 109

Paharganj xi, 35, 36, 37–40, 41n2
Pawar, Maya 79, 86, 91–2, 94, 95
People's Action 168–70
perceived spaces 13, 14
performative interpretation 111
Phoenix project 85–6, 87
pickpockets 35–6, 37–40
planetary urbanization 8–11, 12
politics, local 166–70
population: Delhi *28*, 56–7, 58, 98n17; Gurgaon 122, *122*, 123, 124, 127
post-Partition refugees 55, 56–7, 122, 123
postcolonial urban theory 18–23
Prakash, Chandra 187, 188
Prakash, Gyan 52–3
pre-sales 140, 163–4
presidential complex, New Delhi **53**
private capital 44, *45*
private developers, Gurgaon 125–32, *128*, 134–5, 136–8, 140, 176–7, 184
property brokers, Gurgaon 139–40, **139**
provincialization 21, 22
public interest litigation 133–4
public land acquisition, Gurgaon 126, 132, 133–4, 135
Punjab Land Alienation Act (1900) 125

Qutab Enclave, Gurgaon xi, 150–2, 166

Raheja Developers Ltd. 85–6
Raheja, Navin 86
Ranciere, Jacques 161, 162

rape 36
Ray, Satyajit 156–7
re-settlement colonies 83, 87–8
refugees, post-Partition 55, 56–7, 122, 123
Residential Welfare Associations (RWAs) 162–4, 167–70, 188
rhythmanalysis 41n13
Robinson, Jennifer 22, 67
Rohini xi, 56
Rubin, Robert 115
Rushdie, Salman 79, 81, 89–90

Sahara Mall, Gurgaon xii, 176, 179, 181, 184–5, 193
Sarasvati Vihar, Gurgaon 190, 196
Sassen, Saskia 6
Scott, Allen 11
Scott, James 90–1
Sen, Jai 58, 78
sensible milieu 206–9
sepoy rebellion (1857) 55, 121
Shadipur xi, 78, 79–81, 83, 84–6, 87, 89–90, 91–7
Shah, Rehman 84, 91, 92, 94, 95–6
Shahjahanabad/Old Delhi xi, 1, **10**, **16**, **19**, 27, 54–5, 56, 71n82, 82, 121
Shapiro, Michael J. 90, 92–3, 206
Shatranj Ke Khiladi (1977) 156–7
Sheppard, Eric 22–3, 177
Shiller, Robert 115
Siegel, Lee 90
Simmel, Georg 43, 49
Singh, Bineeta 160–1, 170
Singh, Chaudhary Raghvendra 126
Singh, Jeelay 183–5, 187, 188
Singh, Kushal Pal (K. P.) 127, 129–31, 132, 134, 137–8, 143n40, 177, 184
skyscrapers 85
Slum Areas (Improvement and Clearance) Act (1956) 82
slum demolitions and re-development 58, 78–97; for Commonwealth Games (2010) 61–3, 66; Emergency period 71n82, 81, 82–3, 87–90; in-situ rehabilitations 84–6; Kathputli Colony xi, 78, 79–81, 83, 84–6, 87, 89–90, 91–7; Master Plan for Delhi (2021) 79, 83, 84–6; Phoenix project 85–6, 87; re-settlement colonies 83, 87–9; *Tomorrow We Disappear* (2015) 91–7; Yamuna Pushta xi, 62–3, 66
slums 56–60; hiding with bamboo walls 65; *jhuggi*, Chakkarpur Village xii, 189–91, **189**; moving slum concept 79–81, 88, 89–90

214 *Index*

social production of space 13–15
Soiza (Chakkarpur resident) 198
Sonal, Shilpa 159–60, 161
South Korea 61
spatial practices 13, 14
speculative ecology 135–40, 163–4
Spivak, Gayatri Chakravorty 64
Storper, Michael 11
"Street Ethnography and Rhythmanalysis: Chakkarpur Gurgaon" (2015) 175
Sukanya, Sumit 164
Sundaram, Ravi 56

Tarlo, Emma 87–9
territorialized conception of cities 11
Tharoor, Shashi 115–16
time-images 5, 24–5, 36, 41n5, 88–9
Times of India 47, 164
Tomorrow We Disappear (2015) 91–7
Town Survey Report of Gurgaon 122, 123–4
trace 149–50
Tsing, Anna 140
Tukral, Latika 163, 164–5

unintended city 56–60, 78; *see also* slum demolitions and re-development; slums
Unitech 126, 131, 135

United States 61; economic crisis 110–11, 112
urban assemblages 15–18, 22–3
urban depth of field 6, 23–5, 40, 88, 149, 157, 209
urban elite *see* middle classes
urban land nexus 11
urban mediation 48, 49–51, 56, 59, 60, 65
urban *metis* 38, 39, 40, 90–1, 96, 97
urban turn 43–4
urbanization 6–8, 12–15; of capital 15; planetary 8–11, 12
Uttaranchal Hotel, Chakkarpur Village xii, 192–4, **192**

Valmiki community 203
Varma, Pavan 165–6, 169
Verma, Praveen 175, 178–9

Wall Street Journal 86
Welles, Orson 24–5
Wirth, Louis 10, 30n26
World Spa Action Group (WSAG) 162–4

Yadav, Sunil 203
Yamuna Pushta xi, 62–3, 66

Zakaria, Fareed 115
zoning laws 57–8, 59–60